Paula Orookbi Hentela Brown

THE COLLECTOR'S ENCYCLOPEDIA OF

Hall China

SECOND EDITION

by

Margaret & Kenn Whitmyer

COLLECTOR BOOKS

A Division of Schroeder Publishing Co., Inc.

The current values in this book should be used only as a guide. They are not intended to set prices, which vary from one section of the country to another. Auction prices as well as dealer prices vary greatly and are affected by condition as well as demand. Neither the Authors nor the Publisher assumes responsibility for any losses that might be incurred as a result of consulting this guide.

Searching for a Publisher?

We are always looking for knowledgeable people considered to be experts within their fields. If you feel that there is a real need for a book on your collectible subject and have a large comprehensive collection, contact us.

COLLECTOR BOOKS
P.O. Box 3009
Paducah, Kentucky 42002 -3009

On the cover:
Top Right: Sales Award Autumn Leaf Electric Percolator. Top Left: "Abbey Meal" Tankard and Mug. Bottom Photo: Crocus Pattern; Front Row: Shakers, "Five Band"; water bottle, "Zephyr"; sugar and creamer, "Meltdown." Back Row: Soup tureen, clover style; coffee pot, "Deco" shape.

Cover design: Beth Summers
Book design: Michelle Dowling

Additional copies of this book may be ordered from:

Collector Books
P.O. Box 3009
Paducah, KY 42002-3009
or
Margaret & Kenn Whitmyer
P.O. Box 30806
Columbus, OH 43230

@$24.95. Add $2.00 for postage and handling.

Copyright: Margaret & Kenn Whitmyer, 1994

Printed by IMAGE GRAPHICS, INC., Paducah, Kentucky

Dedication

This book is dedicated to Dan Tucker and Lorrie Kitchen who still have the almost fatal "Hall China Collection Syndrome" after all these years. Harmless to humans, but deadly for the pocketbook; the collecting is fun. This book is also dedicated to the many collectors who have joined them over the past ten years — how are the unenlightened surviving?

ACKNOWLEDGMENTS

The second edition of *The Collector's Encyclopedia of Hall China* has been made possible through the efforts of many faithful collectors and dealers who have been willing to share their knowledge and information with us. We want to thank all of our readers who have sent us pictures and other information which has helped to verify the existence of the many new pieces listed in this book. Due to the volume of mail, we have not been able to respond personally to all of your letters, but we have tried to answer as many as possible. We apologize if you have written to us and have not received an answer. However, we want you to know your letter has been read and the information or suggestions in it have been appreciated.

We appreciate the kindness of Dan Tucker and Lorrie Kitchen who have again provided us with the opportunity to photograph much of the rare Hall China they have acquired over the last few years. They have allowed us to borrow anything and have never questioned its safety or hinted that maybe we had kept something long enough that we might be trying to forget where it came from.

Several people again opened up their homes and allowed us to invade their privacy for our seemingly unending photography sessions. The contributions of Pansy and Billie Ramsey, Woody Griffith, Jerry Macke, and Linda and Elvin Heck were especially appreciated.

We are also very grateful to the following people who either helped with pricing, or supplied us with much needed information: Ken and Carol Baker, Dennis and Rosemary Billings, Ronald Binkley, Joyce and Parke Bloyer, Don and Irma Brewer, Bob Brushaber, Sam and Becky Collings, Jim and Betty Cooper, Sally Davis, Don and Joyce DeJong, Shirley Easley, Krystol Ellis, Ronald and Linda Ellis, Anne Fleming, Gene Florence, Leonard and Shirley Graff, Joyce Guilmire, Jerry Harris, Mr. and Mrs. Johnson, Harriet Kurshadt, Mr. and Mrs. Joseph Lockard, Merle and Dee Long, Robert and Bernadette Ludwig, Nancy Maben, Janet and Wendell Martin, Paula Darden Moeller, Jerry and Connie Monarch, Mrs. W. H. Morgan, Benjamin Moulton, Naomi's Antiques To Go, Tom and Jean Niner, Eugene and Jewel Payton, Bill and Sharon Phillips, Mr. and Mrs. Charles Reed, Patsy Schoemaker, Bonnie Scherrer, Millie Smith, Sue Switzer, Lee Wagner, Ray and Carolyn Wagner, Joel Wilson, Virginia Wilson, and Delmar and Mary Lou Youngen.

Perhaps one of the hardest working, and least recognized, persons on a book of this type is the photographer. He's the silent one behind the camera, upon whom the outcome of the entire project depends. Our photographer, Siegfried Kurz, has the patience to endure the seemingly unending and often unorganized sessions, and the ability to provide us with outstanding results. For this we are grateful.

Hopefully, we have included everyone, but if someone's name has mysteriously been lost in our mountain of papers, please understand that we are not unappreciative of your co-operation. We do try to keep track of where the information is coming from, but sometimes finding names at the moment you need them is a problem.

CONTENTS

PART II: KITCHENWARE

KITCHENWARE PATTERNS

PART III: REFRIGERATOR WARE

PART IV: TEAPOTS AND COFFEE POTS

PART V: OTHER HALL PRODUCTS

PART VI: RE-ISSUES AND NEW PRODUCTS

FOREWORD

The purpose of this book is to provide collectors with a usable guide to the most popularly collected items produced by the Hall China Company of East Liverpool, Ohio. The greatest emphasis will be placed upon the most collectible patterns, but many of the more obscure pieces will also be identified and examined. Currently, the greatest collector interest in the production of the Hall China Company lies in the pieces produced between the early 1930s and the late 1960s. We have tried to illustrate and identify as many items from this period as possible.

In the eight years since the introduction of our first book, many new discoveries have been unearthed. We appreciate the efforts of the numerous collectors who have taken the time to share their discoveries and collections with us. Much of the new information in this book is a direct result of these collectors who have been willing to share their knowledge with us.

Many of the articles from Hall's institutional line have not been included in this guide, since there is still not very much collector interest in most of these items. Some people, who like the superior durability of the ware, are currently buying some of these institutional pieces to use in their kitchens but most of these items have very little collectible value. The possible exceptions are institutional items with a colorful art glaze finish and the very large black tea servers which may be seen in some fast food chains and restaurants. Older tea servers, especially those embossed with unusual advertising, are finding homes with collectors.

Many metal, glass, and wooden items which match Hall patterns, but were not produced by Hall, are also included in this guide. A great number of collectors are now incorporating these matching accessory pieces into their collections.

To provide more convenient reference, Hall collectibles have been divided into several major categories. Arrangement of patterns and items in each area is essentially alphabetical. The major divisions are as follows:

1. Dinnerware Patterns.
   A. Styles C, D, and ruffled -D dinnerware arranged alphabetically.
   B. E-shape dinnerware.
   C. Century shape dinnerware.
   D. Classic shape dinnerware.
2. Kitchenware.
   A. Basic kitchenware shapes.
   B. Kitchenware patterns.

3. Refrigerator Ware.
4. Teapots and Coffee Pots.
5. Advertising and Specialty Items.

To properly identify a piece of Hall China, more than one name is often necessary. Most items, especially if they have a decal, will have a pattern name, such as Autumn Leaf or Red Poppy. In addition to the pattern name, individual pieces in a pattern will also usually have a shape name. The shape name helps to distinguish like items in the same pattern from each other. For example, if someone tells you they have a teapot in the pattern Red Poppy, you still don't know exactly what they have since there are two different teapots in this pattern. Therefore, the shape name — Aladdin — or New York — is used to distinguish between the two similar items in the same pattern. The items in the pictures will be identified by using the name of the pattern where necessary (when more than one pattern is shown in a single photo). This will be followed by the identifying name of the piece, followed by the shape name or color name. Examples are the following:

1. More than one pattern per photo: Acacia (pattern name); jug (item name); "Radiance" (shape name).
2. One pattern per photo: Jug (item name); "Radiance" (shape name).
3. Kitchenware shapes: Teapot (item name); Chinese red (color name).
4. Teapot section: Aladdin (shape name); green (color name).

A lot of the names for the colors, patterns, and shapes used in this book are the ones designated by Hall China. However, Hall did not have names for every piece they made. In the event an official Hall name could not be determined for an item, we have taken the liberty of providing one of our own. These new names we have used will be found in quotation marks. Also, over the years, other names have been introduced and accepted by collectors for the identification of some pieces. We have attempted to use those names in this book wherever possible. In some cases certain pieces have evolved with a dual identity. Therefore, a cross reference of multiple names has been included to aid collectors in their attempts to use other references.

PRICING

The prices in this book represent retail prices for mint condition pieces. Items which are excessively worn or chipped or cracked will only bring a fraction of the listed price. A price range has been included to help account for regional differences in prices. Also, be aware that certain currently rare items which are now valued at several hundred dollars, may prove hard-to-sell if a quantity of these items is discovered. The value of a few items, which are currently one-of-a-kind, may be omitted from the price guide if a retail value has not been established. In these cases, the letters "UND" for undetermined will be used to indicate an unestablished value.

All items are priced each, including shakers. Items which have lids are priced complete. Any exceptions to this will be noted in the individual listing. Prices of solid color kitchenware items, refrigerator items, teapots, and coffee pots may vary considerably according to color. Wherever possible, an attempt has been made to reflect these different valuations. However, any attempt to list and price the dozens of colors in which some of the pieces may be found is impossible in a guide of this type. An effort has been made to give the reader general guidelines about rarity and desirability of various pieces and colors. Thoughtful consideration of these guidelines should produce a qualitative value for most any item.

Pricing information has been obtained from dealer listings, flea market and show observations, trade publications, and from collectors. Remember, prices in this guide should only be used as a reference. Prices may vary in the marketplace and it is not the intention of the authors to establish or control prices.

RE-ISSUES

Hall China introduced a new retail line to buyers at the Housewares Show held in Chicago in March, 1985. The new line was called Hall American and was designed for the retail market to be sold through gourmet shops and department stores.

In addition to some casseroles, bakers, jugs, and teapots which were still in production, Hall revived some shapes from its past. The total number of new shapes available ranged to the mid-sixties, but only a few of these shapes which reflect the past are of particular interest to collectors. Noteworthy shapes, in the re-introduction are the Airflow, Rhythm, and square T-Ball teapots; the Donut and Streamline jugs; a square-based "Sundial" batter bowl; and the "Nora" and "Hercules" water servers.

Generally, this new line was only available in six standard colors in the retail outlets. The new colors were red, black, white, Sandust (tan), Oxford Grey, and Marine Blue. However, any of Hall's colors could be special ordered, and some individual customers have had various pieces produced in their own unique colors. Therefore, do not be surprised to find new pieces in such colors as lavender, rose, or orange.

Fortunately, Hall has considered the concerns of collectors and all the new production was supposed to be marked with the rectangular backstamp which has been in use since 1970.

Hall China has produced a number of collector oriented limited edition items for several organizations or individuals over the last few years. Specifically, new items which are causing the most concern are in the Autumn Leaf, Red Poppy, Crocus, and "Silhouette" patterns. Also, new issues of some of the novelty teapots have been produced. Currently, all of the new items are being marked with special backstamps. However, it is possible to remove some of these backstamps, especially on the re-issued novelty teapots. If an automobile or football teapot is found without a Hall backstamp, proceed cautiously and look for other distinguishing features of the new issues. For more information on new items see the chapter on Re-issues at the back of this book.

COLORS

Hall China produced the widest variety of colored glazes of any china company. Many of the colors are very close, with some only varying by a shade. Due to this small difference, we have tried to reproduce some of the most frequently encountered colors in the accompanying color chart. Even with the help of the chart, it may still be difficult to identify some of the colors.

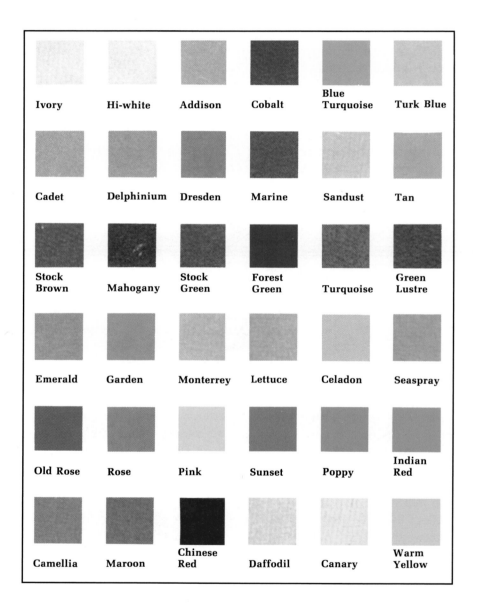

HISTORY OF THE HALL CHINA COMPANY

The Hall China Company was established on August 14, 1903, as a result of the dissolution of the East Liverpool Potteries Company. This company had been formed in 1901, as a result of the merger of five East Liverpool potteries. Robert Hall bought one of the companies — the former East Liverpool Pottery Company — located in the old West, Hardwick, and George building at Fourth and Walnut Streets in East Liverpool, Ohio. Initially, thirty-eight potters were employed at three kilns to produce spittoons and combinets and a limited amount of dinnerware. In 1904, Robert Hall died and his son, Robert Taggert Hall, became manager.

Robert T. Hall kept the plant operating by producing primarily toilet sets, jugs, and other white ware. At the same time he experimented endlessly to rediscover a lost process from the Ming Dynasty (A.D. 1368-1644) in China, which would allow him to produce non-lead glazed china with a single-fire process. This single-firing would allow the glaze to penetrate the unfired body, creating a craze-proof finish. Robert T. Hall experimented from 1904 until 1911 before he finally achieved success. His new process created a colorfully glazed china which was strong, non-porous, and craze-proof. The new technique fused together the white body, color, and glaze when it was fired at a temperature of 2400°F. The resulting product was very dense, did not absorb moisture, and held heat well.

Hall China experimented briefly with dinnerware from 1908 until 1911, but then chose to concentrate on institutional wares. As the company grew, and the institutional line expanded, two more plants were added in East Liverpool. The successful addition of their Gold Decorated Teapot Line in the 1920s pushed the capacity of these plants to the limit. By 1923, Hall claimed the title of "the largest manufacturer of fireproof cooking china in the world." In 1930, a new plant was built on the east side of East Liverpool and the three old plants were abandoned. This new plant enjoyed numerous expansions during the thirties and early forties as production boomed with the intense concentration on decal dinnerware and kitchenware patterns.

The Hall China Company is still operating in this plant today. Once again, production is targeted primarily at institutional and commercial customers. However, in 1985, Hall re-introduced some of its old kitchenware and teapot shapes for the retail trade. Also, of great interest to many collectors are the limited edition Autumn Leaf pieces which are currently being made for both a private company and the National Autumn Leaf Collector's Club. In many ways Hall China has remained viable by adapting to meet the special needs of its customers.

The China Process

The manufacture of Hall China begins with a secret powdered mixture of flint, feldspar, and several different clays. These ingredients are mixed with water in a machine. The resulting slip is passed through separators which remove metals and other foreign objects.

The mixture is then pumped into presses which squeeze out the water, leaving clay in a cake form. The cakes of clay are then aged and pressed through pug mills which remove air from the clay.

The clay is then shaped by a "jiggerman" on a potter's wheel to form flat pieces and bowls. To produce pieces such as teapots or jugs, water is added to the clay, and the resulting slip is poured into a mold. The raw ware is allowed to dry for twenty-four hours at about 100°F. Then the special leadless glaze is applied by either spraying or hand-dipping. The glazed items are placed on cars which move slowly through a kiln. The temperature of the ware is slowly increased to 2400°F. This intense heat causes chemical changes in the body and glaze materials which allows the color to set.

The fired china is then inspected for defects and the good pieces are sent on to the decorating department. Decorating is done by either hand-painting or by transferring decals or prints to the ware. The finished product is then refired in a smaller oven at a lower temperature. Decals were a very popular method of decoration during the thirties and forties. Since only pieces of larger decals were sometimes used on smaller items in a pattern, it is sometimes difficult to associate these pieces with the rest of the items in the pattern. Careful comparison will usually result in a positive identification.

IDENTIFICATION OF HALL CHINA

#1

#2

#3

#4

#5

Pictured here are the general backstamps which may be found on the bottom of most collectible Hall China. Certain other backstamps which are peculiar to a particular pattern will be found illustrated in the section portraying the individual pattern.

Backstamp #1 is a very early mark. This mark was used until the early teens and will not be found on much "collectible" Hall China. Examples of the type of wares found with this mark are shown on page 15.

Backstamp #2 was used primarily from the early teens until the late twenties. "Made in U.S.A." is sometimes missing. Early Gold Decorated Line teapots produced during this period will often bear this mark.

Mark #3 is the backstamp which appears most frequently on items of interest to today's collector. The words "Made in U.S.A." will sometimes appear below the circle. Registration of the mark occurred on February 10, 1930, and use of the mark began in October 1930. This mark was used extensively from the early 1930s until the 1970s and will be found on most items except kitchenware and dinnerware. These two categories have special backstamps.

Mark #4 was used on kitchenware produced after 1932. This mark was usually stamped in gold, but will also be found in black, blue, green, and perhaps a few other colors. Occasionally a pattern name will also appear in conjunction with this mark.

Backstamp #5 was reserved for Hall dinnerware. This mark was modified slightly for use with the dinnerware produced for the Jewel Tea Company and for the Orange Poppy and Wildfire patterns of The Great American Tea Company. Autumn Leaf will have "Tested and Approved by MARY DUNBAR — JEWEL HOMEMAKERS INSTITUTE" in the circle. Orange Poppy has the Great American Golden Key symbol inside the circle and the Wildfire mark acknowledges the 100th anniversary of Great American.

Fortunately for collectors, most of Hall's items have an identifying backstamp. With the exception of shakers, lamps, and some coffee pots, most of the unmarked pieces of Hall were seconds and never reached the decorating room.

In addition to the above printed backstamps, some items will be found with "Hall" impressed in large block letters. Many of the kitchenware pieces with this mark will date to the early 1930s or before. Many institutional pieces will also be marked in this manner.

Numerous other special identifying marks were reserved for certain pieces, patterns, or companies for which Hall produced china. We will show as many special marks as space permits throughout the book. Certain special marks have also been used on limited edition pieces of collector interest produced for such organizations as the National Autumn Leaf Collector's Club and private companies such as China Specialties. For more about these specific backstamps see the section on Reissues at the back of this book.

Paper labels were also used for identification by Hall China. However, since most items were used heavily, not much Hall China is found with paper labels still intact. Paper labels are helpful in identifying lamps which Hall made for the White Lamp Company and others. The only way to identify these lamps as Hall is by their paper label, since there is no backstamp.

Much of the Hall China produced since the early 1970s has backstamp #6. This mark was registered on February 20, 1969, and use of it began January 6, 1969.

#6

EARLY HALL

Although examples are scarce today, some highly collectible pieces of Hall China were made during the early years. All the items shown here were made in the early 1900s.

The large white pitcher with gold trim is part of a chamber set which was made by the East Liverpool Potteries Company around the turn of the century. The pitcher is 12" tall and set in a large bowl about 16" in diameter. Other pieces in this type of set often included a smaller water pitcher, a toothbrush holder, and a covered soap dish.

In the photo below the larger pitcher on the right is 7½" tall and was produced by the East Liverpool Potteries Company. The backstamp (shown below) on this pitcher was used prior to August 1903, when the principals, which included Robert Hall, chose to dissolve the company. Robert Hall took over one of the abandoned buildings and formed the Hall China Company.

The smaller pitcher is 6¾" tall and bears the #1 Hall backstamp.

Backstamp of East Liverpool Potteries Company.

PART I: DINNERWARE

Row 1: C-style; D-style; Ruffled D-style. Row 2: E-style; Century style; Tomorrow's Classic style.

Hall began producing decal pattern dinnerware in 1936 with the introduction of an Autumn Leaf breakfast set. During the next twenty years many different patterns and several different shapes of dinnerware were produced. The dinnerware patterns and shapes will be identified and evaluated in this section. Styles of dinnerware found in this guide include:

D-style. This was the most commonly used shape of dinnerware. The plates and bowls are round and the cups and gravy boat have ear-shaped handles. Although there are some minor modifications in the different patterns, the basic dinnerware service consists of the following pieces:

Bowl, 5¼" fruit	Plate, 6"
Bowl, 6" cereal	Plate, 8"
Bowl, 8½" flat soup	Plate, 9"
Bowl, 9" vegetable	Platter, 11¼" oval
Cup	Platter, 13¼" oval
Gravy boat	Saucer

Some patterns of D-style dinnerware will also have a 10" dinner plate.

C-style. The C-style pieces have the same round shape as the D-style. However, all the C-style dinnerware is embossed with the "Radiance" design. The cup does not have an ear-shaped handle and there is no gravy boat. The only pattern which has been found with this shape dinnerware is Orange Poppy.

Ruffled D-style. This is a modified D-style. The flat pieces and the bowls have a scalloped edge instead of just being plain round. Two additional sizes of plates — a 10" dinner and a 7¼" salad — were also included in the set. This shape is exclusive to the Autumn Leaf pattern.

E-style. The E-style dinnerware shape was designed by J. Palin Thorley and was produced during the forties and early fifties. Many of the patterns which use this shape were produced for Sears, but several non-Sears products were also made.

Century Shape. The Century shape was designed in the fifties by Eva Zeisel. The shape of the plates is slightly oval with a prominent tab handle. Bowls and platters have two distinct tab handles.

Tomorrow's Classic shape. Tomorrow's Classic is another shape designed by Eva Zeisel in the fifties. It is similar in style to the Century shape. However, the plates are slightly oval and lack a tab handle and the bowls and platters feature a single tab handle. There are other minor differences among the other serving pieces in the two shapes, but the butter dish and the gravy boat are the same shape in both lines.

Arrangement of the dinnerware patterns in this chapter is alphabetical in three separate sections. The first section includes a combined listing of all C, D, and Ruffled-D shape dinnerware. This is followed by an alphabetical listing of the E-style dinnerware. The final section presents a listing of the Century and Tomorrow's Classic shapes designed by Eva Zeisel.

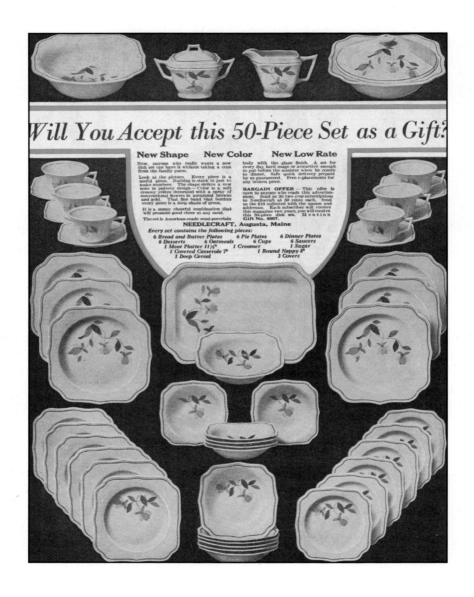

AUTUMN LEAF INTRODUCTION

Hall China with the Autumn Leaf decal first appeared in 1933 with the introduction of a large 9" mixing bowl. By Christmas of the same year, two smaller size bowls were added to complete the three-piece utility set. These three basic pieces remained in the line until Autumn Leaf was discontinued in 1976. Hall produced this pattern exclusively for the Jewel Tea Company of Barrington, Illinois. In the early years the pattern was referred to as the Autumn design and pieces were offered to Jewel customers as premiums for the purchase of other products.

Since Autumn Leaf developed as a premium line, new items were added regularly, and old pieces were discontinued periodically. This gave customers an incentive to buy more products to obtain the premiums while they were still available. Items which were not popular with the housewife of the day were short lived and are difficult for modern-day collectors to find. Metal shortages during World War II also caused the premature departure of some of the metal accessories associated with the line. As a result, collectors are having difficulty obtaining many pre-war tins. Although, all pieces of Autumn Leaf were discontinued in 1976, a number of items reappeared briefly in 1978. Items included in the re-issue are the 10" plate, 7¼" plate, tea cup and saucer, 13½" oval platter, 5½" fruit bowl, 8½" flat soup, oval vegetable bowl, round 10 ounce French baker, two-handle bean pot, and Newport teapot. In addition, 106 of the long spout "Rayed" teapots were produced. These were given by Jewel as awards to outstanding sales people. Most pieces in this short re-introduction will have a backstamp as shown below which includes the date 1978. Certain other premium pieces such as the newer Newport teapot and the two-handled bean pot also have slight decorative differences from the older versions which enable a knowledgeable collector to differentiate between the two issues.

In the last few years, limited edition pieces of Autumn Leaf have been made available to collectors. Thus far the new china pieces have been restricted to items which were not in the original Autumn Leaf line. For more information on these new items see the Re-issues section at the back of this book.

As the hobby of collecting the Autumn Leaf pattern has matured, it has been possible to determine that certain items are truly rare. Pieces in this category are generally sample items submitted to Jewel by Hall. If the item was not approved for production, the few samples were offered for sale through Jewel's employee store. Many of these pieces have now reached the collectible market and some collectors are paying very high prices for them. As a word of caution, there are numerous private entrepreneurs who have made a variety of Autumn Leaf products over the years. Therefore, the history of all purchases of extremely expensive rarities should be carefully examined. As a general guideline, most of the sample items we have seen have had the Mary Dunbar backstamp.

Although the Autumn Leaf decal became a Jewel Tea exclusive, other non-Hall china pieces may be found with this decal. Prior to 1933, the decal was used on a set of china which Needlecraft magazine promoted as a premium. This china was produced by the Crooksville China Company of Crooksville, Ohio, and is shown in the photo to the left. The entire set could be obtained by selling twenty two-year subscriptions to the magazine for fifty cents each. Other companies which are known to have produced pieces using the Autumn Leaf decal include: Columbia, Crown, Harker, American Limoges, Paden City, and Vernon of California. Although some items may have been submitted to Jewel by Hall's rivals in an attempt to gain their business, many of these pieces are far too common to have been mere samples. Most, like the ones in the Needlecraft ad, were probably made prior to 1933. A lot of the non-Hall items will not have a backstamp to identify the manufacturer. However, the shape of the piece will usually reveal the identity of the maker. Pieces of non-Hall Autumn Leaf are often crazed and discolored and do not generally approach the quality of Hall pieces. Today, some collectors are enthusiastically pursuing non-Hall items, and the prices are rising with the corresponding increased demand.

Autumn Leaf Kitchenware Backstamp.

Autumn Leaf Dinnerware Backstamp.

Autumn Leaf 1978 Dinnerware Backstamp.

AUTUMN LEAF DINNERWARE

Abundant supplies of reasonably priced Autumn Leaf basic dinnerware pieces have enticed many people to begin collecting this pattern. Many collections have blossomed from the cheap acquisition of a few pieces at a garage sale, flea market, or auction. Other collectors have gotten their starts through the inheritance of a few pieces from a close relative. Natural curiosity and the thirst for knowledge have driven them to pursue the elusive Autumn Leaf motif. How many of them would have begun if they had realized the vast number of accessory pieces available and the enormous sums of money required to acquire them?

Most dinnerware articles were made for a long period of time − from the thirties and forties until the mid-seventies. Therefore, most of these items are readily available at a moderate price and collectors should expect to be able to purchase pieces which are in excellent condition. The only dinnerware pieces which appear to be in short supply are the cream soups and the 10" plates. Even these can be found by most collectors without extreme effort.

Although the crazing problem with this china is minimal, extensive use will result in abnormal wear and damage to the gold rim. Dinnerware which is scratched or dull will bring only a fraction of the listed prices. Some collectors, who want to use their china, buy these slightly worn pieces to use for everyday in order to preserve the value of the pieces in their collections.

Although Autumn Leaf kitchenware was made earlier, the first dinnerware appeared in 1936. Jewel ads of the time promoted this as the first dinnerware ever produced by Hall China and expounded on its beauty and durability. The new dishes were "manufactured from the best imported and domestic clays. The china has been tested for an hour under 100 pounds of pressure at a temperature of 212 degrees and then doused with cold water. No cracks or crazes developed." The initial offering consisted of a 24-piece set which included four of each of the following: 9" breakfast plates, 5½" deep fruit bowls, and cups and saucers. The complete set sold for $4.95.

Two sizes of oval platters were added to the dinnerware line in 1938. The 11" platter sold for sixty-five cents and the 13" platter was listed at one dollar.

The small 7 ounce custard cup shown on the right side of the middle photograph was one of numerous items added to the Autumn Leaf line in 1936. The custard was Jewel's Item No. 303 and was sold as a set of six for one dollar.

	Item	Introduced	Discontinued	Price
Top Photo:				
Row 1:	Plate, 10"	1938	1976*	$12.00 − 14.00
	Plate, 9"	1936	1976	$8.00 − 9.00
	Plate, 8"	1938	1976	$10.00 − 12.00
Row 2:	Plate, 7¼"	1938	1976	$6.00 − 7.00
	Plate, 6"	1938	1976	$4.00 − 5.00
	Platter, 9" oval	1942	1976	$18.00 − 20.00
Row 3:	Platter, 13½" oval	1938	1976*	$22.00 − 25.00
	Platter, 11½" oval	1938	1976	$20.00 − 22.00
Middle Photo:				
	Bowl, 8½" flat soup	1938	1976*	$11.00 − 14.00
	Bowl, 6½" cereal	1938	1976	$9.00 − 11.00
	Bowl, 5½" fruit	1936	1976*	$4.00 − 5.00
	Custard, "Radiance"	1936	1976	$5.00 − 6.00

*Re-issued in 1978.

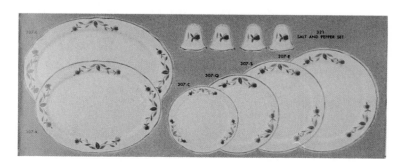

Page from a Jewel Premium book.

AUTUMN LEAF CUPS, BOWLS, SUGARS, AND CREAMERS

The difference between the old style and new style sugar and creamer is shown in the top row. The older style sugar and creamer first appeared with the No. 300 coffee service in 1936. The handles and the vertical rays match the shape and style of the other kitchenware pieces from this period. The newer sugar and creamer was introduced in 1940. The shape of the handles on this set matches the shape of the handles on the dinnerware pieces. The "Rayed" set was made for a much shorter period and is harder to find than the Ruffled-D set. Significant differences also exist between the two styles of sugar lids. The old style lid is flatter and has a "bud" knob with rays. The newer lid is more sloped and has a "bud" knob which lacks rays. Beware of buying lids which have had their knobs glued back on.

The second row pictures the mugs and cups and saucers available in the Autumn Leaf pattern. The first cup and saucer shown is the regular dinnerware style. This set was called the breakfast cup and saucer in Jewel ads. The larger cup and saucer represents a style referred to as St. Denis. This cup and saucer is sometimes called the "he man" style. It was introduced in 1942, and the original price was forty-five cents for a cup and saucer. By the time these pieces were discontinued in 1976, the price of the cup had increased to $2.50 and the saucer was listed at $1.25.

The conic mug was listed in Jewel catalogs as a 10 oz. beverage mug. The introductory price was $6.95 for a set of four in 1966. This same 1966 catalog also heralded the introduction of the Irish coffee mugs which "let you serve coffee in a new and different way...eliminates use of saucers." The

original price of these mugs was $7.95 for a set of four. When they were discontinued in 1976, beverage mugs were selling for $22.00 for a set of four, and four Irish coffee mugs cost $27.00. The Irish coffee mugs, which are now selling for more than ten times their last cost through Jewel, have appreciated considerably since they were discontinued.

The two quart salad bowl is shown on the left side of the third shelf. It was introduced in 1937 as Jewel's Item No. 312, and cost ninety-five cents. When the bowl was discontinued in 1976, it cost $4.95. The long run of this bowl has produced a bountiful supply, thus, the current price is moderate.

The salad fork with the Autumn Leaf decal is very rare. The quality of this piece suggests it may have been made by Hall for Jewel. However, it appears to have been a sample or a sales award item. So few have been found there are doubts that it was ever offered for sale.

The 9" vegetable bowl appears on the right side of the third shelf. This bowl was only made for a few years, between 1937 and 1939. Therefore, it is rather difficult to find and has become expensive.

The two styles of oval bowls are shown on the bottom row. The bowl on the left is divided and is much harder to find than the undivided style. The divided bowl was designed to serve two vegetables in the same bowl and was available from 1957 through 1976. In 1976, the oval bowl sold for $7.95 and the divided bowl sold for $10.95. Today, the value of the divided bowl is about four times that of the regular oval bowl.

	Item	Introduced	Discontinued	Price
Top Photo:				
Row 1:	Sugar and lid, "Rayed"	1934	1940	$20.00 – 25.00
	Creamer, "Rayed"	1934	1940	$15.00 – 18.00
	Sugar and lid, ruffled-D	1940	1976	$15.00 – 18.00
	Creamer, ruffled-D	1934	1940	$9.00 – 12.00
Row 2:	Cup, ruffled-D	1936	1976	$5.00 – 6.00
	Saucer, ruffled-D	1936	1976	$1.00 – 1.50
	Cup, St. Denis	1942	1976	$18.00 – 22.00
	Saucer, St. Denis	1942	1976	$6.00 – 8.00
	Mug, conic	1966	1976	$50.00 – 60.00
	Mug, Irish coffee	1966	1976*	$90.00 – 120.00
Bottom Photo:				
Row 3:	Bowl, salad	1937	1976	$16.00 – 18.00
	Fork, salad			$400.00 – 500.00
	Bowl, 9" round	1937	1939	$75.00 – 85.00
Row 4:	Bowl, oval divided	1957	1976	$80.00 – 90.00
	Bowl, oval	1939	1976*	$18.00 – 20.00

*Re-issued in 1978.

22

AUTUMN LEAF DINNERWARE AND ACCESSORIES

There is no proof the cake lifter shown in the top photo was made by Hall. However, many collectors are searching for these accompanying pieces to enhance their collections. Although quite a few of the more advanced collectors own one, this cake lifter with the Autumn Leaf decal is not easily found. Another cake lifter (shown below) with a large Autumn Leaf decal in the center and a long gold stripe on the handle may also be found. Since this lifter is usually found with Harker cake plates, this style lifter was probably made by Harker. Neither of these cake lifters bears an identifying backstamp and some confusion has resulted in distinguishing these two old lifters from the new ones which are being made by a private individual. The new lifters are thicker and more square at the area where the blade rises toward the handle.

The round 9½" cake plate is one of the most commonly found pieces of Autumn Leaf. The cake plate was added to the line in 1937 and was discontinued in 1976. This was a truly multi-purpose item and was priced at seventy-five cents in 1937. It was designed to fit perfectly into the previously introduced metal cake carriers and could also be used as a serving plate or as a tile under the casseroles or coffee servers. In addition, the two raised rings on the underside allowed it to become a cover for the utility bowls.

The small two handled round bowl on the right side of the top row is a cream soup. It is shown here sitting on the breakfast cup saucer which is often used as an underplate for this piece.

The oval covered vegetable dish shown on the second row was introduced in 1940 and discontinued in 1976. Jewel's price for this piece in 1949 was $2.75. As with many other Jewel items, replacement of a damaged part was simple since the top and the bottom could be purchased separately.

The gravy boat was also introduced in 1940 and was discontinued in 1976. It is shown here sitting on the 8½" oval pickle dish which also doubles as the underplate for the gravy boat. The oval pickle was added to the line in 1942. In 1949, the gravy boat was priced at $1.25 and the cost of the pickle dish was .75¢.

Item	Introduced	Discontinued	Price
Top Photo:			
Row 1: Cake server			$500.00 – 550.00
Cake plate	1937	1976	$14.00 – 16.00
Cream soup	1950	1976	$25.00 – 28.00
Row 2: Dish, oval covered	1940	1976	$40.00 – 45.00
Gravy boat	1940	1976	$22.00 – 25.00
Gravy boat underplate	1942	1976	$18.00 – 20.00
Photo Below:			
Cake Server, Harker			$400.00 – 450.00

Harker cake lifter.

Page from a Jewel premium book.

JEWEL CHINA BOWL SET — ITEM NO. 313

JEWEL CHINA BOWL SET — ITEM NO. 313

JEWEL CHINA BOWL SET . . . . . ITEM NO. 313

Three bowls of four-fold purpose—mixing, baking, serving, or storing. Not affected by oven heat or refrigerator cold. Non-absorbent, and decorated in the exquisite, exclusive Jewel pattern. The 1, 2, and 3½ quart bowls measure 6¾, 7½ and 8¾ inches across, respectively. They nest conveniently for storage.

20

An Appealing Dessert . . . Prepared and Served in a Jewel China Bowl

RICE PUDDING

2 eggs	½ cup sugar
2 cups milk	⅛ teaspoon Jewel Cinnamon
½ cup raisins	¾ teaspoon salt
1¼ cups cooked Jewel Rice	1 tablespoon powdered sugar

Separate eggs, beat yolks, and add two tablespoons of the milk. Place remaining milk in double boiler, add washed raisins, and cook until raisins are soft (about 15 minutes). Add the rice, cook five minutes, then stir in egg yolks, sugar, spice, and salt. Mix well, cook for three minutes. Pour into medium size Jewel China bowl. Beat egg whites, add powdered sugar, and spread over top of pudding. Bake in slow oven (325°F.) until delicately brown.

Page from a Jewel premium book.

AUTUMN LEAF KITCHENWARE

Two styles of Autumn Leaf bean pots are pictured on the top shelf — one handle and two handle. Of the two, the one handle variety is much harder to find. The two handle version was introduced in 1960, but was re-issued in 1978. There are slight differences between the two issues. The major difference is in the gold decoration on top of the handles. The older one has three gold lines and the newer one has a single gold stripe on the handle. Although the lids for both the one handle and two handle bean pots are the same size, they are not interchangeable. The lid to the two handle pot simply has a gold band around the knob, while the lid to the other one has the gold band plus an Autumn Leaf flower in the center of the knob. The newer two handle bean pot has closed the gap in price with the older one and generally seems to be bringing about $20.00 to $25.00 less.

Three different sizes of fluted bakers are shown on the second row. The largest holds three pints and sold for .85¢ in 1939. The one in the middle holds two pints and the smallest one holds ten ounces. The two pint fluted baker is not easy to find and the price of this size baker is rising steadily. The small baker is commonly found and was re-issued in 1978. The newer baker is about ¼" larger than the original baker.

The covered family casserole was introduced as a special premium for Jewel's 36th anniversary in 1935. The price of this item in 1939 was $1.75. The pie baker, which is shown in the center of row three baked a 9½" pie and was guaranteed to heat evenly. This resulted in a perfectly baked pie with "no burnt crusts." The shallow oval bowl on the right side of the third row holds twelve ounces and is often called a Fort Pitt oval baker. It was a convenient item since it held individual size portions and allowed the food to be baked and served in the same dish. However, as the high price indicates, these are difficult to find today.

The oval baker pictured below is similar in shape to the Fort Pitt baker, but it is larger. This baker holds two pints and measures 10" long by 7½" wide by 2¼" deep. At the present time, only a few of these have been found.

The three piece utility bowl set was introduced in 1939. If the number available today is any indication, this must have been one of Jewel's more successful offerings. The set cost $2.65 when it was introduced and had only increased to $4.95 by 1960. The three-piece set consisted of a large 3½ quart bowl, a medium-sized 2 quart bowl, and a small 1 quart bowl. They were advertised as being ideal for mixing, baking, serving, and storing.

	Item	Introduced	Discontinued	Price
Row 1:	Bean pot, 1-handle, 2¼ qt.			$550.00 − 675.00
	Bean pot, 2-handle	1960	1976*	$180.00 − 225.00
Row 2:	Baker, French, 3 pt.	1936	1976	$16.00 − 18.00
	Baker, French, 2 pt.	1966	1976	$90.00 − 110.00
	Baker, French, 4½" (not pictured)	1978	1978*	$25.00 − 30.00
	Baker, French, 4⅛"	1966	1976	$5.00 − 7.00
Row 3:	Casserole, round, 2 qt.	1935	1976	$25.00 − 30.00
	Pie baker	1937	1976	$25.00 − 27.00
	Baker, Fort Pitt, 12 oz.	1966	1976	$125.00 − 135.00
Row 4:	Bowl, 9", "Radiance"	1933	1976	$20.00 − 22.00
	Bowl, 7½", "Radiance"	1933	1976	$14.00 − 16.00
	Bowl, 6", "Radiance"	1933	1976	$10.00 − 12.00

*Re-issued 1978

Rare 10" Autumn Leaf oval baker.
Price
$325.00 − 375.00

AUTUMN LEAF KITCHENWARE

The modern-style cookie jar with the two big ear-like handles was added to the Autumn Leaf line in 1957. Jewel liked to call these handles "easy-grip" and sold the cookie jar for $3.00. The shape of the jar came from a line designed by Eva Zeisel and many collectors call this style "Zeisel" to distinguish this cookie jar from the earlier shape cookie jar which is shown in the center of the top row.

The old style cookie jar was introduced for Christmas 1936. It was a dual purpose item since it could also be used as a bean pot. This cookie jar sold for $1.50 and was only offered for three years.

The Autumn Leaf four-piece stack set is pictured on the right side of the top row. It was called the stackette set in Jewel's ads and consists of three separate stacking containers and one lid. Each of the stacking units is a different size. The bottom one holds 34 ounces; the center one 24 ounces; and the top one 18 ounces. The complete set sold for $5.25 in 1960.

The ball-shaped, beverage jug was an outstanding success for Jewel. This may be seen by the availability of this item today at shows and flea markets. It has a 5½ pint capacity and was designed with an ice lip to trap ice cubes while pouring.

An Autumn Leaf batter jug is shown in the center of the second row. Not much is known about when this piece was made. It may have been a special promotion since it is quite rare to find one today.

The 2½ pint utility pitcher was introduced in 1937. It was a multi-purpose kitchen item which was convenient for either beverages or batter.

Tidbit trays made an appearance in 1954. These trays were made from plates in the regular dinnerware line. However, plates which were selected for use in the trays do not have a backstamp in the normal position. The large 10¼" plates have an off-center backstamp so the holes for the center handle were not drilled through the backstamp. Also, the smaller plates which are used in the tidbit have no backstamp. The three-tiered tidbit offered in the 1960 catalog sold for $4.00. At various times a two-tiered tidbit was also available.

	Item	Introduced	Discontinued	Price		
Row 1:	Cookie jar, Zeisel	1957	1969	$150.00	–	175.00
	Cookie jar, "Rayed"	1936	1939	$150.00	–	175.00
	Stack set	1951	1976	$75.00	–	90.00
Row 2:	Ball jug, #3	1938	1976	$25.00	–	30.00
	Batter jug, "Sundial"			$1,800.00	–	2,200.00
	Jug, 2½ pt., "Rayed"	1937	1976	$14.00	–	16.00
Row 3:	Tidbit, 3-tier	1954	1969	$85.00	–	95.00
	Tidbit, 2-tier	1954	1969	$45.00	–	55.00

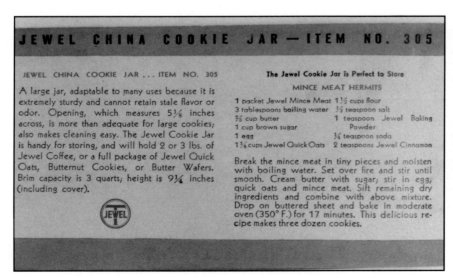

Jewel pamphlet describing "Rayed" cookie jar and suggesting a recipe.

AUTUMN LEAF COFFEE POTS AND TEAPOTS

The first Autumn Leaf coffee pot appeared in 1934. It was a nine-cup server introduced as part of a complete coffee service set which also included the oval 18¾" metal tray, an asbestos hot pad, and the old style sugar and creamer. The price of the complete set was $5.25 in 1937. The coffee server was also sold with an optional metal dripper made by the West Bend Aluminum Company. This dripper had also been used on previous Jewel all-metal coffee pots. The nine-cup server remained in the line until 1949.

In November 1936, Jewel added another coffee server to the Autumn Leaf line. This was an eight-cup maker and was lauded in their ads as being "improved for the making of perfect coffee and modernized in appearance." The lid of this pot would not fit the metal dripper. The new dripper was designed to "aid in the flow of water and to simplify coffee making." Apparently this new concept was short-lived. Ads for the eight-cup coffee server from late 1937 indicate the dripper was redesigned. The new dripper had the Autumn Leaf motif and was made so the cover of the coffee server also fit the dripper. On occasion, glass drippers will be found with some coffee servers. Coffee servers with glass drippers are illustrated in Jewel News publications during the early 1940s. The wartime restrictions during World War II necessitated this alteration. In later years, the eight-cup coffee pot came complete with a measuring spoon and an asbestos pad. This style set sold for $6.25 in the 1960 Jewel catalog.

The introduction of another coffee maker was also prompted by wartime restrictions. The five-cup all-china coffee maker made an appearance in 1942. The new design was implemented to meet the government's request to conserve coffee and also eliminated the need for the use of any metal in its manufacture. According to the ads the china dripper conserved coffee since it was designed "to bring out the maximum flavor so less than the usual amount of coffee is needed to brew a cup of normal strength."

The ultimate in automation in coffee brewing was achieved in 1957 when the automatic electric percolator was added to the line. It featured a safety-lock top, switched automatically to warming heat after brewing, and was guaranteed for a full year against any defects in workmanship. The retail price of this marvel was only $19.95.

Teapots played an important role in the early development of the Autumn Leaf line. The first teapot, the Newport shape, was introduced in 1933. It was a square 7-cup teapot which sold for $1.50. Two years later, it was replaced by a combination tea/coffee pot. This was the familiar long-spout pot which could be used to make either seven cups of tea or four cups of coffee. A small metal dripper was provided to institute the conversion from a teapot to a coffee pot. This new pot was also priced at $1.50. In 1978, a special issue of 106 long spout teapots was made by Hall China for Jewel to be given as sales awards.

The Newport teapot was re-issued in 1978. There are several differences between the old version and the newer one. The old teapot has no gold around the tip of the spout and the decal is larger than the decal on the later teapot. The teapot from 1978 has gold around the tip of the spout and has a decal with a pink leaf. The two lids are also different. The hole in the older lid is to the side of the knob while the hole in the newer lid is in front of the knob.

The advent of the seven-cup Aladdin teapot in 1942 with the china tea strainer eliminated the need for the metal tea ball. Judging from the number of Aladdins seen today, the success of this teapot must have been phenomenal. Autumn Leaf purists collect two different versions of this teapot — long spout and short spout. The difference here was probably not intentional. Instead, the variation appears to be the result of slight mold variations. The Aladdin teapot was listed in a 1960 catalog for $4.25.

	Item	Introduced	Discontinued	Price
Row 1:	Coffee pot, 9-cup, "Rayed"	1934	1949	$55.00 – 65.00
	Coffee pot, 8-cup, "Rayed" / open drip (not shown)	1936	1937	$32.00 – 37.00
	Coffee pot, 8-cup, "Rayed"	1937	1976	$50.00 – 60.00
Row 2:	Electric Percolator	1957	1969	$280.00 – 320.00
	Drip coffee, all-china	1942	1945	$240.00 – 260.00
	Teapot, "Rayed" long spout	1935	1942	$50.00 – 60.00
Row 3:	Teapot, 1930s Newport	1933	1935	$155.00 – 175.00
	Teapot, 1970s Newport	1978	1978	$110.00 – 130.00
	Teapot, Aladdin	1942	1976	$55.00 – 65.00

AUTUMN LEAF CANISTERS, CONDIMENT SETS, SHAKERS, AND WARMERS

A few of the pieces pictured on the opposite page are among the scarcest in the Autumn Leaf pattern. The "Medallion" style shakers shown in the middle photo are the only ones that have been found as of this writing. The sugar and tea canisters have now been joined by a coffee canister. If anyone can offer any assistance in finding the fourth canister to complete the canister set, I'm sure they would make the owner of these three lonely canisters very happy. Another partial set of canisters has been found. These canisters have decals which are arranged differently from those in the photo. These sample items came from former employees who got them from Jewel's employee store. A few other sample items have shown up in recent years, but it seems likely that most of these rarities are out of the attics now.

The ruffled base shakers were designed to be used with the Autumn Leaf dinnerware service. According to sources at Hall, the small-size version was introduced first. However, these were too small to be practical and they were soon replaced with the larger size shakers. The first pair of ruffled base shakers shown on the second row is the normal-size pair. They were first offered in 1939, and were priced at four pairs for $1.00. The pair shown next to them is smaller — just 2" high — and only a few pairs of this size have been found. For a more distinct comparison between the two see the top photo.

The handled shakers and drip jar comprise the range set which was introduced in 1936. The price of the complete set in 1939 was $1.50. Many of the drip jars were used for other purposes, such as soup bowls or lidless butters. Therefore, a surplus of bottoms exists today.

The first warmer shown is not actually Autumn Leaf since it lacks the decal. However the attractive gold decoration on this piece makes it desirable as a go-along item. The oval warmer in the center was designed for use with the Aladdin shape teapot. The round warmer on the right was used with the coffee servers or the round casserole. Both shapes contain a built-in candleholder in the center and came boxed with four candles. The selling price of both warmers in 1960, the year they were discontinued, was $2.25.

Three different style condiment jars are pictured on the bottom row. In answer to a lot of questions, no china spoons were provided for these jars by either Jewel or Hall. The larger jar on the left is a marmalade and the one in the center is a mustard. Both of these items made their appearance in 1938, and disappeared the following year. Even though both were only produced for a short time, collectors seem to have only moderate difficulty in obtaining them. Notice the underplates are different sizes. The diameter of the marmalade underplate is 6" and the diameter of the mustard underplate is 4¾". The 3½" tall condiment jar on the right is not commonly found. Very little is known about this jar and it is believed to have been a sample submitted by Hall in about 1941. Jewel must have rejected this design, and since it was never put into regular production, very few collectors will ever experience the joy of owning one.

Item	Introduced	Discontinued	Price
Middle Photo:			
Row 1: Canister			$1,000.00 – 1,200.00
Shaker "Medallion"			$600.00 – 750.00
Row 2: Shaker, regular size, ruffled, ea.	1939	1976	$11.00 – 13.00
Shaker, miniature, ruffled, pr.	1939	1939	$550.00 – 650.00
Shaker, range, ea.	1936	1976	$12.00 – 14.00
Shaker, left hand			$18.00 – 22.00
Drip jar	1936	1976	$15.00 – 18.00
Bottom Photo:			
Row 3: Warmer, no decal			$25.00 – 30.00
Warmer, oval	1955	1960	$125.00 – 140.00
Warmer, round	1956	1960	$110.00 – 120.00
Row 4: Condiment, marmalade	1938	1939	$65.00 – 75.00
Condiment, mustard	1938	1939	$60.00 – 70.00
Condiment, experimental			$800.00 – 1,000.00

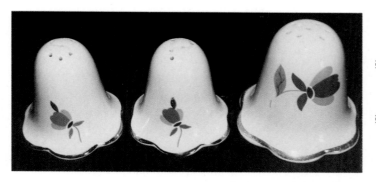

Comparison of rare miniature shakers with normal ruffled shakers.

AUTUMN LEAF BUTTER DISHES

Two sizes of butter dishes were made for Jewel by Hall – one pound and one-quarter pound. As may be seen from the photo, there are several different styles of each size butter. A quick glance at the prices indicates none of these butters is common. However, one style in each size will be obtainable for the average collector with a little diligent searching.

The first butter dish listed in the Jewel catalog was the one pound dish shown in the center of the second row. It was introduced in 1959, and sold for $3.25. Its design proved to be inconvenient and this butter was discontinued after only one season. This style of pound butter was in very short supply until a quantity was discovered in a warehouse in the early eighties. This find has been slowly absorbed by collectors and the price of this butter has been steadily rising as its availability decreases.

The other two one pound butter dishes are probably experimental designs submitted by Hall as improvements to the original version. Both are the same shape as the original, but they have a knob which is easier to grip. The only difference between these two butters is the one on the right has a bud knob with rays and the one on the left has the same style knob without the rays. The lid without the rays is 5/16" taller than the one with the rays. The underplate for all three styles is the same.

The replacement for the pound butter was introduced in 1961 in the form of the one-quarter pound butter shown on the left side of the top row. Another variety of one-quarter pound butter, the wings style, shown in the center of the top row, was also introduced the same year. Judging from their availability today, this shape must not have been very popular. The other one-quarter pound butter with the smooth top grip is found frequently enough to suggest it was more than a mere sample item. It is possible this may have been a sales award item. The underplate for the first and third butters is the same, while the underplate for the wings style butter is more deeply curved.

The photo at the bottom of the next page shows an unusual Zephyr shape one pound butter with the Autumn Leaf decal. This butter was never offered to Jewel customers and only a few examples are known.

Item	Introduced	Discontinued	Price
Top Photo:			
Row 1: Butter, ¼ pound, regular	1961	1976	$175.00 – 225.00
Butter, ¼ pound, wings	1961		$900.00 – 1,200.00
Butter, ¼ pound, smooth top grip			$500.00 – 600.00
Row 2: Butter, one pound, bud knob			$1,200.00 – 1,400.00
Butter, one pound, regular	1959	1960	$300.00 – 350.00
Butter, one pound, bud "rayed" knob			$800.00 – 1000.00
Bottom Photo:			
Zephyr shape butter			$2,000.00 – 2,500.00

AUTUMN LEAF ACCESSORIES

The coaster and demitasse cup and saucer in the top photo were purchased by a Jewel employee at the employee store. Jewel never made these items available to the public.

An Autumn Leaf clock was introduced in 1956. A clock which still has its original movement will have the name "HALL" stamped on its face. Clocks could be hung on the wall or set upright on a shelf with the use of an attached wire stand. The clock shown on the left is the style which is normally found. Two other styles of clocks, which have been produced from the regular Autumn Leaf cake plate may be found. One version is a salesman's award clock which was given as a prize to outstanding sales personnel by Jewel. An example of this clock is illustrated in our first book, *The Collector's Guide to Hall China*. The other type is a clock which is currently being produced for sale by a private individual. This clock is shown on the right in the picture. An easy way to tell the difference between the two cakeplate-style clocks is to look at the size and placement of the numbers. The salesman's award clock has small numbers placed a few inches from the edge of the cakeplate, similar in position to the standard Jewel clock. The numbers on the clock which is currently being made are larger and are arranged near the edge of the cakeplate. The cost of this new clock is $65.00.

So few morning tea sets, shown on the second shelf, have been found that it can be assumed they were never a regular production item. This set is the same style as other morning sets which were made in some of Hall's kitchenware patterns. The teapot is identical to the teapot used in the No. 1 tea set. However the sugar and creamer were restyled and feature the addition of handles. Also new is a lid for the sugar which matches the style of the teapot lid.

Two varieties of bud vases are shown. Variations in size and location of the decal are common occurrences in the Autumn Leaf pattern and these two vases are an excellent example. The more commonly found vase is the one with the larger decal shown on the right.

The two large vases shown on the top row of the bottom picture have no backstamp to indicate they were made by Hall. Nor is there any evidence to associate them with Jewel Tea. However, they are striking examples of pieces with the Autumn Leaf decal and exhibit the same excellent quality in both pottery and glaze which other Hall pieces possess.

The footed cakestand and the footed candy were both introduced in 1959. The metal base could be unscrewed from the china piece and used as a candle holder. Originally, each piece sold for $4.95. Today, the footed cakestand is found much more readily than the footed candy.

The covered candy jar shown in the center of the bottom row is probably an experimental one-of-a-kind piece. Sources indicated that it was made by Hall and submitted to Jewel as a sample, but was never put into production.

	Item	Introduced	Discontinued	Price
Top Photo:				
	Coaster			UND
	Cup/saucer, demi			UND
Middle Photo:				
Row 1:	Clock	1956	1959	$400.00 – 500.00
	Clock, new	1980		$65.00
	Clock, salesman's award (not shown)	1980	1980	$300.00 – 350.00
Row 2:	Sugar and lid, morning			$350.00 – 450.00
	Teapot, morning			$900.00 – 1,100.00
	Creamer, morning			$300.00 – 400.00
	Candleholder, 4"			$700.00 – 1,000.00
Bottom Photo:				
Row 1:	Vase, small decal	1940		$175.00 – 195.00
	Vase, regular decal	1940		$175.00 – 195.00
	Vase or lamp base, 11"			$850.00 – 950.00
	Vase, 7¾"			$850.00 – 950.00
Row 2:	Cakestand, metal base	1958	1969	$120.00 – 135.00
	Candy jar, experimental			$1,500.00 – 1,800.00
	Candy, metal base	1958	1969	$450.00 – 500.00

AUTUMN LEAF PAPER AND PLASTIC ARTICLES

Many different styles of hotpads have been found associated with the Autumn Leaf pattern. Some are readily identifiable with the pattern and some which were supplied with the coffee servers lack the pattern and are not commonly thought of as Autumn Leaf. The black asbestos hotpads shown on the top shelf were supplied with coffee service sets during the 1930s. A cream color cardboard hotpad with a tin back was introduced in 1937. Another type of hotpad with a creamy wax-like coating and a green or red felt backing was introduced later.

The holiday fruit cake tin is from the late 1970s, but some collectors who like to have an example of everything in Autumn Leaf are adding these to their collections. The wooden bowl shows a lot of age and the enameled design appears to be original. No information is available on its history.

Plastic covers for appliances and bowls were introduced in 1950. An eight piece set of bowl covers in assorted sizes with a drawstring holder sold for $1.00 in 1950. In 1960 a seven piece set which included a toaster cover and six bowl covers in assorted sizes sold for .98¢. The bowl covers ranged in size from five inches to thirteen inches. Other plastic covers included a Mary Dunbar mixer cover and a standard-size mixer cover.

Two styles of playing cards were introduced in 1943. Attractively boxed sets of pinochle decks or regular double deck sets were available. The price of a box of regular cards in 1943 was $1.50. Collectors should be aware that new decks of playing cards are currently on the market. Careful examination of these cards will reveal an almost microscopic date on the reverse side of each card. Also new decks are complete with a 1992 calendar card.

Item	Introduced	Discontinued	Price
Coaster, 3⅛"			$4.00 — 6.00
Hotpad, 10¾", oval			$10.00 — 13.00
Hotpad, 7¼", felt back	1946		$12.00 — 14.00
Hotpad, 7¼", tin back	1937		$8.00 — 10.00
Mixer cover, standard	1950	1961	$40.00 — 50.00
Mixer cover, Mary Dunbar	1950	1961	$40.00 — 50.00
Plastic bowl covers, 8 pc. set	1950	1961	$90.00 — 100.00
Playing cards, regular deck	1943	1946	$140.00 — 160.00
Playing cards, pinochle deck	1943	1946	$150.00 — 175.00
Toaster cover	1950	1961	$30.00 — 40.00
Tin, holiday fruit cake			$9.00 — 10.00
Wooden bowl			$300.00 — 350.00

AUTUMN LEAF CLOTH AND PAPER ARTICLES

An Autumn Leaf blanket was released by Jewel in 1979. It was made by Martex and came in three sizes and two colors. The twin size retailed for $22.99; the full size for $29.99; and the Queen/King size for $46.99. Another version, in addition to the standard color, is shown in the picture. This one has green leaves and lilac Autumn Leaf-style flowers.

Shelf paper was a premium which was offered in 1945. This issue of shelf paper had the pattern only on the edge and was available in sheets 9 feet long and 9¼ inches wide. In 1956 shelf paper was again offered. This newer shelf liner was 13" wide. It was made of plastic, came in rolls twelve feet long, and had an all-over design.

Magnetic note holders are a Jewel premium and have been offered for many years. The set consists of five different holders. One pictures a brown panel truck, another shows an Autumn Leaf cup and saucer, a third features a coffee grinder. The remaining two depict a horse drawn vending cart and an early Jewel delivery truck.

Mary Dunbar cookbooks are a favorite collectible of many Autumn Leaf collectors. They were produced for many years. Besides the excellent recipes, they feature many pieces of Autumn Leaf.

An 18" by 30" rubber backed fatigue mat was listed in a 1958 catalog. This was intended to be used by the busy housewife to stand on while ironing or doing dishes. To date only a few of these have been reported.

Item	Introduced	Discontinued	Price
Blanket, standard color, twin-size	1979		$140.00 – 160.00
Blanket, standard color, full-size	1979		$150.00 – 175.00
Blanket, standard color, king-size	1979		$150.00 – 175.00
Blanket, lilac color, full-size	1979		$100.00 – 125.00
Cookbook, Mary Dunbar			$12.00 – 15.00
Magnetic holders, set			$7.00 – 8.00
Pickle fork			$10.00 – 12.00
Shelf paper, pattern on edge, sheet	1945		$35.00 – 45.00
Shelf paper, all-over pattern, roll	1956	1957	$125.00 – 150.00

Item not pictured:

Fatigue mat			$450.00 – 550.00

Colorful Jewel cookbooks with Autumn Leaf china used in the illustrations.

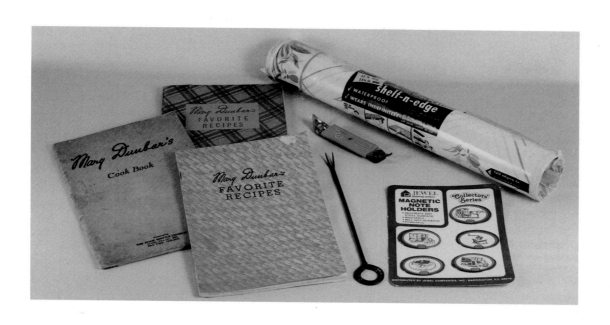

AUTUMN LEAF LINEN AND SILVERWARE

The items shown here were not made by Hall. However they are the Autumn Leaf design and were made for the Jewel Company to compliment their existing china pattern. Many collectors of china are finding these accessories attractive additions to their collections.

Most Autumn Leaf linens, like many other collectible linens, have been subjected to many years of daily use and abuse. As a result, the availability of quality Autumn Leaf lines is limited, and prices are slowly creeping upward as more collectors are striving to add these treasures to their collections. Pieces which are stained, torn, or badly faded will only bring a fraction of the prices listed on the following page.

The muslin tablecloth and napkins were introduced as a set in 1937. The Autumn Leaf design ran just above a row of stripes along the edge and was repeated again in the center of the cloth. This set was discontinued in 1942.

In 1950, another tablecloth was offered. This tablecloth was plastic-coated cotton and came in two sizes. Both sizes had an all-over Autumn Leaf design and were discontinued in 1953.

The last tablecloth introduced was made of cotton sailcloth and appeared in 1955. There were two official sizes — 54" x 54" and 54" x 72". However, a 54" x 62" tablecloth also is appearing frequently. These were decorated with a border design featuring a gold stripe below an Autumn Leaf motif.

The history of the tablecloth with the aqua, purple, and yellow colors is unknown. It is an interesting find and only a few of these have been reported.

Curt-towels served a dual purpose. They could be used as dish towels, or curtain rods could be inserted in their wide hems to produce cafe curtains. In the photo the curt-towel is the article with the Autumn Leaf design, the cup and saucer, and the clock.

In 1958, Jewel offered a silverplate flatware service made by the International Silver Company. The sets were offered in a 24-piece service for six and a 50-piece service for eight. Serving pieces including a gravy ladle, meat fork, berry spoon, and sugar shell were also available as open stock items. Autumn silverplate pieces were no longer offered after 1959, but 1960 catalogs indicate special orders would still be accepted. In the photo on page 43, the silver plate knife and fork are on the right side; the silverplate spoon is at the bottom. Notice the silverplate pieces have square ends at the handle and the stainless ends are curved.

Autumn pattern stainless steel tableware made by the International Silver Company craftsmen became available in 1960. Sets were available in both 24-piece and 50-piece services. A 24-piece service sold for $19.95 in 1960. A six-piece place setting included a teaspoon, a soup spoon, a tablespoon, a dinner knife, a dinner fork, and a salad fork. Open stock items included a sugar shell, a solid serving spoon, a slotted serving spoon and a butter knife. Recently, a private company has revived the Autumn pattern stainless. A five-piece place setting of stainless tableware is being produced from the old International Silver silverplate dies. Thus, the new stainless differs in style from that of the old. Also, the backstamp on the new stainless is "C & C Collectible® 93."

A Jewel tablecloth with a modernistic design using Autumn Leaf colors is shown in the photo at the bottom of page 43. Due to the color similarities, some Autumn Leaf collectors are beginning to search for this style tablecloth.

Jewel's Autumn pattern stainless.

Item	Introduced	Discontinued	Price
Curt-towels, ea.	1957	1959	$40.00 – 50.00
Napkin, 16" square	1937	1942	$35.00 – 40.00
Silverware, 5 piece silverplate setting	1958	1959	$140.00 – 160.00
Silverware, 6 piece stainless setting	1960	1968	$125.00 – 145.00
Silverware, silverplate or stainless serving items			$40.00 – 60.00
Tablecloth, 56" x 81", muslin	1937	1942	$150.00 – 175.00
Tablecloth, 54" x 54", plastic	1950	1953	$125.00 – 145.00
Tablecloth, 54" x 72", plastic	1950	1953	$125.00 – 145.00
Tablecloth, 54" x 54", sailcloth	1955	1958	$85.00 – 95.00
Tablecloth, 54" x 62", sailcloth			$90.00 – 110.00
Tablecloth, 54" x 72", sailcloth	1955	1958	$110.00 – 125.00
Tea towel, 16" x 33"	1956	1957	$35.00 – 40.00
Tablecloth, modernistic			UND

AUTUMN LEAF TIN ACCESSORIES

During the last several years many new Autumn Leaf collectors have joined the ranks. These new collectors have joined with the more advanced collectors in focusing more attention on non-Hall and non-china Autumn Leaf pieces. As a result the demand for tin accessories has increased dramatically. Collectors still prefer to buy pieces in mint condition so care should be exercised when attempting to clean metal items with a lacquered finish. The finish practically dissolves when subjected to washing with water. Dealers should also remember that any pricing labels which are placed on the lacquered surface will cause damage to the finish.

The rectangular-shaped canisters on the top shelf are a four-piece set. They have plastic handles on their lids which are easily damaged. The so-called "chip resistant baked on enamel finish" is a little tougher than the coating on some of the earlier tinware, but it can also be damaged if handled carelessly.

The cleanser can is quite a prize. Any of these which are offered for sale seem to find a new home immediately.

The tin canister set in the center consists of three different size canisters. The large canister appeared in 1935, and the other two sizes followed the next year. The introduction of the smallest canister preceded the arrival of the medium-size canister by a few months. The original canister was designed to hold three pounds of coffee and sold for .50¢ in 1936. The price of the three piece set was $1.00 in 1939. None of the canisters has a label to designate its contents. There are two slight variations of these sets. One style is marked "TINDECO" on the bottom and has gold lacquered insides and gold bottoms. The other style is unmarked and has a gold bottom and silver insides. The smallest canister is the most plentiful.

The round four-piece canister set introduced in 1960 had a "chip-resistant baked enamel finish" and Coppertone finished lids with black plastic knobs. The sugar and flour each hold five pounds and the coffee and tea hold 1½ pounds. The set retailed for $3.98 when it was introduced.

The picnic thermos is hard-to-find in good condition. Many have been destroyed by rust through the negligence of an uncaring owner. This, coupled with a war-shortened production of only one year due to the scarcity of tin, has caused many collectors to search a long time to obtain one. The thermos has an outer jacket made of tin with a lacquered finish bearing the Autumn Leaf motif. The heavy weight of the thermos is due to the thick stoneware lining which is used for insulation.

A metal kitchen chair with a folding step was listed in a 1941 catalog. The retail price was $2.75. The chair had a baked enamel finish with the Autumn Leaf decal on the front of the backrest. Wartime restrictions on the use of metals probably resulted in the production of very few of these chairs.

	Item	Introduced	Discontinued	Price
Row 1:	Canister, 8¼", sugar	1959		$35.00 – 40.00
	Canister, 8¼", flour	1959		$35.00 – 40.00
	Canister, 4", tea	1959		$32.00 – 37.00
	Canister, 4", coffee	1959		$32.00 – 37.00
	Cleanser can			$250.00 – 300.00
Row 2:	Canister, round, 8¼"	1935	1942	$25.00 – 30.00
	Canister, round, 7"	1935	1942	$20.00 – 22.00
	Canister, round, 6"	1935	1942	$12.00 – 14.00
	Sifter			$350.00 – 400.00
Row 3:	Canister, round, tall, (copper-color lid)	1960	1962	$33.00 – 37.00
	Canister, round, short, (copper-color lid)	1960	1962	$25.00 – 27.00
	Thermos	1941	1941	$300.00 – 350.00
Metal accessories not pictured:				
	Chair, kitchen	1939	1942	$500.00 – 550.00
	Waste basket	1951	1951	$225.00 – 250.00

45

AUTUMN LEAF TIN ACCESSORIES

The lacquer finish on metal accessories was easily damaged through use and by washing. Any damage drastically reduces the desirability and value of a piece. Most collectors are seeking these metal items in almost mint condition.

Glass serving trays are difficult to find in good condition. They were only made for a short time, therefore they only turn up infrequently. However, to complicate matters, the design, which is painted on the reverse side of the glass, is easily damaged by water. If care is not taken in cleaning these trays, and water gets between the glass and the backing, the paint will become wrinkled and the value of the tray will decrease substantially.

The bread box is a very desirable item for an Autumn Leaf collector to own. It was introduced in 1936, and was a casualty of the tin shortages of World War II. Bread boxes were designed to hold three regular-size loaves or two larger sandwich loaves. Since they opened conveniently from the front they could be easily fit between two cabinet shelves. In 1938, the price of the bread box was $1.45.

According to Jewel ads the metal coffee dispenser "released the exact measure for one cup of coffee with each pull of the lever." The price of the dispenser was $2.50 in 1942, when it was discontinued. The dispenser was designed to be wall mounted and featured a glass window so the remaining quantity of coffee could be determined easily. Its war curtailed production has caused this item to be in short supply today.

Two different styles of cake safes are available to the collector. The older one was released in 1935, and has the Autumn Leaf pattern on top as well as on the side of the lid. It sold for $1.25 in 1936. The newer one was issued in 1950, and lacks the pattern on the top of the lid. Both cake safes were equipped with a locking handle and were designed to carry a standard 9" cake placed on the matching Jewel Autumn Leaf cakeplate. Notice also, the lighter color of the older cakesafe, which is characteristic of the pre-war tinware.

	Item	Introduced	Discontinued	Price
Row 1:	Glass tray			$110.00 – 135.00
Row 2:	Bread box	1937	1941	$200.00 – 225.00
	Coffee dispenser	1941	1941	$150.00 – 175.00
Row 3:	Cake safe	1950	1953	$22.00 – 25.00
	Cake safe	1935	1941	$35.00 – 40.00
Below:	Tray, 18¾", oval	1934	1938	$45.00 – 55.00

Complete coffee service first offered in 1934.

AUTUMN LEAF MISCELLANEOUS GLASS AND PLASTIC

Jewel's attempt, in 1960, to market Melmac with an Autumn Leaf pattern appears to have been half-hearted. Many of the pieces offered in the Melmac Autumn Leaf sets lacked the pattern. For example, in the 16-piece starter set only the 10" dinner plates and the saucers had the pattern; the cups and fruit dishes were plain Melmac pieces. Also, in the larger 45-piece service, the sugar, creamer, soups, cups, and vegetable dish lacked decoration. The only decorated pieces of Melmac which collectors will find available are 10" dinner plates, 8" salad plates, saucers, and a 14" platter.

The Linoettes (placemats) are from the early 1940s. They have scalloped edges and the Autumn Leaf pattern in the corners. The plastic apron is not easy to find. The few that have surfaced have attracted a lot of attention from collectors.

The insulated mug and tumbler were sample items which were bought in Jewel's employee store. Undoubtedly, there were some advantages to working for Jewel, even if the former employees did not realize it at the time.

The Royal Glasbake articles shown on the two shelves below are part of a short-lived bakeware set introduced in 1961. The set consists of a divided oval bowl, two sizes of covered casseroles, and a four piece bowl set. These items were not very popular and were only offered for one season.

Below:	Price:
Casserole, Glasbake	$15.00 – 18.00
Divided bowl, Glasbake	$12.00 – 15.00
Bowl set, 4-pc., Glasbake	$30.00 – 35.00
Insulated mug	UND
Insulated tumbler	UND
Plastic apron	$450.00 – 550.00
Placemat, plastic	$35.00 – 40.00

(Not shown) Melmac:	
Bowl, soup	$5.00 – 7.00
Creamer	$7.00 – 9.00
Cup/saucer	$6.00 – 8.00
Plate, 7" salad	$5.00 – 7.00
Plate, 10" dinner	$7.00 – 9.00
Platter, 14"	$16.00 – 18.00
Sugar	$7.00 – 9.00

Autumn Leaf place mats.

Insulated cup and tumbler bought from Jewel's employee store.

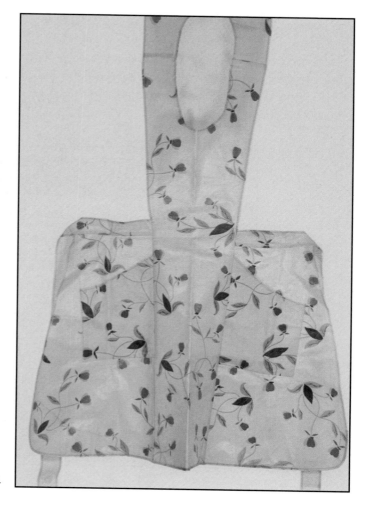

Hard-to-find plastic apron.

PORCELAIN-CLAD STEEL COOKWARE AND BAKEWARE

Autumn design porcelain-clad steel cookware was a Jewel exclusive introduced in 1979. The cookware set consists of seven pieces. It includes a 1½-quart covered saucepan, a 2-quart covered saucepan, a 5-quart covered Dutch oven, and a 9½" open skillet. The Dutch oven cover also fits the skillet. Retail price for this set was $59.95. Also, offered at the same time was a matching teakettle which sold for $16.95. By the next year the price of the teakettle had increased to $18.99.

In 1980, Jewel added three new sets to compliment its original offering. All were made of the familiar enameled porcelain metal which was supposed to be chip resistant and easy to clean.

A three-piece mixing bowl set consisted of bowls in the 1⅓-quart, 2-quart, and 2⅔-quart sizes. This set and a 2-quart fondue set were priced at $29.99 each. The fondue set consisted of a 2-quart pot with a brown metal cover, a metal rack with a fork stand, 6 color-coded forks, a chrome-plated burner, and a brown metal tray.

The rectangular pieces of the bakeware/casserole set came in 1-quart, 2-quart, and 3-quart sizes. They were conveniently designed so the same dish could be utilized for cooking, serving, and storing leftovers. The casseroles had tab handles for easy handling and featured plastic storage lids which snapped on tightly to ensure the safekeeping of leftovers.

	Cookware/Bakeware	Price
Row 1:	Dutch oven, 5-quart	$90.00 – 110.00
	Fondue set	$175.00 – 200.00
Row 2:	Saucepan, 2-quart	$50.00 – 60.00
	Saucepan, 1½-quart	$50.00 – 60.00
	Saucepan	$35.00 – 45.00
Row 3:	Mixing bowl, 2⅔-quart	$25.00 – 30.00
	Mixing bowl, 2-quart	$20.00 – 25.00
	Mixing bowl, 1⅓-quart	$12.00 – 17.00
Row 4:	Teakettle	$175.00 – 225.00
	Bakeware/casserole set, 3-piece	$150.00 – 185.00
Not pictured:	Skillet, 9½"	$85.00 – 95.00
Below:	Metal tray with red border	$45.00 – 55.00

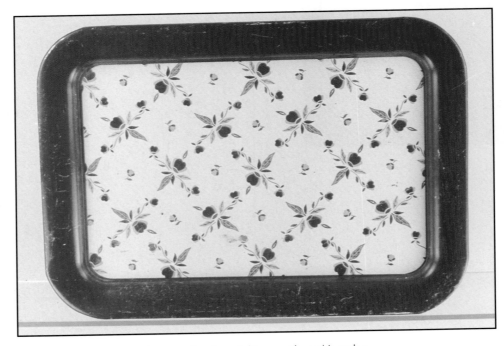

Autumn Leaf metal tray with red border.

AUTUMN LEAF GLASS AND METAL ACCESSORIES

Glassware with the Autumn Leaf motif continues to be popular among collectors. The most desirable items are those pictured on the top row, however the Douglas pieces are becoming increasingly collectible although many collectors are finding them prohibitively expensive.

The exciting news in this area is the discovery of a new style frosted tumbler. It is a 6½" tall pilsner-shaped tumbler with frosted sides and a clear bottom. The bottom has the Libbey "L" mark and the sides have the all-over Autumn design. The bad news for collectors is that this is a sample item which was never offered for sale by Jewel. Therefore, only a handful of collectors can ever hope to own one of these pieces.

The frosted tumblers on the first row were made for Jewel by Libbey. The tumbler with the bands at the bottom is the hardest to find. Of the two frosted tumblers with the Autumn Leaf motif, the large one is the easiest to find. A set of six of the large tumblers sold for $1.98 in 1949.

The clear tumblers on the top shelf with the Autumn-like design were made by Brockway. The tumblers were offered in three sizes and disappeared quickly from Jewel's catalog after a short trial in the mid-seventies. As a result of the short run, these tumblers are not easy to find and they are expensive for a newer item.

The clear tumblers on the second shelf were made for Jewel by Libbey in the early sixties. These tumblers were

advertised as having "an all-over Autumn pattern in 22K gold and etched frost motif with Safedge Gold rims which defy chipping." The four pieces offered consisted of two sizes of heavy bottom tumblers, a footed goblet, and a footed sherbet. A set of eight tumblers sold for $3.98, and sets of sherbets or goblets for $5.98.

The first Autumn pattern Douglas piece — a combination coffee percolator, carafe, and candle warmer — appeared in Jewel's 1960 catalog. It had a 22K gold fused design, a Bakelite handle, and an anodized aluminum lid and collar. Like many other Jewel items this was a multi-purpose piece. It was presented as an 8-cup percolator, or a 12-cup instant coffee maker, tea maker, or beverage server. Other Douglas pieces introduced the following year included a sauce dish and hurricane lamp with a goldtone metal base. Several collectors have reported finding an unlisted ice-lip style pitcher similar in shape and size to the 8-cup coffee maker. This pitcher is shown at the bottom of the opposite page. To positively identify the Douglas Autumn pattern items look for the name Douglas stamped in gold near the bottom of the piece.

Jewel customers remember the metal canisters with the plastic lids coming filled with old fashioned hard Christmas candy. The goldtone candlesticks pictured on the third shelf are also used as the base for the footed cakeplate and footed candy shown on page 37.

	Item	Introduced	Discontinued	Price
Row 1:	Tumbler, banded			$25.00 – 27.00
	Tumbler, 5½", frosted	1940	1949	$18.00 – 20.00
	Tumbler, 3¾", frosted	1950	1953	$22.00 – 25.00
	Tumbler, 16 oz., Brockway	1975	1976	$45.00 – 50.00
	Tumbler, 13 oz., Brockway	1975	1976	$42.00 – 47.00
	Tumbler, 9 oz., Brockway	1975	1976	$42.00 – 47.00
Row 2:	Tumbler, 15 oz., Libbey	1960	1961	$50.00 – 55.00
	Tumbler, 10 oz., Libbey	1958	1961	$40.00 – 45.00
	Goblet, 10 oz., Libbey	1960	1961	$50.00 – 55.00
	Sherbet, 6½ oz., Libbey	1960	1961	$50.00 – 55.00
	Sauce dish, Douglas	1961	1962	$125.00 – 150.00
	Warmer base	1960	1962	$25.00 – 30.00
Row 3:	Percolator, Douglas	1960	1962	$200.00 – 225.00
	Canister, brown/gold			$9.00 – 11.00
	Canister, white plastic lid			$8.00 – 10.00
	Candlestick, pair			$60.00 – 70.00
Bottom:				
	Pitcher, Douglas, ice lip			$400.00 – 500.00
	Tumbler, pilsner-style			UND
Not pictured:				
	Hurricane lamp, Douglas, pair	1961	1962	$300.00 – 350.00

Douglas ice-lip water pitcher.

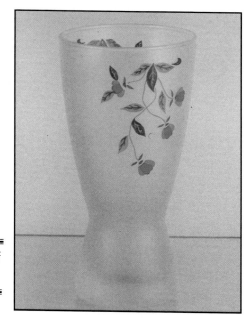

Rare frosted Autumn Leaf
pilsner-style tumbler.

BLUE BOUQUET

Hall China produced this decal line for the Standard Coffee Company of New Orleans, therefore, Blue Bouquet is a pattern which is found more frequently in the southeastern states. Production began in the early fifties and continued into the mid-sixties. All pieces of the D-style dinnerware can be found. Many china kitchenware pieces exist, and there are a limited number of metal accessories available.

Among the more frequently found pieces are the large salad bowl, the drip jar, the handled shakers, sugars and creamers, and the #3 "Medallion" jug. Hard-to-find pieces include the New England bean pot, the pretzel jar, the electric percolator, both leftovers, the soup tureen, and the spoon. Notice the special heating element on the electric percolator which fits between the base and the china dripper.

Metal kitchen items with the Blue Bouquet decal include canisters, coasters, shakers, a coffee dispenser, and a rectangular tray.

The photo below shows tumbler prototypes with the Blue Bouquet decal. The tumblers were found in the Toledo area which is the home of Libbey. Yellow markings on the tumblers suggest their former home may have been in the company's sample department. The two tumblers to the left are frosted. However, the one on the left has a narrow clear band around the top. The tumbler in the center is clear and the one on the right is frosted on the bottom half and clear on the top. Since other tumblers are not being found it is probably safe to assume these samples did not meet with approval and were never put into production.

The photo in the center of page 56 pictures a "Kadota" style all-china coffee pot and the 6-cup Boston teapot. Both pieces are hard to find. New items to the listing since the last book include a "Sundial" batter bowl, a "Five Band" cookie jar, and a #3 "Radiance" jug.

D-style Dinnerware	Price
Bowl, 5½", fruit	$5.00 – 7.50
Bowl, 6", cereal	$9.00 – 11.00
Bowl, 8½", flat soup	$15.00 – 20.00
Bowl, 9¼", round vegetable	$25.00 – 30.00
Cup	$10.00 – 12.00
Gravy boat	$25.00 – 30.00
Plate, 6"	$4.00 – 5.00
Plate, 7¼"	$7.00 – 8.00
Plate, 8¼"	$9.00 – 10.00
Plate, 9"	$12.00 – 14.00
Platter, 11¼", oval	$20.00 – 24.00
Platter, 13¼", oval	$25.00 – 27.00
Saucer	$1.50 – 2.50

Prototype Blue Bouquet tumblers made by Libbey.

Left to right: 1. Lower ¾ frosted, top ¼ clear; 2. Entire tumbler frosted; 3. Entire tumbler clear, 4. Bottom ½ frosted with clear bands, top ½ clear.

Row 1: Sugar and creamer, Boston; salad bowl, 9"; sugar and creamer, modern.
Row 2: Drip jar, "Thick Rim"; salt and pepper, handled; cup and saucer.
Row 3: Bowl, flat soup; bowl, 6" cereal; bowl, 5½" fruit.
Row 4: Plate, 9" dinner; plate 8¼"; plate, 6".
Row 5: Platter, 13" oval; bowl, 7¾" flared; custard, "Thick Rim."

Blue Bouquet

Kitchenware	Price	Kitchenware	Price
Baker, French, fluted	$15.00 – 18.00	Drip jar, "Thick Rim"	$25.00 – 30.00
Ball jug, #3	$50.00 – 75.00	Electric percolator	$250.00 – 295.00
Batter bowl, "Sundial"	UND	Jug, "Medallion," #3	$14.00 – 18.00
Bean pot, New England, #4	$100.00 – 125.00	Jug, "Radiance"	$60.00 – 70.00
Bowl, 7¾", flared	$30.00 – 35.00	Leftover, rectangular	$40.00 – 45.00
Bowl, 9", salad	$15.00 – 17.00	Leftover, square	$50.00 – 60.00
Bowl, 6", "Radiance"	$12.00 – 14.00	Pie baker	$27.00 – 32.00
Bowl, 7½", "Radiance"	$16.00 – 18.00	Pretzel jar	$95.00 – 125.00
Bowl, 9", "Radiance"	$22.00 – 27.00	Shakers, teardrop, ea.	$14.00 – 17.00
Bowl, 6", "Thick Rim"	$15.00 – 18.00	Shakers, handled, ea.	$14.00 – 17.00
Bowl, 7½", "Thick Rim"	$18.00 – 22.00	Spoon	$95.00 – 110.00
Bowl, 8½", "Thick Rim"	$25.00 – 30.00	Soup tureen	$220.00 – 250.00
Cakeplate	$22.00 – 27.00	Sugar and lid, Boston	$18.00 – 22.00
Casserole, "Radiance"	$30.00 – 35.00	Sugar and lid, modern	$18.00 – 22.00
Casserole, "Thick Rim"	$35.00 – 45.00	Teapot, Aladdin	$100.00 – 125.00
Coffee pot, "Five Band"	$50.00 – 60.00	Teapot, Boston	$110.00 – 145.00
Coffee pot, "Terrace"	$50.00 – 60.00		
Cookie jar, "Five Band"	UND	*Metal Accessories*	
Creamer, Boston	$10.00 – 12.00	Canister	$10.00 – 12.00
Creamer, modern	$10.00 – 12.00	Coaster	$4.00 – 5.00
Custard, "Thick Rim"	$11.00 – 13.00	Coffee dispenser	$20.00 – 25.00
Drip coffee pot, "Kadota,"		Shakers, ea.	$7.00 – 9.00
all china	$185.00 – 210.00	Tray, rectangular	$25.00 – 30.00

Left: Drip coffee pot, "Kadota" shape all china.
Right: Boston teapot.

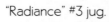

"Radiance" #3 jug.

Row 1: Pretzel jar; bean pot, New England #4; coffee pot, "Terrace."
Row 2: Ball jug #3; teapot with infuser, Aladdin; coffee pot, "Five Band."
Row 3: Soup tureen; jug, "Medallion" #3; casserole, "Thick Rim."
Row 4: Electric percolator; coffee dispenser; metal canisters.

CROCUS

Crocus is a Hall dinnerware pattern which was introduced in the mid-thirties. Assembling the multitude of pieces available in this pattern presents a challenge to even the most dedicated collector. Obtaining basic dinnerware pieces, which appear to be in short supply, is frustrating to some of the collectors who do not have access to major shows or flea markets. The 10" dinner plate has become virtually extinct.

The list of kitchenware shapes appearing with the Crocus decal is almost endless. Even some veteran Hall collectors have been astounded by some of the discoveries in this pattern. Some of the more interesting new pieces include a "Radiance" canister set, "Five Band" shakers, and a "Deco" style coffee pot. Unusual pieces of high desirability include the Donut shape teapot, the "Teardrop"-style shakers, the Aladdin teapot, the Streamline teapot, and the "Meltdown" sugar and creamer. In addition, just to keep collectors interested and to add a little confusion, there are two styles of all-china drip coffee pots, two different shape beverage mugs, and at least five different shapes of coffee pots with the Drip-O-lator backstamp. One of these is a shape called "Kadota" which we have only seen with a china dripper. The other four have a metal dripper which usually has the Crocus decal embossed on it. The "Five Band" coffee pot also will be found with a glass dripper which contains an electric heating element.

The New York teapot is most commonly found in the 6-cup size, but it has also been found in the 2-cup, 4-cup, 8-cup, and 12-cup sizes with the Crocus decal.

Several "Zephyr" style one-pound butter dishes and leftovers have been reported since the last book, but these pieces are still lacking from many collections. The matching water bottle is not being found as frequently. Notice the two different shapes of beverage mugs — 8 ounce flagon and tankard style. The lid to the tureen may be found smooth or with an embossed clover shape.

Metal pieces include a coffee dispenser, a soap dispenser, a round canister set, a bread box, a cake safe, and an oval tray.

Hall is again making selected limited edition pieces with the Crocus decal for a private company. All of the new issue is clearly marked with a special backstamp and no old shapes are being reproduced. For more information see the section on Re-issues in the back of the book.

D-style Dinnerware	Price
Bowl, 5½", fruit	$5.00 – 7.00
Bowl, 6", cereal	$12.00 – 14.00
Bowl, 8½", flat soup	$18.00 – 22.00
Bowl, 9¼", round vegetable	$27.00 – 32.00
Bowl, oval	$25.00 – 30.00
Cup	$12.00 – 15.00
Gravy boat	$25.00 – 30.00
Plate, 6"	$4.00 – 6.00

D-style Dinnerware	Price
Plate, 7¼"	$6.00 – 7.00
Plate, 8¼"	$8.00 – 9.00
Plate, 9"	$12.00 – 16.00
Plate, 10"	$35.00 – 45.00
Platter, 11¼", oval	$20.00 – 22.00
Platter, 13¼", oval	$25.00 – 30.00
Saucer	$1.50 – 2.50
Tidbit, 3-tier	$47.00 – 52.00

Mug, beverage (flagon style); teapot, Streamline; teapot, Aladdin; shakers, "Teardrop" style.

Row 1: Drip coffee pot, "Kadota"; ball jug #3.
Row 2: Bowl, 9" round; cup and saucer.
Row 3: Custard, "Radiance"; leftover, square; bowl, 5½" fruit.
Row 4: Plate, 6"; Plate, 9"; bowl, flat soup.
Row 5: Tray, oval, metal.

Crocus

Row 1: Drip coffee, "Jordan"; coffee pot, "Meltdown." Row 2: Coffee pot, "Waverly," teapot, Donut.

Kitchenware	Price	Kitchenware	Price
Baker, French, fluted	$20.00 – 22.00	Leftover, rectangular	$35.00 – 45.00
Ball jug, #3	$75.00 – 95.00	Leftover, square	$50.00 – 60.00
Bean pot, New England, #4	$95.00 – 115.00	Leftover, "Zephyr"-style	$175.00 – 225.00
Bowl, 9", salad	$16.00 – 18.00	Mug, flagon style	$42.00 – 47.00
Bowl, 6", "Radiance"	$10.00 – 12.00	Mug, tankard style	$37.00 – 42.00
Bowl, 7½", "Radiance"	$16.00 – 18.00	Pie baker	$27.00 – 32.00
Bowl, 9", "Radiance"	$20.00 – 25.00	Pretzel jar	$90.00 – 110.00
Butter, one-pound, "Zephyr"-style	$500.00 – 600.00	Saucer, St. Denis	$8.00 – 10.00
Cakeplate	$22.00 – 27.00	Shakers, handled, ea.	$7.00 – 8.00
Canister, "Radiance"	UND	Shakers, "Five Band," ea.	$27.00 – 32.00
Casserole, "Radiance"	$27.00 – 32.00	Shakers, handled, ea.	$16.00 – 18.00
Coffee pot, "Deco"	$400.00 – 500.00	Shakers, "Teardrop," ea.	$14.00 – 17.00
*Coffee pot, "Five Band"	$50.00 – 60.00	Soup tureen, "Thick Rim"	$250.00 – 300.00
Coffee pot, "Medallion"	$45.00 – 55.00	Soup tureen, clover lid	$250.00 – 300.00
Coffee pot, "Meltdown"	$90.00 – 110.00	Stack set, "Radiance"	$125.00 – 150.00
Coffee pot, "Terrace," (two sizes)	$40.00 – 55.00	Sugar and lid, Art Deco	$25.00 – 30.00
Coffee pot, "Waverly," (Drip-O-lator)	$45.00 – 55.00	Sugar and lid, "Medallion"	$20.00 – 25.00
Creamer, Art Deco	$18.00 – 22.00	Sugar and lid, "Meltdown"	$55.00 – 65.00
Creamer, "Medallion"	$14.00 – 16.00	Sugar and lid, modern	$20.00 – 25.00
Creamer, "Meltdown"	$35.00 – 40.00	Sugar and lid, New York	$22.00 – 27.00
Creamer, modern	$10.00 – 12.00	Teapot, Aladdin	$550.00 – 650.00
Creamer, New York	$12.00 – 14.00	Teapot, Boston	$150.00 – 175.00
Cup, St. Denis	$35.00 – 40.00	Teapot, Donut	UND
Custard	$12.00 – 14.00	Teapot, "Medallion"	$80.00 – 95.00
Drip coffee pot, "Jordan"	$200.00 – 250.00	Teapot, New York, 2 or 4 cup	$150.00 – 175.00
Drip coffee pot, "Kadota"	$175.00 – 200.00	Teapot, New York, 6 cup	$110.00 – 135.00
Drip jar, #1188, open	$30.00 – 35.00	Teapot, New York, 8 or 12 cup	$180.00 – 200.00
Drip jar and lid, "Radiance"	$18.00 – 22.00	Teapot, Streamline	$285.00 – 325.00
Jug and cover, "Radiance," #3, #4	$60.00 – 70.00	Teapot, two cup, "Terrace"	$150.00 – 175.00
Jug and cover, "Radiance," #5, #6	$80.00 – 95.00	Water bottle, "Zephyr"-style	$400.00 – 500.00
Jug, "Simplicity"	$120.00 – 140.00	*With glass dripper	$75.00 – 90.00

Row 1: Gravy boat; bean pot, New England #4; sugar and creamer, Art Deco style.
Row 2: Butter, "Zephyr"; leftover, "Zephyr"; leftover, rectangular.
Row 3: Drip jar, "Radiance"; shakers, handled; mug, beverage.
Row 4: Teapot, New York; soup tureen, "Thick Rim"; tidbit, 3-tier.

Crocus

Metal Accessories	Price
Bread box	$35.00 – 40.00
Cake safe	$25.00 – 30.00
Canister set, round, 4-piece	$55.00 – 60.00
Coffee dispenser	$20.00 – 25.00
Coffee dispenser with glass window	$30.00 – 35.00
Soap dispenser	$25.00 – 30.00
Tray, oval	$22.00 – 25.00
Tray, round	$18.00 – 22.00

Crocus metal cake safe.

"Radiance" jug and cover.

Crocus metal bread box.

Front: Shakers, "Five Band"; water bottle, "Zephyr"; sugar and creamer, "Meltdown."
Rear: Soup tureen, clover style; coffee pot, "Deco" shape.

HOMEWOOD

The Homewood pattern was made for the Eureka Tea Company of Chicago. The availability of pieces in this pattern is limited to a few kitchenware pieces and some of the D-style dinnerware.

D-style Dinnerware	*Price*
Bowl, 5½", fruit	$4.50 – 5.50
Bowl, 8½", flat soup	$8.00 – 10.00
Cup	$6.00 – 7.00
Plate, 9"	$7.00 – 9.00
Saucer	$1.00 – 1.50

Kitchenware	*Price*
Bowl, 6", "Radiance"	$9.00 – 11.00
Bowl, 7½", "Radiance"	$12.00 – 15.00
Bowl, 9" "Radiance"	$16.00 – 20.00
Coffee pot, "Terrace"	$45.00 – 55.00
Creamer, Art Deco	$18.00 – 22.00
Drip coffee pot, "Kadota"	$70.00 – 80.00
Drip jar, "Radiance"	$20.00 – 25.00
Sugar, Art Deco	$20.00 – 25.00
Shakers, handled, ea.	$16.00 – 18.00

Left to Right: Drip coffee pot, "Kadota"; drip jar, "Radiance"; shaker, handled.

MUMS

Mums is a pink floral decal which appears to be most prevalent in the Wisconsin and Minnesota areas. The earliest references to this decal date to the late 1930s. Many people seem to be confusing this decal with another similar decal — Pastel Morning Glory. There are substantial differences between the two decals if care is taken to look at them closely. Even if the obvious difference between the two types of flowers is ignored, Mums does not have the sprigs of blue flowers which are present on the Pastel Morning Glory pieces.

The dinnerware is D-shape. Although the kitchenware listing is continuing to expand, this pattern is almost impossible to collect unless you live in one of the two states mentioned above.

New discoveries include "Radiance" canisters, a "Medallion" coffee pot, and a large-size "Terrace" coffee pot. The New York six cup teapot, the "Simplicity" jug, and the pretzel jar are difficult pieces for many collectors to find. The large-size "Medallion" teapot is shown in the photograph. We have not heard any reports of the smaller one appearing with this decal.

D-style Dinnerware	Price
Bowl, 5½", fruit	$4.50 – 5.50
Bowl, 6", cereal	$8.00 – 9.00
Bowl, 8½", flat soup	$14.00 – 16.00
Bowl, 9¼", round	$22.00 – 27.00
Bowl, 10¼", oval	$22.00 – 27.00
Cup	$10.00 – 12.00
Gravy boat	$22.00 – 27.00
Plate, 6"	$2.50 – 3.50
Plate, 8¼"	$5.50 – 6.50
Plate, 9"	$9.00 – 10.00
Platter, 11¼", oval	$16.00 – 18.00
Platter, 13¼", oval	$20.00 – 25.00
Saucer	$1.50 – 2.50

Kitchenware	Price
Bowl, 9", salad	$18.00 – 22.00
Bowl, 6", "Radiance"	$9.00 – 11.00
Bowl, 7½", "Radiance"	$14.00 – 16.00
Bowl, 9", "Radiance"	$18.00 – 22.00
Bowl, 9½", ruffled, tab handled, "Medallion"	$45.00 – 55.00
Canister, "Radiance"	UND
Casserole, "Medallion"	$35.00 – 40.00
Casserole, "Radiance"	$32.00 – 37.00

Kitchenware	Price
Coffee pot, "Medallion"	$60.00 – 70.00
Coffee pot, "Terrace"	$60.00 – 70.00
Creamer, Art Deco	$15.00 – 18.00
Creamer, "Medallion"	$14.00 – 16.00
Creamer, New York	$14.00 – 16.00
Custard, "Medallion"	$14.00 – 16.00
Custard, "Radiance"	$8.00 – 10.00
Drip jar, #1188, open	$30.00 – 35.00
Drip jar and cover, "Medallion"	$22.00 – 27.00
Jug, #3, "Medallion"	$25.00 – 30.00
Jug, "Simplicity"	$110.00 – 125.00
Mug, beverage	$37.00 – 42.00
Pie baker	$25.00 – 30.00
Pretzel jar	$90.00 – 110.00
Shakers, handled, ea.	$14.00 – 16.00
Stack set, "Radiance"	$70.00 – 90.00
Sugar and lid, Art Deco	$20.00 – 25.00
Sugar and lid, "Medallion"	$18.00 – 22.00
Sugar and lid, New York	$18.00 – 22.00
Teapot, "Medallion"	$90.00 – 110.00
Teapot, New York	$125.00 – 150.00
Teapot, "Rutherford"	$140.00 – 160.00

Row 1: Teapot, "Terrace"; teapot, "Medallion"; teapot, "Rutherford."
Row 2: Bowl, tab-handled "Medallion"; bowl, 9¼", round.
Row 3: Shakers, handled; mug, beverage; creamer and sugar, "Medallion."

Left to Right: Pretzel jar; jug, "Simplicity"; drip jar, #1188, open.

No. 488

Numerous kitchenware shapes with this decal and the discovery of the existence of Hall dinnerware have made this pattern more attractive to collect. All of the dinnerware seems to be concentrated in the Wisconsin and Minnesota areas, while kitchenware seems to be found both there and in eastern Pennsylvania. Although it is not rare, a complete set of dinnerware will be difficult to assemble.

Interesting new kitchenware finds include the #691 drip coffee pot and the "Terrace" coffee pot. Numerous other items such as the French fluted baker, the 9" salad bowl, the one-handled cocette, and the "Meltdown" and

New York sugar and creamer are new to the listing in this book.

Notice in the picture the "Teardrop" shakers may be difficult to identify since they only have a small part of the No. 488 decal. The lids to all the sizes of "Radiance" jugs exist, but it will take diligent searching to find both the largest and the smallest.

The handled shakers may be found on either an ivory or an eggshell body. We have only seen the salad bowl on an eggshell body. The Tom & Jerry punch bowl is difficult to find, but the mugs have been appearing more frequently.

D-style Dinnerware	Price
Bowl, 5½", fruit	$5.50 – 6.50
Bowl, 8½", flat soup	$18.00 – 22.00
Bowl, 9¼", round	$30.00 – 35.00
Cup	$12.00 – 14.00
Plate, 7"	$7.00 – 9.00
Plate, 8¼"	$8.00 – 10.00
Plate, 9"	$11.00 – 14.00
Platter, 11¼", oval	$18.00 – 22.00
Platter, 13¼", oval	$20.00 – 25.00
Saucer	$1.50 – 2.50

Row 1: Teapot, "Radiance"; drip coffee pot, "Radiance"; jug and cover, #6 "Radiance."

Row 2: Jug and cover, #5 "Radiance"; jug and cover, #4 "Radiance"; jug and cover, #3 "Radiance"; jug and cover, #2 "Radiance."

Row 3: Drip jar, "Radiance"; casserole, "Radiance"; butter, 1# "Zephyr."

Row 1: Stack set, "Radiance"; condiment jar, "Radiance"; cookie jar, "Five Band"; pretzel jar.

Row 2: Bowl, 7½" "Radiance"; custard, "Radiance"; shaker set of four, "Novelty Radiance."

Row 3: Leftover, square with ridged lid; casserole #4 "Sundial"; casserole, "Thick Rim."

Kitchenware	Price
Baker, French	$20.00 – 25.00
Ball jug, #3	$85.00 – 95.00
Bean pot, New England, (#3, #4, #5)	$90.00 – 115.00
Bowl, 9", salad	$20.00 – 22.00
Bowl, 5", "Radiance"	$18.00 – 20.00
Bowl, 6", "Radiance"	$12.00 – 14.00
Bowl, 7½", "Radiance"	$14.00 – 16.00
Bowl, 9", "Radiance"	$18.00 – 20.00
Bowl, 10", "Radiance"	$20.00 – 25.00
Bowl, 8½", "Thin Rim"	$30.00 – 37.00
Butter, 1 lb., "Zephyr"	$400.00 – 450.00
Canister, "Radiance"	$125.00 – 150.00
Casserole, "Five Band"	$35.00 – 40.00
Casserole, "Medallion"	$32.00 – 37.00
Casserole, "Radiance"	$27.00 – 32.00
Casserole, "Sundial"	$45.00 – 55.00
Casserole, "Thick Rim"	$37.00 – 45.00
Cocette, handled	$25.00 – 30.00
Coffee pot, "Meltdown"	$95.00 – 110.00
Coffee pot, "Terrace"	$80.00 – 10.00
Condiment jar, "Radiance"	$250.00 – 350.00
Cookie jar, "Five Band"	$125.00 – 150.00
Creamer, Art Deco	$14.00 – 16.00
Creamer, "Meltdown"	$27.00 – 32.00
Creamer, modern	$12.00 – 14.00
Creamer, New York	$18.00 – 20.00
Custard "Radiance"	$10.00 – 12.00

Kitchenware	Price
Drip coffee pot, #691	$200.00 – 225.00
Drip coffee pot, "Radiance"	$200.00 – 225.00
Drip jar, #1188, open	$25.00 – 30.00
Drip jar and cover, "Medallion"	$22.00 – 27.00
Drip jar and cover, "Radiance"	$22.00 – 27.00
Jug, "Medallion"	$50.00 – 65.00
Jug and cover, "Radiance," (#1, #2, #3)	$55.00 – 65.00
Jug and cover, "Radiance," (#4, #5, #6)	$75.00 – 85.00
Jug, "Rayed"	$30.00 – 35.00
Jug, "Simplicity"	$90.00 – 110.00
Leftover, square	$65.00 – 75.00
Mug, Tom & Jerry	$14.00 – 16.00
Pretzel jar	$120.00 – 135.00
Punch bowl, Tom & Jerry	$600.00 – 800.00
Shakers, handled, ea.	$16.00 – 20.00
Shakers, "Medallion," ea.	$20.00 – 25.00
Shakers, "Novelty Radiance," ea.	$25.00 – 30.00
Shakers, "Teardrop," ea.	$16.00 – 18.00
Shirred egg dish	$30.00 – 35.00
Soup tureen	$200.00 – 250.00
Stack set, "Radiance"	$80.00 – 100.00
Sugar and lid, Art Deco	$25.00 – 30.00
Sugar and lid, "Meltdown"	$35.00 – 40.00
Sugar and lid, modern	$18.00 – 22.00
Sugar and lid, New York	$22.00 – 27.00
Teapot, New York	$125.00 – 150.00
Teapot, "Radiance"	$175.00 – 225.00

Row 1: Coffee pot, "Terrace"; jug, "Simplicity"; ball jug #3.
Row 2: Bean pot, New England #4; bean pot, New England #3; Shaker set of four, handled.
Row 3: Drip jar, #188 open; dish, shirred egg; cocette, handled; shakers, "Teardrop."

Row 1: Punch bowl, Tom & Jerry; mug, Tom & Jerry; teapot, New York.
Row 2: Soup tureen; sugar and creamer, Art Deco.
Row 3: Sugar and creamer, modern; bowl, 9¼" round vegetable.

ORANGE POPPY

Orange Poppy is a decal dinnerware line which was introduced in 1933. Production continued through the fifties and the pattern was used as a premium for the Great American Tea Company.

Until recently, C-style dinnerware appeared to be abundant, but newer collectors are reporting shortages of plates, cups, and saucers. One problem collectors of this pattern encounter is crazing of the dinnerware pieces. Items which are hardest to find include the canister style shakers and the Bellvue shape teapot and coffee pot. Other desirable pieces which many collectors are still seeking are the canister set and the Melody and Donut teapots. Other pieces which are rapidly disappearing into collections are the Streamline, Boston, and Windshield teapots.

The few metal accessories available in this pattern are not abundant, but most collectors, who are patient and persistent, will be able to find these items. Notice the canister set in the photo is square, but a round set is also available. The cake safe has a metal cover and a wooden base.

C-style Dinnerware	Price
Bowl, 5½", fruit	$6.00 – 7.00
Bowl, 6", cereal	$13.00 – 15.00
Bowl, 8½", flat soup	$18.00 – 20.00
Bowl, 9¼", round vegetable	$27.00 – 32.00
Cup	$14.00 – 16.00
Plate, 6"	$5.00 – 6.00
Plate, 7¼"	$7.00 – 8.00
Plate, 9"	$12.00 – 14.00
Platter, 11¼", oval	$20.00 – 22.00
Platter, 13¼", oval	$25.00 – 30.00
Saucer	$2.50 – 3.00

Row 1: Canister set, "Radiance."

Row 2: Jug, #5 "Radiance"; shakers, canister-style; leftover, loop handle.

Row 3: Shaker, handled salt; drip jar, "Radiance"; shaker, handled pepper; shakers, "Novelty Radiance"; mustard.

Kitchenware	Price		Kitchenware	Price	
Baker, French, fluted	$16.00 –	18.00	Drip jar and cover, "Radiance"	$18.00 –	22.00
Ball jug, #3	$60.00 –	70.00	Jug #4, "Radiance"	$32.00 –	37.00
Bean pot, New England, #4	$85.00 –	95.00	Jug #5, "Radiance"	$25.00 –	27.00
Bowl, 6", "Radiance"	$10.00 –	12.00	Leftover, loop handle	$40.00 –	45.00
Bowl, 7½", "Radiance"	$16.00 –	18.00	Mustard and liner	$50.00 –	57.00
Bowl, 9", "Radiance"	$20.00 –	22.00	Pie baker	$30.00 –	32.00
Bowl, 10", "Radiance"	$24.00 –	28.00	Pretzel jar	$85.00 –	95.00
Bowl, 9", salad	$13.00 –	15.00	Shakers, "Teardrop," ea.	$20.00 –	25.00
Cakeplate	$22.00 –	25.00	Shakers, handled, ea.	$14.00 –	16.00
Canister, "Radiance"	$100.00 –	125.00	Shakers, canister-style, "Radiance," ea.	$85.00 –	100.00
Casserole, 8", oval	$42.00 –	47.00	Shakers, "Novelty Radiance," ea.	$22.00 –	27.00
Casserole, 11¾", oval	$65.00 –	75.00	Spoon	$50.00 –	60.00
Casserole, 13", oval	$80.00 –	90.00	Sugar and lid, "Great American"	$18.00 –	20.00
Casserole #76, round	$35.00 –	40.00	Teapot, 2-cup, Bellvue	$400.00 –	500.00
Coffee pot, 2-cup, Bellvue	$400.00 –	500.00	Teapot, Boston	$140.00 –	160.00
Coffee pot, "Great American"	$45.00 –	55.00	Teapot, Donut	$310.00 –	350.00
Coffee pot, S-lid	$47.00 –	57.00	Teapot, Melody	$240.00 –	260.00
Condiment jar, "Radiance"	$250.00 –	300.00	Teapot, Streamline	$240.00 –	260.00
Creamer, "Great American"	$14.00 –	16.00	Teapot, Windshield	$225.00 –	260.00
Custard	$6.00 –	7.00			

Left: Teapot, Bellvue; Right: Coffee pot, Bellvue.

Row 1: Coffee pot, S-lid; coffee pot, Bellvue; coffee pot, "Great American."
Row 2: Teapot, Windshield; teapot, Donut; teapot, Boston.
Row 3: Teapot, Streamline; teapot, Melody.

Row 1: Pretzel jar; bean pot, New England #4; ball jug #3. Row 2: Custard, "Radiance"; casserole, #76 round; creamer, sugar and lid, "Great American." Row 3: Casserole, "Radiance"; casserole, 8" oval; baker, French fluted.

Metal Accessories	Price
Bread box	$35.00 – 45.00
Cake safe	$25.00 – 30.00
Canister set, round, 4-piece	$40.00 – 50.00
Canister set, square, 4-piece	$40.00 – 50.00
Coffee dispenser	$25.00 – 30.00
Match safe	$22.00 – 27.00
Shakers, ea.	$9.00 – 11.00
Sifter	$35.00 – 45.00
Soap dispenser	$35.00 – 45.00
Tray, 14¼" x 18½"	$25.00 – 30.00
Waste basket	$35.00 – 45.00

Row 1: Bowl, 9" salad; cakeplate; plate, 9" dinner. Row 2: Spoon; cup and saucer; salt and pepper, metal. Row 3: Canister set, 4 pc. square metal.

PASTEL MORNING GLORY

The Pastel Morning Glory pattern provides an attractive dinnerware service. The decal features a prominent pink morning glory accented with tiny blue floral sprigs and green leaves. This decal appears to be of late thirties origin and the pattern was distributed primarily in upper Michigan, Wisconsin, and Minnesota. Collectors living in these areas seem to find an ample supply of items; those in other parts of the country have trouble finding even the most common pieces.

Some interesting items have appeared since the last book. Among these are the "Radiance" canister set, the "Radiance" teapot, and the round tea tile. The Donut jug, which is rarely found with any decal, and the square and rectangular leftovers are also prize pieces. Covered "Radiance" jugs are still in short supply, but more are turning up.

D-style Dinnerware	Price
Bowl, 5½", fruit	$5.00 – 6.00
Bowl, 6", cereal	$9.00 – 10.00
Bowl, 8½", flat soup	$16.00 – 18.00
Bowl, 9¼", round	$25.00 – 30.00
Bowl, oval	$20.00 – 25.00
Cup	$9.00 – 11.00
Gravy boat	$22.00 – 27.00
Plate, 6"	$3.50 – 4.50
Plate, 8¼"	$5.00 – 6.50
Plate, 9"	$8.00 – 10.00
Plate, 10"	$22.00 – 25.00
Platter, 11¼"	$18.00 – 20.00
Platter, 13¼"	$20.00 – 25.00
Saucer	$1.50 – 2.50

Row 1: Ball jug #3; pretzel jar; gravy boat.
Row 2: Bowl, 6" "Radiance"; sugar and creamer, modern; cup and saucer.
Row 3: Casserole, "Radiance"; tea tile; custard, "Radiance"; bowl, 5½" fruit.

Pastel Morning Glory

Kitchenware	Price	Kitchenware	Price
Ball jug, #3	$75.00 – 85.00	Jug and cover, #4, #5, #6, "Radiance"	$65.00 – 85.00
Bean pot, New England, #4	$95.00 – 110.00	Leftover, rectangular	$45.00 – 55.00
Bowl, 9", salad	$16.00 – 18.00	Leftover, square	$55.00 – 65.00
Bowl, 6", "Radiance"	$11.00 – 13.00	Pie baker	$25.00 – 30.00
Bowl, 7½", "Radiance"	$12.00 – 15.00	Pretzel jar	$95.00 – 115.00
Bowl, 9", "Radiance"	$18.00 – 22.00	Saucer, St. Denis	$6.00 – 7.50
Bowl, 10", "Radiance"	$22.00 – 27.00	Shakers, handled, ea.	$14.00 – 16.00
Cakeplate	$18.00 – 22.00	Shakers, "Novelty Radiance," ea.	$25.00 – 30.00
Canister, "Radiance"	UND	Shakers, "Teardrop," ea.	$12.00 – 15.00
Casserole, "Medallion"	$27.00 – 32.00	Stack set, "Radiance"	$85.00 – 95.00
Casserole, "Radiance"	$30.00 – 35.00	Sugar and lid, Art Deco	$22.00 – 27.00
Coffee pot, "Terrace"	$60.00 – 70.00	Sugar and lid, modern	$18.00 – 22.00
Creamer, Art Deco	$16.00 – 18.00	Sugar and lid, New York	$18.00 – 22.00
Creamer, modern	$12.00 – 14.00	Teapot, Aladdin	$195.00 – 225.00
Creamer, New York	$12.00 – 14.00	Teapot, "Medallion"	$165.00 – 185.00
Cup, St. Denis	$30.00 – 35.00	Teapot, New York	$125.00 – 150.00
Custard	$9.00 – 11.00	Teapot, "Radiance"	$200.00 – 250.00
Drip jar and lid, "Radiance"	$22.00 – 27.00	Teapot, "Rutherford"	$125.00 – 150.00
Drip jar, #1188, open	$27.00 – 32.00	Tea tile	$45.00 – 55.00
Jug, Donut	$110.00 – 135.00		

Row 1: Coffee pot, "Terrace"; teapot, "Medallion."
Row 2: Teapot, New York; bean pot, New England #4; shakers, handled.
Row 3: Leftover, square; leftover, rectangular; drip jar, #1188 open;
shakers, "Teardrop."

RED POPPY

Hall's Red Poppy pattern consists of a red floral decal accented with black leaves using an ivory body as a background. Additionally, each piece is highlighted with a narrow silver band. Production of this pattern began in the mid-thirties and continued for about twenty years. The Grand Union Tea Company, which used this pattern as a premium, was the primary recipient of this lengthy production.

With the exception of the 10" dinner plate, the D-style dinnerware pieces are generally available for moderate prices, although both the quantity and quality of available items appear to be shrinking. The serving pieces have become especially popular and usually sell very quickly. The gravy boat lacks an underplate and is not an easily found item. Cups may be found with their decal on either the inside or on the outside. Collectors are experiencing a lot of frustration trying to locate 10" dinner plates. The 9" dinner plate is the most commonly found size of plate.

D-style Dinnerware	Price
Bowl, 5½", fruit	$4.50 – 5.50
Bowl, 6", cereal	$10.00 – 12.00
Bowl, 8½", flat soup	$16.00 – 18.00
Bowl, 9¼", round	$25.00 – 30.00
Bowl, 10¼", oval	$20.00 – 25.00
Cup	$11.00 – 13.00
Gravy boat	$25.00 – 30.00
Plate, 6"	$4.00 – 5.00
Plate, 7¼"	$5.00 – 6.50
Plate, 8¼"	$6.00 – 7.50
Plate, 9"	$9.00 – 11.00
Plate, 10"	$30.00 – 35.00
Platter, 11¼"	$18.00 – 22.00
Platter, 13¼"	$25.00 – 30.00
Saucer	$2.00 – 3.00

"Daniel" coffee pot with metal dripper.

Hard to find pretzel jar.

Red Poppy

China kitchenware accessory pieces in Red Poppy appear to be limited to the "bare essentials." There does not appear to be the variety of shapes and sizes of such premium articles like coffee pots, teapots, or cookie jars which are found in some of the other popular Hall patterns. Also, while interesting pieces are being uncovered in other patterns, only one new china piece has been reported in this pattern in the last four years. This is the pretzel jar shown in the photo on the preceding page. In the photo below there are two sizes of the "Daniel" cream pitcher. The taller one is sometimes called a milk jug or syrup by collectors.

Notice the slight difference in color of the Aladdin teapot and the French baker in comparison to the other pieces in the photo. On these two articles, the Red Poppy decal has been placed on a Hi-white body. This deviation from the use of an ivory body may indicate that these two items were made for some company other than Grand Union.

Kitchenware	Price
Baker, French, fluted	$14.00 – 16.00
Ball jug, #3	$40.00 – 45.00
Bowl, 9", salad	$12.00 – 14.00
Bowl, 6", "Radiance"	$11.00 – 14.00
Bowl, 7½", "Radiance"	$14.00 – 16.00
Bowl, 9", "Radiance"	$16.00 – 18.00
Cakeplate	$20.00 – 22.00
Casserole, "Radiance"	$22.00 – 27.00
Coffee pot, "Daniel"	$42.00 – 47.00
Creamer, "Daniel"	$12.00 – 15.00
Creamer, modern	$12.00 – 15.00
Custard	$9.00 – 11.00
Drip jar, #1188, open	$32.00 – 37.00

Kitchenware	Price
Drip jar and cover, "Radiance"	$16.00 – 20.00
Jug, 4", "Daniel," milk or syrup	$42.00 – 47.00
Jug, #5, "Radiance"	$22.00 – 27.00
Leftover, square	$65.00 – 80.00
Pie baker	$25.00 – 30.00
Pretzel jar	UND
Shakers, "Teardrop," ea.	$12.00 – 14.00
Shakers, handled, ea.	$11.00 – 15.00
Sugar and lid, "Daniel"	$18.00 – 22.00
Sugar and lid, modern	$18.00 – 22.00
Teapot, Aladdin	$80.00 – 95.00
Teapot, New York	$75.00 – 85.00

Row 1: "Daniel" creamer; "Daniel" milk jug or syrup. Row 2: Cake safe; look-alike waffle iron.

Row 1: Coffee pot, "Daniel"; sugar and creamer, "Daniel"; jug, "Radiance" #5.
Row 2: Teapot, New York; teapot, Aladdin; salt, handled; drip jar, "Radiance"; pepper, handled.
Row 3: Casserole, "Radiance"; baker, French; drip jar, #1188 open; custard, "Radiance."
Row 4: Bowl, "Radiance" #5; bowl, "Radiance" #4; bowl, "Radiance" #3.

Glass accessory items in the Red Poppy pattern consist of a 10 ounce frosted tumbler with two styles of decal, a clear tumbler, and a one gallon canister. Of these glass items, the clear tumbler is the hardest to find. The gallon canister is a square clear glass jar with a screw lid and red poppies painted on the outside with enamel. This jar is also sometimes found with green enameled poppies. Two styles of frosted tumblers are shown in the picture on page 80. One style is slightly taller than the other, the flower is a little different and the bands around the top are different colors — one has red bands, the other has black.

Metal accessories with the Red Poppy decal are relatively abundant. Many were available through Montgomery Ward mail order catalogs in the 1940s. Metal pieces are subject to dents through abuse and damage to their enamel finish from improper cleaning. Most collectors are still resisting the temptation to buy metal items which are in poor condition. Three different styles of bread boxes have been reported. None of these is easy to find. Other hard-to-find items include the dustpan and soap dispenser. There are two different styles of coffee dispensers. One type has a glass window like the Autumn Leaf dispenser and the other style has no window.

Plastic accessories include an 8-piece bowl cover set, appliance covers, a teapot-shaped clock, and a tablecloth.

Reports of a waffle iron produced in the Red Poppy pattern always seem to lead to a decal which is similar to and goes well with Hall's Red Poppy decal. This decal has red poppy-like flowers which are much smaller than the ones on Hall pieces. Also, the stem of the flower on the waffle iron has both black and green leaves. The Hall Red Poppy decal has only black leaves. The waffle iron has a metal base and metal lid which contains the decaled china insert. The back of the waffle iron is marked "SAMSON NO E128; Samson United Corp., Rochester, NY." A picture of this waffle iron is shown in the photo at the bottom of page 76. A dinnerware set with this decal also exists. The set was made by AVCO China Co. of Alliance, Ohio.

Glass Accessories	Price
Canister, gallon	$25.00 – 28.00
Tumbler, clear	$27.00 – 30.00
Tumbler, frosted, 2 styles	$18.00 – 22.00

Metal Accessories	Price
Bread box, three styles	$30.00 – 40.00
Cake safe	$30.00 – 35.00
Canister set, round, 5 pc.	$35.00 – 45.00
Canister set, square, 4 pc.	$35.00 – 40.00
Clock, metal, teapot shape	$65.00 – 75.00
Coffee dispenser	$22.00 – 27.00
Coffee dispenser with glass window	$30.00 – 35.00
Dust pan	$32.00 – 37.00
Hot pad	$9.00 – 11.00
Match safe	$30.00 – 35.00
Recipe box	$30.00 – 35.00
Shakers, ea.	$9.00 – 11.00
Sifter	$30.00 – 35.00

Metal Accessories	Price
Soap dispenser	$30.00 – 40.00
Tray, rectangular	$25.00 – 30.00
Tray, round	$22.00 – 27.00
Waste can, 12½", oval	$30.00 – 35.00
Waste can, round, 15½" tall	$40.00 – 45.00
Waste can, step-on	$50.00 – 60.00
Wax paper dispenser	$32.00 – 37.00

Plastic Accessories	Price
Bowl covers, 8-pc set	$55.00 – 65.00
Clock, teapot shape	$55.00 – 65.00
Mixer cover	$22.00 – 24.00
Tablecloth, 54" x 100"	$80.00 – 95.00
Toaster cover	$22.00 – 24.00

Miscellaneous Accessories	Price
Cutting board, wooden	$30.00 – 35.00
Silverware box, wooden	$40.00 – 50.00
Tablecloth, cotton	$90.00 – 125.00

Left: Waste can, round metal, 15½" tall;
Right: bread box.

Row 1: Cutting board; coffee dispenser; sifter.
Row 2: Canister set, square; shaker, round, metal; hotpad.
Row 3: Canister set, round; matchholder.
Row 4: Waxed paper dispenser; tablecloth; recipe box.
Row 5: Tray, round; tray, rectangular.

Row 1: Shakers, "Teardrop"; creamer, modern; gravy boat; tumblers, 10 oz., frosted.
Row 2: Cup and saucer (pattern outside); cup and saucer (pattern inside); bowl, 9" salad; bowl, 9", round.
Row 3: Pie baker; cakeplate; bowl, 8½" flat soup.
Row 4: Plate, 6"; plate, 7"; plate, 9".
Row 5: Platter, 13¼"; bowl, 6", cereal; bowl, 5½", fruit.

SERENADE

The autumn-colored floral Serenade pattern was made for the Eureka Tea Company of Chicago. The complete D-style dinnerware is available, although most pieces are not easy to find. A growing list of kitchenware pieces has sparked collectors' interest, but availability is still a problem. The "Kadota" style all-china drip coffee maker is pictured. In addition another style all-china coffee pot has been found. The latest discovery is the same "Jordan" shape as the one found in the Autumn Leaf pattern.

Basic kitchenware items such as mixing bowls, bakers, casseroles, and handled shakers are found frequently. Hard to find items include the pretzel jar, New York teapot, New England bean pot, and the all-china drip coffee pot.

Row 1: Drip coffee pot, "Kadota"; ball jug #3.
Row 2: Teapot, New York; sugar and creamer, Art Deco.
Row 3: Pie baker; bowl, 5½", fruit; cup.

D-style Dinnerware	Price
Bowl, 5½", fruit	$4.50 – 5.50
Bowl, 6", cereal	$6.50 – 7.50
Bowl, 8½", flat soup	$11.00 – 13.00
Bowl, 9¼", round	$18.00 – 22.00
Bowl, oval	$18.00 – 20.00
Cup	$8.00 – 9.00
Gravy Boat	$20.00 – 25.00
Plate, 6"	$3.00 – 4.00
Plate, 8¼"	$4.00 – 5.50
Plate, 9"	$6.00 – 8.00
Platter, 11¼"	$16.00 – 18.00
Platter, 13¼"	$18.00 – 22.00
Saucer	$1.00 – 2.00

Kitchenware	Price
Baker, French, fluted	$12.00 – 14.00
Ball jug, #3	$55.00 – 65.00
Bean pot, New England, #4	$70.00 – 85.00
Bowl, 9", salad	$14.00 – 16.00
Bowl, 6", "Radiance"	$9.00 – 11.00

Kitchenware	Price
Bowl, 7½", "Radiance"	$10.00 – 12.00
Bowl, 9", "Radiance"	$14.00 – 16.00
Casserole, "Radiance"	$22.00 – 27.00
Coffee pot, "Terrace"	$40.00 – 45.00
Creamer, Art Deco	$14.00 – 16.00
Creamer, modern	$9.00 – 11.00
Creamer, New York	$10.00 – 12.00
Custard	$6.00 – 8.00
Drip coffee pot, "Jordan," all-china	UND
Drip coffee pot, "Kadota," all-china	$110.00 – 135.00
Drip jar and cover, "Radiance"	$18.00 – 22.00
Pie baker	$20.00 – 25.00
Pretzel jar	$80.00 – 95.00
Shakers, handled, ea.	$14.00 – 16.00
Sugar and lid, Art Deco	$18.00 – 22.00
Sugar and lid, modern	$11.00 – 13.00
Sugar and lid, New York	$12.00 – 14.00
Teapot, New York	$95.00 – 110.00

"SILHOUETTE"

The "Silhouette" pattern was introduced in the 1930s. This all-black decal contains two figures seated at a table on two high-back, bench-like chairs. Individual pieces are highlighted with the use of silver trim. Both Hall China and Taylor, Smith, and Taylor produced numerous items with this decal for Cook Coffee and Standard Coffee to use as premiums.

The dinnerware shape in this pattern consists of the D-style. Collectors are finding a general lack of availability of all pieces of Hall "Silhouette" dinnerware. Therefore, some collectors are mixing Hall and non-Hall pieces in their collections.

Collectors have the opportunity to obtain two all-china drip coffee pots in this pattern — "Medallion" and "Kadota." Some other items which are unusual and of particular interest to collectors include the handled shakers, the "Radiance" stack set, and the St. Denis cup and saucer.

In addition to the two companies listed above, Harker also made some items with the same "Silhouette" decal. Two of their most popular pieces with collectors include the china rolling pin and pie lifter. A similar decal was used by the Crooksville China Company. However, this decal featured a seated dog at the foot of the table. The Hall items do not contain a dog in the decal.

Glass, metal, and wooden accessories are numerous, but many of these are not easily found. A gallon-size screw lid jar with green enameled figures may be found.

D-style Dinnerware	Price	D-style Dinnerware	Price
Bowl, 5½", fruit	$6.50 – 8.00	Plate, 6"	$5.00 – 6.50
Bowl, 6", cereal	$9.00 – 11.00	Plate, 8¼"	$7.00 – 8.50
Bowl, 8½", flat soup	$18.00 – 20.00	Plate, 9"	$16.00 – 18.00
Bowl, 9¼", round vegetable	$25.00 – 30.00	Platter, 11¼", oval	$18.00 – 22.00
Bowl, oval	$22.00 – 27.00	Platter, 13¼", oval	$25.00 – 30.00
Cup	$12.00 – 14.00	Saucer	$1.50 – 2.50
Gravy Boat	$25.00 – 30.00		

Left to Right: Coffee pot, "Medallion," all china drip; teapot, "Medallion."

Kitchenware	Price	Kitchenware	Price
Baker, French, fluted	$16.00 – 18.00	Drip coffee pot, "Medallion"	$185.00 – 215.00
Ball jug, #3	$80.00 – 95.00	Drip jar and cover, "Medallion"	$22.00 – 28.00
Bean pot, New England, #4	$110.00 – 125.00	Jug, #2, "Medallion"	$18.00 – 22.00
Bowl, 3⅝", flared	$10.00 – 12.00	Jug, #3, "Medallion"	$22.00 – 27.00
Bowl, 7¾", flared	$30.00 – 35.00	Jug, #4, "Medallion"	$25.00 – 30.00
Bowl, 9", salad	$16.00 – 18.00	Jug, "Simplicity"	$115.00 – 130.00
Bowl, 6", "Medallion"	$12.00 – 14.00	Leftover, rectangular	$35.00 – 45.00
Bowl, 7½", "Medallion"	$14.00 – 16.00	Leftover, square	$45.00 – 55.00
Bowl, 8½", "Medallion"	$18.00 – 22.00	Mug, beverage	$37.00 – 42.00
Bowl, 6", "Radiance"	$13.00 – 15.00	Pie baker	$25.00 – 30.00
Bowl, 7½", "Radiance"	$16.00 – 18.00	Pretzel jar	$100.00 – 125.00
Bowl, 9", "Radiance"	$20.00 – 22.00	Saucer, St. Denis	$8.00 – 10.00
Casserole, "Medallion"	$30.00 – 40.00	Shakers, "Five Band," ea.	$14.00 – 16.00
Coffee pot, "Five Band"	$45.00 – 55.00	Shakers, "Medallion," ea	$20.00 – 25.00
Coffee pot, "Five Band",		Shakers, handled, ea.	$40.00 – 50.00
(glass dripper)	$80.00 – 90.00	Sugar and lid, "Medallion"	$18.00 – 22.00
Coffee pot, "Medallion"	$90.00 – 110.00	Sugar and lid, modern	$18.00 – 22.00
Creamer, "Medallion"	$12.00 – 15.00	Teapot, "Medallion"	$60.00 – 80.00
Creamer, modern	$12.00 – 15.00	Teapot, New York	$195.00 – 225.00
Cup, St. Denis	$30.00 – 35.00	Teapot, Streamline	$200.00 – 250.00
Drip coffee pot, "Kadota," all-china	$175.00 – 195.00	Tea tile, 6"	$85.00 – 95.00

Handled shakers.

Row 1: Teapot, New York; coffee pot, "Five Band"; Coffee pot, "Medallion."
Row 2: Pretzel jar; sugar and creamer, "Medallion"; jug, #3, "Medallion."
Row 3: Leftover, square; leftover, rectangular; tea tile; bowl, 9", salad.
Row 4: Bowl, #5, "Medallion"; bowl, #4, "Medallion"; bowl, #3, "Medallion"; custard, flared.

Row 1: Drip coffee, "Kadota"; jug, "Simplicity."
Row 2: Beverage mug; shakers, "Five Band"; salt, "Medallion"; drip jar, "Medallion"; pepper, "Medallion."

Other Accessories	Price
Bread box	$65.00 – 75.00
Cake safe	$30.00 – 35.00
Canister, one gallon glass with green decal	$22.00 – 27.00
Canister set, 4-pc., metal	$40.00 – 50.00
Clock, electric	$70.00 – 75.00
Coffee dispenser	$60.00 – 70.00
Coaster	$5.00 – 6.00
Double boiler, enamel	$40.00 – 45.00
Kitchen utensils, wooden handled, ea.	$10.00 – 12.00
Match safe	$30.00 – 35.00
Metal tray, oval	$28.00 – 32.00
Metal tray, rectangular	$25.00 – 28.00
Mirror	$65.00 – 75.00

Other Accessories	Price
Pitcher, crystal, Federal	$100.00 – 120.00
Pitcher, crystal, Macbeth-Evans style	$110.00 – 125.00
Rolling pin, china, (not Hall)	$95.00 – 110.00
Sifter	$45.00 – 55.00
Soap dispenser	$35.00 – 45.00
Shakers, lg. metal, ea.	$12.00 – 14.00
Shelf paper (30 ft pack)	$40.00 – 50.00
Silverware box	$60.00 – 65.00
Tumbler, 9 oz., crystal	$30.00 – 35.00
Tumbler, 10 oz., crystal	$27.00 – 30.00
Waffle iron	$95.00 – 110.00
Waste basket	$45.00 – 55.00
Wax paper dispenser	$35.00 – 45.00

SPRINGTIME

The Springtime decal consists of a floral sprig with a prominent grayish-white flower accented by numerous smaller red and yellow flowers. All pieces in the pattern are also trimmed with a silver band. The dinnerware line is comprised of the entire number of D-style items. However, some pieces of dinnerware appear to be eluding the efforts of some collectors to obtain them within a reasonable amount of time.

Some of the Springtime kitchenware items appear on the market quite frequently. Among these are the cakeplate, covered drip jar, ball jug, and the casserole. The all-china drip coffee pot is the hardest item to locate — and probably the most expensive. Newer items with the Springtime decal include several sizes of the Washington shape coffee pot.

D-style Dinnerware	Price
Bowl, 5½", fruit	$4.50 – 5.50
Bowl, 6", cereal	$5.00 – 7.00
Bowl, 8½", flat soup	$11.00 – 13.00
Bowl, 9¼", round	$18.00 – 22.00
Bowl, oval	$18.00 – 20.00
Cup	$6.00 – 7.50
Gravy boat	$18.00 – 22.00
Plate, 6"	$3.00 – 4.00
Plate, 7¼"	$5.00 – 6.00
Plate, 8¼"	$5.00 – 6.00
Plate, 9"	$7.50 – 9.50
Platter, 11¼", oval	$12.00 – 15.00
Platter, 13¼", oval	$18.00 – 20.00
Platter, 15", oval	$20.00 – 25.00
Saucer	$1.50 – 2.50

Kitchenware	Price
Ball jug, #3	$45.00 – 55.00
Bowl, 9", salad	$12.00 – 14.00
Bowl, 6", "Thick Rim"	$9.00 – 11.00
Bowl, 7½", "Thick Rim"	$12.00 – 14.00
Bowl, 8½", "Thick Rim"	$15.00 – 17.00
Cakeplate	$14.00 – 16.00
Casserole, "Thick Rim"	$22.00 – 27.00
Coffee pot, Washington	$30.00 – 35.00
Creamer, modern	$9.00 – 11.00
Custard	$5.00 – 7.00
Drip coffee pot, "Kadota", all-china	$85.00 – 95.00
Drip jar and cover, "Thick Rim"	$18.00 – 22.00
Jug, #6, "Radiance"	$20.00 – 25.00
Pie baker	$18.00 – 20.00
Shakers, handled, ea.	$12.00 – 14.00
Sugar and lid, modern	$16.00 – 18.00
Teapot, French	$65.00 – 75.00

Row 1: Ball jug #3; teapot, French; shaker, handled; bowl, 5½", fruit.
Row 2: Casserole, "Thick Rim"; cakeplate; cup and saucer.

Row 1: Bowl, 9", round; bowl, oval. Row 2: Plate, 8¼"; gravy boat; plate, 6".

TULIP

The Tulip decal is a budding lavender and pink floral representation on an ivory body with platinum trim. This pattern was used as a premium by the Cook Coffee Company. The dinnerware shape is D-style with the addition of a 10" dinner plate and the omission of the 8¼" plate. Other potteries such as Harker and Paden City also used this same decal on some of their wares.

The "Perk" coffee pot pictured on the top row and the "Kadota" all-china drip coffee pot both have the Drip-O-lator backstamp of Enterprise Aluminum Company. The "Perk" coffee pot will also be found in colored glazes without a decal, but this and "Shaggy Tulip" are the only decal lines in which this shape pot has been found.

Collectors seem to be having the most trouble finding the "Radiance" stack set and the St. Denis cups and saucers. Obtaining Hall dinnerware also seems to be more difficult than finding Harker dinnerware. Although there are numerous Hall shapes to collect in this pattern, many collectors are mixing in pieces made by other companies. The rolling pin and pie server made by Harker are especially desirable.

Metal accessories include a waffle iron and a 4-piece canister set with glass knobs.

D-style Dinnerware	Price
Bowl, 5½", fruit	$5.50 – 6.50
Bowl, 6", cereal	$11.00 – 14.00
Bowl, 8½", flat soup	$16.00 – 18.00
Bowl, 9¼", round	$25.00 – 30.00
Bowl, oval	$22.00 – 27.00
Cup	$11.00 – 13.00
Gravy boat	$22.00 – 27.00
Plate, 6"	$4.00 – 5.00
Plate, 7"	$6.00 – 7.00
Plate, 9"	$9.00 – 11.00
Plate 10"	$20.00 – 25.00
Platter, 11¼", oval	$16.00 – 18.00
Platter, 13¼", oval	$22.00 – 25.00
Saucer	$1.50 – 2.50
Tidbit, 3-tier	$35.00 – 45.00

Kitchenware	Price
Baker, French, fluted	$16.00 – 18.00
Bowl, 9", salad	$14.00 – 16.00
Bowl, 6", "Radiance"	$9.00 – 11.00
Bowl, 7½", "Radiance"	$12.00 – 14.00

Kitchenware	Price
Bowl, 9", "Radiance"	$18.00 – 22.00
Bowl, 6", "Thick Rim"	$10.00 – 12.00
Bowl, 7½", "Thick Rim"	$14.00 – 16.00
Bowl, 8½", "Thick Rim"	$25.00 – 30.00
Casserole, "Radiance"	$30.00 – 35.00
Casserole, "Thick Rim"	$30.00 – 40.00
Coffee pot, "Perk"	$50.00 – 60.00
Creamer, modern	$10.00 – 12.00
Cup, St. Denis	$30.00 – 35.00
Custard	$8.00 – 10.00
Drip coffee pot, "Kadota", all-china	$85.00 – 95.00
Drip jar and cover, "Thick Rim"	$18.00 – 22.00
Saucer, St. Denis	$8.00 – 9.00
Shakers, handled, ea.	$12.00 – 15.00
Stack set, "Radiance"	$75.00 – 85.00
Sugar and lid, modern	$18.00 – 20.00

Metal Accessories	Price
Canister set, 4-pc	$40.00 – 50.00
Waffle iron	$65.00 – 75.00

Row 1: Coffee pot, "Perk"; shakers, handled. Row 2: Creamer and sugar, modern; cup and saucer.
Row 3: Bowl 9", round; bowl, 9", "Radiance." Row 4: Plate, 6"; plate, 9". Row 5: Platter, 13¼", oval; baker, French.

WILDFIRE

The Wildfire pattern was used as a premium by the Great American Tea Company during the 1950s. The dinnerware is D-style, but the 8¼" plate was not used and a 10" dinner plate, a 7¼" salad plate, a 3-tier tidbit, and an oval bowl were added.

There is a sunken handle "Thick Rim" casserole with a cadet base to go along with the cadet "Thick Rim" bowl in the picture. The base does not have the Wildfire pattern and is interchangeable with those of other patterns such as Royal Rose and Morning Glory. Sets of utility bowls in both the straight-sided and "Thick Rim" styles have been found with cadet exteriors and white interiors. On these bowls the decal is on the inside, whereas it is on the outside of the regular white bowls.

Two styles of Aladdin teapots with the Wildfire decal have been reported — round opening and oval opening. Infusors may be obtained for both styles. The S-lid coffee pot has been found with an electric heating element and glass dripper. Rarely found pieces include the egg cup, "Pert" shakers, "Pert" jug, "Pert" teapot, and Boston teapot.

The exciting news in this pattern is the discovery of a Streamline teapot. At this time it is the only one known.

D-style Dinnerware	Price
Bowl, 5½", fruit	$5.00 – 6.00
Bowl, 6", cereal	$8.00 – 10.00
Bowl, 8½", flat soup	$14.00 – 16.00
Bowl, 9¼", round	$22.00 – 27.00
Bowl, oval	$18.00 – 22.00
Cup	$12.00 – 14.00
Gravy boat	$20.00 – 25.00
Plate, 6"	$3.00 – 4.00
Plate, 7"	$5.50 – 7.50
Plate, 9"	$8.00 – 10.00
Plate 10"	$18.00 – 22.00
Platter, 11¼", oval	$18.00 – 22.00
Platter, 13¼", oval	$20.00 – 25.00
Saucer	$1.50 – 2.50
Tidbit, 3-tier	$45.00 – 55.00

Kitchenware	Price
Baker, French, fluted	$16.00 – 18.00
Bowl, 9", salad	$14.00 – 16.00
Bowl, 6", straight-sided	$10.00 – 12.00
Bowl, 7½", straight-sided	$14.00 – 16.00
Bowl, 9", straight-sided	$18.00 – 22.00
Bowl, 6", "Thick Rim"	$12.00 – 15.00
Bowl, 7½", "Thick Rim"	$16.00 – 18.00
Bowl, 8½", "Thick Rim"	$20.00 – 25.00
Cakeplate	$18.00 – 22.00

Kitchenware	Price
Casserole, tab-handled	$28.00 – 32.00
Casserole, "Thick Rim"	$25.00 – 30.00
Coffee pot, S-lid	$45.00 – 55.00
Coffee pot, S-lid (glass dripper)	$75.00 – 85.00
Creamer, modern	$11.00 – 13.00
Creamer, "Pert"	$25.00 – 30.00
Custard	$7.00 – 9.00
Drip jar, tab-handled	$18.00 – 22.00
Drip jar and cover, "Thick Rim"	$18.00 – 22.00
Egg cup	$50.00 – 60.00
Jug, 5", "Pert"	$60.00 – 70.00
Jug #5, "Radiance"	$32.00 – 37.00
Pie baker	$25.00 – 30.00
Shakers, handled, ea.	$12.00 – 15.00
Shakers, "Pert," ea.	$25.00 – 30.00
Shakers, "Teardrop," ea.	$12.00 – 14.00
Sugar and lid, modern	$18.00 – 22.00
Sugar, "Pert"	$25.00 – 30.00
Teapot, Aladdin	$80.00 – 90.00
Teapot, Boston	$125.00 – 150.00
Teapot, 6-cup, "Pert"	$110.00 – 140.00
Teapot, Streamline	UND

Metal Accessories	Price
Coffee dispenser	$18.00 – 22.00

Row 1: Jug, #5, "Radiance"; jug, 5", "Pert"; teapot, Aladdin. Row 2: Teapot, "Pert"; sugar and creamer, "Pert"; shakers, "Teardrop." Row 3: Bowl, 6", straight-sided; shaker, handled; drip jar, "Thick Rim"; bowl with cadet exterior, 6", "Thick Rim."

Streamline teapot.

YELLOW ROSE

Yellow Rose was produced for the Eureka Tea Company of Chicago. Distribution of this pattern was regional, and collectors are having very little success finding any outside of the northern midwest area.

The "Norse" shape coffee pot, sugar, and creamer are found frequently in this pattern, but this shape has not been found in other decal lines. Finding the "Radiance" stack set and the all-china drip coffee is proving to be a challenge for collectors.

D-style Dinnerware	Price
Bowl, 5½", fruit	$4.50 – 5.50
Bowl, 6", cereal	$6.50 – 7.50
Bowl, 8½", flat soup	$12.00 – 14.00
Bowl, 9¼", round vegetable	$18.00 – 20.00
Cup	$7.00 – 9.00
Gravy boat	$20.00 – 25.00
Plate, 6"	$2.50 – 3.50
Plate, 8¼"	$6.00 – 7.00
Plate, 9"	$8.00 – 9.00
Platter, 11¼", oval	$14.00 – 16.00
Platter, 13¼", oval	$18.00 – 22.00
Saucer	$1.50 – 2.00

Kitchenware	Price
Baker, French, fluted	$14.00 – 16.00
Bowl, 9", salad	$14.00 – 16.00
Bowl, 6", "Radiance"	$10.00 – 12.00
Bowl, 7½", "Radiance"	$12.00 – 14.00
Bowl, 9", "Radiance"	$16.00 – 18.00
Casserole, "Radiance"	$22.00 – 27.00
Coffee pot, "Dome"	$30.00 – 35.00
Coffee pot, "Norse"	$55.00 – 65.00
Coffee pot, "Waverly"	$30.00 – 37.00
Creamer, "Norse"	$12.00 – 15.00
Custard	$8.00 – 10.00
Drip coffee pot, "Kadota"	$90.00 – 100.00
Drip jar and cover, "Radiance"	$18.00 – 22.00
Onion soup	$25.00 – 32.00
Shakers, handled, ea.	$14.00 – 16.00
Stack set, "Radiance"	$85.00 – 95.00
Sugar and lid, "Norse"	$18.00 – 22.00
Teapot, New York	$75.00 – 85.00

Row 1: Drip coffee pot, "Norse"; teapot, New York; creamer and sugar, "Norse."
Row 2: Salt, handled; drip jar or covered onion soup; pepper, handled; platter, 11¼", oval.
Row 3: Bowl, 6", cereal; bowl, 5½", fruit; bowl, 8½", flat soup.
Row 4: Plate, 9", dinner; plate, 8¼"; cup

CAMEO ROSE

Cameo Rose is an E-style dinnerware pattern which was made exclusively for the Jewel Tea Company. According to their catalog, the pattern "features a single rose, framed by a rosebud and leaf wreath, accented in gold." It was lauded as a "superior quality hand fired semi-porcelain dinnerware that would never fade or craze." Cameo Rose was first offered in the fifties and remained available until the early seventies.

Services were offered as a 16-piece "breakfast starter set, " a 16-piece "dinner starter set, " and a "53-piece service for eight." Individual pieces could also be bought from open stock.

Today most pieces of Cameo Rose can be readily found. However, a few items require diligent searching. The piece we have found to be the hardest to acquire is the cream soup. This is followed by the 15½" oval platter

and the butter. These last two pieces were not made for the entire time and this may explain their scarcity.

A decal variation of the sugar and creamer has been reported. The commonly found sugar and creamer are pictured on the opposite page. Another form exists with the large rosebud decal in the center of the side (like the teapot).

Several other rare pieces have been reportedly purchased from a former Jewel employee. These were probably one-of-a-kind sample items which found their way to the employee's home through the employee store. These items include a "wings" style butter dish which is shaped like the "wings" butter in the Autumn Leaf pattern and a clock fashioned from a dinner plate. There is also a covered round vegetable bowl with tab handles on both the base and the lid.

Cameo Rose	Price
Bowl, 5¼", fruit	$5.00 – 6.50
Bowl, 6¼", cereal	$7.00 – 9.50
Bowl, 5", cream soup	$75.00 – 85.00
Bowl, 8", flat soup	$10.00 – 12.00
Bowl, covered vegetable	$40.00 – 45.00
Bowl, 9", round vegetable	$18.00 – 22.00
Bowl, 10½", oval	$18.00 – 22.00
Butter, quarter pound	$40.00 – 50.00
Butter, quarter pound, "wings" top	UND
Clock	UND
Creamer	$7.00 – 9.00
Cup	$7.50 – 9.00
Gravy boat and underplate	$27.00 – 32.00

Cameo Rose	Price
Plate, 6½"	$3.00 – 4.00
Plate, 7¼"	$5.50 – 6.50
Plate, 8"	$7.00 – 8.50
Plate, 9¼"	$8.00 – 9.00
Plate, 10"	$9.00 – 11.00
Platter, 11¼", oval	$14.00 – 16.00
Platter, 13¼", oval	$16.00 – 18.00
Platter, 15½", oval	$20.00 – 25.00
Saucer	$1.00 – 1.50
Shakers, pr	$20.00 – 25.00
Sugar and lid	$14.00 – 16.00
Teapot, 8-cup	$50.00 – 60.00
Tidbit tray, 3-tier	$37.00 – 42.00

Left: Bowl, cream soup; Right: Bowl, 6¼", tab-handled cereal.

Row 1: Sugar and lid; creamer; gravy boat; shakers. Row 2: Teapot; bowl, covered vegetable.
Row 3: Cup and saucer; bowl, 5¼", fruit; bowl, 10½", oval.

Left: Butter, quarter pound "wings" top; Right: clock.

CHRISTMAS TREE AND HOLLY

The discovery of dinnerware with this decorative holiday pattern has peaked collector interest. E-style dinnerware and selected kitchenware items are available in this combination of Christmas tree and holly decals. Plates and serving pieces will generally bear the Christmas tree decal. The cups, saucers, sugar and creamer, and some of the kitchenware pieces are decorated with the holly decal. In some cases, as with the coffee pot shown, a piece may be found decorated with either decal.

The #1091, 4½" plum pudding bowl will often be found decorated with a holly decal with light green leaves. These bowls usually have gold lettering on the reverse side which reads "Keen's English Chop House, New York City." Notice two variations of the holly decal on the coffee set sugars and creamers in the photo on the opposite page.

Dinnerware	Price
Bowl, oval	$25.00 – 30.00
Cup	$16.00 – 18.00
Plate, 7¼"	$9.00 – 11.00
Plate, 10"	$22.00 – 25.00
Platter, 15½"	$27.00 – 32.00
Saucer	$3.00 – 4.00
Tidbit, 2-tier	$45.00 – 55.00

Accessories	Price
Bowl, 4½", plum pudding	$12.00 – 14.00
Coffee pot	$125.00 – 145.00
Cookie jar, Zeisel	$165.00 – 195.00
Creamer, coffee set	$16.00 – 18.00
Mug, 3 oz. Irish coffee	$18.00 – 22.00
Sugar, coffee set	$16.00 – 18.00

Front and rear of 4½" #1091 plum pudding bowl.

Row 1: Cookie jar, Zeisel; coffee set coffee pot with Christmas tree decal; coffee set coffee pot with holly decal. Row 2: Bowl, oval; tidbit, 2-tier. Row 3: Mug, 3 oz. Irish coffee; creamers and sugars, coffee set.

Left to right: Plate, 10"; cup and saucer; plate, 7¼".

GAME BIRD

The Game Bird decal features scenes with two different birds. One decal depicts an ascending male and female pheasant. The other shows a pair of geese in flight. Some pieces will have only one decal while other pieces may have both decals — one on each side. This decal is more commonly associated with the electric percolator than with a dinnerware pattern. However, some pieces of E-style dinnerware are surfacing. The most popular pieces found with this decal are the New York and Windshield teapots.

A matching metal saucepan has been found with the Ernest Sohn backstamp. Ernest Sohn was a Hall China customer and a picture of an electric percolator marketed by Sohn will be found in the section on electric percolators.

Dinnerware	Price
Bowl, 5½", fruit	$7.00 – 8.00
Bowl, oval	$25.00 – 30.00
Creamer	$12.00 – 15.00
Cup	$12.00 – 14.00
Plate, 6½"	$8.00 – 10.00
Plate, 10"	$18.00 – 22.00
Platter	$27.00 – 32.00
Saucer	$3.00 – 4.00
Sugar and lid	$20.00 – 25.00

China Accessories	Price
Bowl, 6" "Thick Rim"	$12.00 – 14.00
Bowl, 7½", "Thick Rim"	$14.00 – 16.00
Bowl, 8½", "Thick Rim"	$18.00 – 22.00
Casserole	$25.00 – 30.00
Cookie jar, Zeisel	$145.00 – 165.00
Mug, coffee	$10.00 – 12.00
Mug, Irish coffee	$16.00 – 18.00
Percolator, electric	$80.00 – 90.00
Teapot, "Grape", Thorley	$95.00 – 125.00
Teapot, New York	$100.00 – 125.00
Teapot, Windshield	$145.00 – 165.00

Left: mug, coffee; Right: mug, Irish coffee.

Electric percolator, geese decal.

Electric percolator, pheasant decal.

Mixing bowl set, "Thick Rim."

HEATHER ROSE

The Heather Rose decal dinnerware used the same E-style blanks used for the Granitetone dinnerware which Hall produced for Sears starting in the 1940s. The decal is a pink rose with green leaves which are interspersed with delicate white baby's breath. Although this dinnerware pattern dates to the fifties and sixties, it is not plentiful. However, most pieces can be found with diligent searching. Cream soups could exist, but we have not seen any and the E-style covered casserole is not plentiful.

Several shapes, other than E-style, sporting this decal include the New York teapot, the Irish coffee mug, the Washington coffee pot, the "Rayed" jug, the "Terrace" coffee pot, and several Flare-shape items. The New York teapot with the Heather decal is probably hard enough to find that it should be considered rare. The Washington coffee pots are of recent vintage and still may be made on occasion if Hall desires. Two sizes

are commonly found. The smaller 12 ounce size can be found with either a knob lid or a sunken lid. The larger six cup coffee pot has only been found with the knob-style lid. The Irish coffee mug is also a newer piece, but we have not seen many. Another new piece is the small open teapot which is Hall's London shape. The "Rayed" jug is one of the more common Heather Rose pieces.

Flare-shape pieces do not appear to be common, but there are probably enough of these out there to satisfy the demand. Three sizes of bowls, a teapot, and a cookie jar have been found. Other Flare-shape pieces with this decal should exist.

Some dealers and collectors are confusing this pattern with a similar Hall pattern — Primrose. Both patterns utilize the same E-style shape and a very similar rose decal, but Primrose does not have the dainty white sprigs of baby's breath.

Heather Rose	Price
Bowl, 5¼", fruit	$3.50 – 5.00
Bowl, 6¼", cereal	$4.50 – 6.00
Bowl, 8", flat soup	$8.00 – 10.00
Bowl, 9", salad	$14.00 – 16.00
Bowl, 9¼", oval	$14.00 – 16.00
Bowl, 6¾", Flare-shape	$9.00 – 11.00
Bowl, 7¾", Flare-shape	$10.00 – 12.00
Bowl, 8¾", Flare-shape	$12.00 – 15.00
Bowl, covered vegetable	$25.00 – 30.00
Cakeplate	$12.00 – 15.00
Coffee pot, "Terrace"	$35.00 – 40.00
Coffee pot, 30 oz., Washington	$35.00 – 45.00
Coffee pot, 12 oz., Washington	$18.00 – 22.00
Cookie jar, Flare-shape	$30.00 – 40.00
Creamer	$7.00 – 9.00
Cup	$5.50 – 6.50
Gravy boat and underplate	$15.00 – 18.00

Heather Rose	Price
Jug, "Rayed"	$12.00 – 14.00
Mug, Irish coffee	$14.00 – 16.00
Pickle dish, 9"	$6.00 – 8.00
Pie baker	$16.00 – 18.00
Plate, 6½"	$2.50 – 3.50
Plate, 7¼"	$3.50 – 5.00
Plate, 9¼"	$6.00 – 7.50
Plate, 10"	$6.50 – 7.50
Platter, 11¼", oval	$10.00 – 12.00
Platter, 13¼", oval	$13.00 – 15.00
Platter 15½", oval	$16.00 – 20.00
Saucer	$1.00 – 2.00
Sugar and lid	$14.00 – 16.00
Teapot, Flare-shape	$35.00 – 45.00
Teapot, London	$20.00 – 25.00
Teapot, New York	$75.00 – 85.00

Row 1: Coffee pot, "Terrace"; teapot, New York; coffee pot, 30 oz., Washington.
Row 2: Bowl, covered vegetable; mug, Irish coffee; teapot, London; bowl, Flare-shape.

Row 1: Bowl, tab-handled cereal; bowl, oval; plate, 6".
Row 2: Bowl, 5¼", fruit; gravy boat and underplate; cup and saucer.

PRIMROSE

Primrose is an E-style dinnerware line with a floral rose decal very similar to that of Heather Rose. However, Primrose lacks the sprigs of baby's breath. Primrose was made for Grand Union during the fifties and early sixties.

In addition to the regular E-style dinnerware, a cakeplate, pie baker, and "Rayed" jug have been found. Other pieces will probably surface eventually.

Primrose backstamp.

Primrose	Price
Ashtray	$8.00 – 10.00
Bowl, 5¼", fruit	$3.00 – 4.50
Bowl, 6¼", cereal	$4.50 – 5.50
Bowl, 8", flat soup	$8.00 – 10.00
Bowl, 9¼", oval	$12.00 – 15.00
Cakeplate	$12.00 – 15.00
Creamer	$6.00 – 8.00
Cup	$6.00 – 7.50
Jug, "Rayed"	$14.00 – 16.00
Pie baker	$18.00 – 22.00
Plate, 6½"	$2.00 – 2.50
Plate, 7¼"	$4.00 – 5.50
Plate, 9¼"	$5.00 – 6.50
Plate, 10"	$6.00 – 8.00
Platter, 13¼", oval	$15.00 – 18.00
Saucer	$1.00 – 1.50
Sugar and lid	$12.00 – 14.00

Row 1: Creamer; pie baker. Row 2: Cakeplate; bowl, oval.

SEARS' ARLINGTON

Left to Right: Creamer and sugar; bowl, covered vegetable.

Arlington is an E-style dinnerware pattern which Hall produced for Sears during the 1950s. Currently, not much of this pattern appears at shows or flea markets. The pattern is characterized by a series of three parallel blue brush-strokes which alternately intersect a winding golden vine. Pieces are nicely accented with gold trim. An example of the backstamp is shown below.

Arlington Dinnerware	Price
Bowl, 5¼", fruit	$3.00 – 4.00
Bowl, 6¼", cereal	$4.50 – 5.50
Bowl, 8", flat soup	$7.00 – 8.00
Bowl, 9¼", oval	$12.00 – 14.00
Bowl, covered vegetable	$25.00 – 28.00
Creamer	$7.00 – 9.00
Cup	$4.00 – 5.00
Gravy boat and underplate	$12.00 – 14.00
Pickle dish, 9"	$4.00 – 5.00
Plate, 6½"	$2.00 – 2.50
Plate, 7¼"	$3.50 – 4.50
Plate, 8"	$3.50 – 4.50
Plate, 9¼"	$4.00 – 5.50
Plate, 10"	$5.00 – 6.00
Platter, 11¼", oval	$12.00 – 14.00
Platter, 13¼", oval	$13.00 – 15.00
Platter, 15½", oval	$18.00 – 20.00
Saucer	$1.00 – 1.50
Sugar and lid	$10.00 – 12.00

Arlington backstamp.

SEARS' FAIRFAX

Fairfax was produced for Sears by Hall during the 1950s and it was sold under the Harmony House label. It has a white floral pattern with brown leaves in the center of the piece and the pattern is repeated in a narrow band along the edge.

Fairfax Dinnerware	*Price*
Bowl, 5¼", fruit	$3.50 – 4.50
Bowl, 6¼", cereal	$4.50 – 6.00
Bowl, 8", flat soup	$7.00 – 9.00
Bowl, 9¼", oval	$12.00 – 15.00
Creamer	$6.00 – 8.00
Cup	$4.00 – 5.00
Plate, 6½"	$2.00 – 3.00
Plate, 7¼"	$3.50 – 4.50
Plate, 8"	$3.50 – 4.50
Plate, 9¼"	$4.50 – 5.50
Plate, 10"	$5.00 – 7.00
Platter, 11¼", oval	$10.00 – 12.00
Platter, 13¼", oval	$12.00 – 14.00
Saucer	$1.00 – 2.00
Sugar and lid	$10.00 – 12.00

Row 1: Plate, 10", dinner; platter, 13¼", oval. Row 2: Creamer, sugar and lid; bowl, 8", flat soup.
Row 3: Bowl, oval; bowl, 5¼", fruit; cup and saucer.

SEARS' MONTICELLO

Row 1: Creamer; sugar and lid; bowl, 6¼", tab-handled cereal. Row 2: Bowl, 8", flat soup; cup and saucer; bowl, covered vegetable. Row 3: Gravy boat and underplate; bowl, 5¼", fruit; bowl, 9¼", oval.

Monticello was introduced in 1941, as a pattern of the Harmony House Granitetone dinnerware line by Sears. This pattern was discontinued in 1959. Granitetone was created for Sears by the noted designer, J. Palin Thorley. The pattern utilized Hall's E-style dinnerware and was named after Thomas Jefferson's Virginia home. According to Sears' ads, it features "flower sprigs in dainty blue, blue-green, pink, and yellow colors scattered in profusion on each piece." A 32-piece service for six sold for $5.79 and was designed to provide the fine china look for a modest price.

Matching style white Granitetone candlesticks without the pattern could also be added to the set. These tall candles sold for $1.69 a pair. Of interest to collectors is a listing in a 1954 Sears' catalog for handled cream soups for $6.25 each. To date, the existence of this item has not been confirmed.

Monticello Dinnerware	Price
Bowl, 5¼", fruit	$4.00 – 5.00
Bowl, 6¼", cereal	$5.00 – 6.50
Bowl, 8", flat soup	$9.00 – 11.00
Bowl, 9¼", oval	$14.00 – 16.00
Bowl, covered vegetable	$27.00 – 32.00
Creamer	$7.00 – 9.00
Cup	$5.00 – 6.00
Gravy boat and underplate	$16.00 – 18.00
Pickle dish, 9"	$5.00 – 6.00
Plate, 6½"	$2.00 – 2.50
Plate, 8"	$3.50 – 4.50
Plate, 9¼"	$5.00 – 6.00
Plate, 10"	$6.00 – 7.00

Monticello Dinnerware	Price
Platter, 11¼", oval	$11.00 – 13.00
Platter, 13¼", oval	$14.00 – 16.00
Platter, 15½", oval	$18.00 – 20.00
Saucer	$1.00 – 1.50
Sugar and lid	$12.00 – 14.00

Monticello backstamp.

Row 1: Sugar and lid; drip coffee, all-china; creamer. Row 2: Cup and saucer; bowl, 8½", flat soup; bowl, 5¼", fruit.

The Mount Vernon pattern was sold under Sears' Harmony House label. This pattern was offered in the catalog from 1941 through 1959. The style was created by designer J. Palin Thorley and the decoration was the most exquisite of the contemporary designs which Hall produced for Sears. The plate design consists of a blue-green and tan leaf border with an inner wreath of pink roses. Edges, handles, knobs, and feet are trimmed in 22K coin gold.

The eight-cup all-china drip coffee maker shown on the top shelf was available in this pattern from 1942 to 1948. The coffee maker and one hundred paper filters were available for $2.89. Also, a three-piece hostess set which included a creamer and covered sugar with the coffee maker could be purchased for $4.65. Plain white 8½" tall candlesticks which matched the style of the dinnerware were available for $1.69 a pair. There is a listing for a two-handled cream soup bowl in this pattern in a 1954 Sears' catalog. They retailed for $7.55 each. We have never seen this item in any collection.

E-style Dinnerware	Price
Bowl, 5¼", fruit	$4.00 – 6.00
Bowl, 6¼", cereal	$6.00 – 7.00
Bowl, 5", cream soup	UND
Bowl, 8", flat soup	$10.00 – 12.00
Bowl, 9¼", oval	$14.00 – 16.00
Casserole and cover	$27.00 – 32.00
Coffee pot, all-china	$95.00 – 125.00
Creamer	$8.00 – 9.00
Cup	$6.00 – 7.00
Gravy boat and underplate	$18.00 – 20.00
Pickle dish, 9"	$6.00 – 8.00
Plate, 6½"	$2.50 – 3.50
Plate, 8"	$3.00 – 4.00
Plate, 9¼"	$4.50 – 6.50
Plate, 10"	$8.00 – 9.00
Platter, 11¼", oval	$12.00 – 14.00
Platter, 13¼", oval	$14.00 – 16.00
Platter 15½", oval	$20.00 – 25.00
Saucer	$1.00 – 2.00
Sugar and lid	$12.00 – 15.00

SEARS' RICHMOND/BROWN-EYED SUSAN

Row 1: Teapot, Aladdin; sugar and lid; creamer. Row 2: Bowl set, "Thick Rim."
Row 3: Baker, French, flute; bowl, 9", round vegetable.

Richmond and Brown-Eyed Susan are two names for Hall dinnerware with the same decal. The decal consists of a cluster of brown, pink, and yellow meadow flowers which are used as a center decoration. The beauty of the design is enhanced by the use of 22K gold trim. The Richmond design, as selected by Sears, was intended to match the floral decoration of some of the Duncan Phyfe fabric of the period. Richmond had a relatively short life with Sears. It was introduced in 1941 and disappeared from their catalog in 1946.

Later, in the 1960s, this pattern was revived by Hall under the name Brown-Eyed Susan for use by trading stamp companies. Pieces from this later issue will not bear the Harmony House backstamp. During this period, Hall also used this decal on some kitchenware shapes. These additional kitchenware items made later in only the Brown-Eyed Susan era will be indicated by (BES) in the listing below.

Richmond/Brown-Eyed Susan	Price
Baker, French, flute (BES)	$12.00 – 15.00
Bowl, 5¼", fruit	$3.50 – 4.50
Bowl, 6¼", cereal	$6.00 – 7.00
Bowl, 8", flat soup	$7.00 – 9.00
Bowl, 9", salad, (BES)	$12.00 – 14.00
Bowl, 9¼", oval	$12.00 – 15.00
Creamer	$7.00 – 9.00
Cup	$5.00 – 6.50
Gravy boat and underplate	$16.00 – 18.00
Jug, "Rayed", (BES)	$12.00 – 15.00
Pickle dish, 9"	$4.00 – 5.00

Richmond/Brown-Eyed Susan	Price
Plate, 6½"	$2.00 – 2.50
Plate, 7¼"	$4.00 – 5.00
Plate, 9¼"	$5.00 – 6.50
Plate, 10"	$6.00 – 7.50
Platter, 11¼", oval	$12.00 – 14.00
Platter, 13¼", oval	$14.00 – 16.00
Platter 15½", oval	$18.00 – 22.00
Saucer	$1.00 – 1.50
Sugar and lid	$12.00 – 14.00
Teapot, Aladdin, (BES)	$60.00 – 75.00

EVA ZEISEL DESIGNS

Eva Zeisel designed the Tomorrow's Classic and Century shapes which were produced by Hall China. She was essentially working as a freelance designer while she held a teaching position at Pratt Institute in the early fifties. In 1952, nine decal patterns were created by Zeisel and her associates and students. The ensuing years resulted in the addition of more patterns. However, production problems at Hall led to the acquisition of the molds by the Hollydale pottery of California in 1957.

The Century shape consists of a dinnerware service which includes twenty-three pieces. There are four different patterns — white and three decal patterns. Plates consist of slightly distended ovals which are elongated into gently arching tips which also serve as handles. Platters and bowls are slightly elongated with the upward sloping tips forming double handles. The shapes of the teapots, jugs, casseroles, and other accessories are equally modernistic.

The Tomorrow's Classic shape consists of forty different pieces which comprised a futuristic-looking dinnerware service. The pieces differ only slightly in style from that used in the Century line. Plates are slight ovals which lack any elongated tips and bowls are essentially ovals which distend to a single elongated tip which forms a handle.

Hallcraft Century backstamp.

CENTURY FERN

The Hallcraft Century Fern pattern consists of twenty-three pieces of stylized china. The decal is comprised of leaf-like shapes in mulberry, green, and pastel blue set on a lace-like gray background. The interiors of the jugs and cups and the tops of the casserole lids, sugar lids, and teapot lids are glazed in pastel blue. Cups may be found both with the decal and without.

Century Fern	Price
Ashtray	$5.00 – 6.00
Bowl, 5¾", fruit	$3.00 – 4.50
Bowl, 8", soup	$6.00 – 7.00
Bowl, 11¾", salad	$12.00 – 14.00
Bowl, 10½", vegetable	$14.00 – 16.00
Bowl, divided vegetable	$16.00 – 18.00
Butter dish	$25.00 – 30.00
Casserole	$20.00 – 25.00
Creamer	$5.00 – 6.00
Cup	$4.00 – 5.00
Gravy boat	$12.00 – 14.00
Jug	$11.00 – 13.00

Century Fern	Price
Ladle	$8.00 – 10.00
Plate, 6"	$2.00 – 3.00
Plate, 8"	$3.50 – 5.00
Plate, 10¼"	$6.00 – 7.50
Platter, 13¾"	$12.00 – 14.00
Platter, 15"	$18.00 – 22.00
Relish, 4-part	$17.00 – 20.00
Saucer	$1.00 – 1.50
Shaker, ea.	$7.00 – 9.00
Sugar and cover	$12.00 – 15.00
Teapot, 6-cup	$50.00 – 60.00

Row 1: Jug; casserole. Row 2: Bowl, 8", soup; bowl, 11¾", salad. Row 3: plate, 8", salad; cup and saucer; bowl, 5¾", fruit.
Row 4: Bowl, divided vegetable; relish, 4-part.

CENTURY SUNGLOW

Row 1: Plate, 8"; platter, 13¾". Row 2: Bowl, divided vegetable; cup and saucer; plate, 6".

The Sunglow pattern of the Hallcraft Century shape consists of a decal which features a thin tree dotted with brilliant yellow leaves. Randomly dispersing yellow leaves also generously adorn the otherwise stark exterior surfaces. The interiors of the jugs and cups and the tops of the casseroles, teapots, and sugar lids are also finished in a matching yellow glaze. Some cups will be found with only the interior yellow glaze, while others will also sport the decal decoration.

Century Sunglow	Price	Century Sunglow	Price
Ashtray	$4.00 – 5.00	Ladle	$8.00 – 10.00
Bowl, 5¾", fruit	$3.50 – 4.50	Plate, 6"	$2.00 – 3.50
Bowl, 8", soup	$7.00 – 9.00	Plate, 8"	$3.50 – 4.50
Bowl, 11¾", salad	$11.00 – 13.00	Plate, 10¼"	$6.00 – 8.00
Bowl, 10½", vegetable	$12.00 – 14.00	Platter, 13¾"	$12.00 – 14.00
Bowl, divided vegetable	$12.00 – 15.00	Platter, 15"	$14.00 – 16.00
Butter dish	$25.00 – 30.00	Relish, 4-part	$18.00 – 22.00
Casserole	$18.00 – 22.00	Saucer	$1.00 – 1.50
Creamer	$6.00 – 8.00	Shaker, ea.	$7.00 – 9.00
Cup	$4.50 – 5.50	Sugar and cover	$12.00 – 14.00
Gravy boat	$12.00 – 14.00	Teapot, 6-cup	$55.00 – 65.00
Jug	$10.00 – 12.00		

Ad for Hallcraft by distributor Midhurst China Company in the
China and Glass Red Book from the mid-fifties.

Hallcraft advertising ashtray.

TOMORROW'S CLASSIC ARIZONA AND BUCKINGHAM

Tomorrow's Classic Arizona pattern features a decal with rust colored leaves set against a white background with traces of fine black lines. The design was originated by Charles Seliger who was an associate of Eva Zeisel. Designer Erik Blegvad was responsible for the creation of the Buckingham pattern. Pieces in this pattern exhibit an iron grill-work fence. The design varies slightly among the various items in the pattern as may be seen in the photograph. The shape of the fence is different and trees will be interspersed in some fences and lacking in others.

Item	Arizona	Buckingham
Ashtray	$5.00 – 6.00	$7.00 – 8.00
Bowl, 5¾", fruit	$4.00 – 5.00	$5.00 – 6.50
Bowl, 6", cereal	$4.50 – 5.50	$6.50 – 7.50
Bowl, 9", coupe soup	$6.00 – 7.50	$7.00 – 9.00
Bowl, 8¾", sq. open vegetable	$10.00 – 12.00	$14.00 – 16.00
Bowl, 14½", large salad	$16.00 – 18.00	$25.00 – 30.00
Bowl, 11 oz., open baker	$9.00 – 11.00	$12.00 – 14.00
Bowl, oval, celery	$11.00 – 13.00	$14.00 – 16.00
Bowl, large, ftd. fruit	$22.00 – 27.00	$27.00 – 32.00
Butter dish	$45.00 – 55.00	$60.00 – 70.00
Candlestick, 4½"	$18.00 – 22.00	$22.00 – 25.00
Candlestick, 8"	$22.00 – 25.00	$27.00 – 32.00
Casserole, 1¼ qt.	$27.00 – 32.00	$30.00 – 35.00
Casserole, 2 qt.	$30.00 – 35.00	$32.00 – 37.00
Coffee pot, 6-cup	$50.00 – 60.00	$65.00 – 75.00
Creamer	$6.50 – 8.00	$9.00 – 12.00
Creamer, a.d.	$6.50 – 8.00	$9.00 – 12.00
Cup	$5.00 – 6.00	$5.00 – 6.00
Cup, a.d.	$8.00 – 10.00	$9.00 – 12.50
Egg cup	$20.00 – 25.00	$27.00 – 30.00
Gravy boat	$12.00 – 15.00	$22.00 – 25.00
Jug, 1¼ qt.	$18.00 – 22.00	$22.00 – 27.00
Jug, 3 qt.	$20.00 – 25.00	$25.00 – 30.00
Ladle	$14.00 – 16.00	$18.00 – 20.00
Marmite and cover	$18.00 – 22.00	$22.00 – 27.00
Onion soup and cover	$20.00 – 25.00	$25.00 – 30.00
Plate, 6"	$2.00 – 2.50	$3.50 – 5.00
Plate, 8"	$3.50 – 4.50	$4.50 – 6.50
Plate, 11"	$7.00 – 9.00	$10.00 – 12.00
Platter, 12¼"	$14.00 – 16.00	$18.00 – 22.00
Platter, 15"	$18.00 – 22.00	$22.00 – 27.00
Platter, 17"	$22.00 – 27.00	$27.00 – 32.00
Saucer	$1.00 – 1.50	$1.50 – 2.50
Saucer, a.d.	$2.00 – 2.50	$2.00 – 2.50
Shaker, ea.	$7.00 – 9.00	$9.00 – 11.00
Sugar and cover	$11.00 – 13.00	$12.00 – 15.00
Sugar, open a.d.	$6.50 – 8.00	$9.00 – 12.00
Teapot, 6-cup	$65.00 – 75.00	$85.00 – 95.00
Vase	$20.00 – 25.00	$27.00 – 32.00
Vinegar bottle	$20.00 – 25.00	$27.00 – 30.00

Left to Right: Gravy boat, Arizona; jug, 1¼ qt., Arizona; marmite, Arizona.

Left to Right: Teapot, Buckingham; jug, 1¼ qt., Buckingham.

TOMORROW'S CLASSIC BOUQUET

Row 1: Shakers; ashtray; marmite; egg cup.
Row 2: Casserole; casserole, "M. J." shape; candlestick, 4½".

The colorful floral Bouquet pattern is beginning to appeal to collectors. This pattern is the most readily available and is the most highly collected of all the Hallcraft designs. In addition to the forty pieces of Classic shape, collectors will also find this decal on a shape designated "M. J." by some researchers. The "M. J." casserole and electric percolator are shown in the photographs.

Bouquet	Price	Bouquet	Price
Ashtray	$8.00 – 10.00	Gravy boat	$20.00 – 25.00
Bowl, 5¾", fruit	$4.00 – 6.00	Jug, 1¼ qt.	$20.00 – 25.00
Bowl, 6", cereal	$5.50 – 7.50	Jug, 3 qt.	$27.00 – 32.00
Bowl, 9", coupe soup	$10.00 – 12.00	Ladle	$14.00 – 16.00
Bowl, 8¾", sq. open vegetable	$16.00 – 19.00	Marmite and cover	$25.00 – 30.00
Bowl, 14½", large salad	$25.00 – 30.00	Onion soup and cover	$30.00 – 35.00
Bowl, 11 oz., open baker	$14.00 – 16.00	Percolator, electric "M. J."	$100.00 –125.00
Bowl, oval, celery	$15.00 – 18.00	Plate, 6"	$2.50 – 3.00
Bowl, large, ftd. fruit	$30.00 – 40.00	Plate, 8"	$6.00 – 7.50
Butter dish	$55.00 – 65.00	Plate, 11"	$12.00 – 15.00
Candlestick, 4½"	$25.00 – 30.00	Platter, 12¼"	$18.00 – 22.00
Candlestick, 8"	$30.00 – 40.00	Platter, 15"	$22.00 – 27.00
Casserole, 1¼ qt.	$30.00 – 35.00	Platter, 17"	$27.00 – 32.00
Casserole, 2 qt.	$37.00 – 42.00	Saucer	$1.50 – 2.50
Casserole, "M. J."	$35.00 – 40.00	Saucer, a.d.	$2.00 – 3.00
Coffee pot, 6-cup	$75.00 – 85.00	Shaker, ea.	$9.00 – 11.00
Creamer	$8.00 – 10.00	Sugar and cover	$12.00 – 15.00
Creamer, a.d.	$8.00 – 10.00	Sugar, open a.d.	$8.00 – 10.00
Cup	$7.00 – 9.00	Teapot, 6-cup	$75.00 – 85.00
Cup, a.d.	$8.00 – 10.00	Vase	$27.00 – 32.00
Egg cup	$25.00 – 28.00	Vinegar bottle	$27.00 – 32.00

Row 1: Coffee pot; electric percolator, "M. J."; teapot. Row 2: Jug, 1¼ qt.; ladle; gravy boat; creamer and sugar. Row 3: Butter; sugar, a.d.; creamer, a.d.; cup and saucer. Row 4: Bowl, 8¾", sq.; bowl, 9"; bowl, 5¾", fruit. Row 5: Plate, 6"; platter, 15".

TOMORROW'S CLASSIC CAPRICE

Caprice is a Tomorrow's Classic leaf and floral design. The colors are pastel pinks, grays, and yellows. Discerning the pattern on some of the smaller pieces is sometimes confusing since only one part of the pattern often appears on the piece.

Caprice	Price
Ashtray	$4.50 – 6.00
Bowl, 5¾", fruit	$4.50 – 5.00
Bowl, 6", cereal	$5.00 – 6.00
Bowl, 9", coupe soup	$8.00 – 9.00
Bowl, 8¾", sq. open vegetable	$13.00 – 15.00
Bowl, 14½", large salad	$17.00 – 19.00
Bowl, 11 oz., open baker	$12.00 – 14.00
Bowl, oval, celery	$13.00 – 15.00
Bowl, large, ftd. fruit	$22.00 – 27.00
Butter dish	$45.00 – 55.00
Candlestick, 4½"	$15.00 – 18.00
Candlestick, 8"	$22.00 – 27.00
Casserole, 1¼ qt.	$18.00 – 22.00
Casserole, 2 qt.	$22.00 – 27.00
Coffee pot, 6-cup	$45.00 – 55.00
Creamer	$7.50 – 9.00
Creamer, a.d.	$8.00 – 10.00
Cup	$4.50 – 6.00
Cup, a.d.	$5.00 – 7.50
Egg cup	$18.00 – 22.00
Gravy boat	$18.00 – 22.00
Jug, 1¼ qt.	$20.00 – 25.00
Jug, 3 qt.	$22.00 – 27.00
Ladle	$10.00 – 12.00
Marmite and cover	$20.00 – 25.00
Onion soup and cover	$22.00 – 27.00
Plate, 6"	$2.50 – 3.50
Plate, 8"	$4.50 – 6.50
Plate, 11"	$10.00 – 12.00
Platter, 12¼"	$15.00 – 18.00
Platter, 15"	$18.00 – 22.00
Platter, 17"	$22.00 – 27.00
Saucer	$1.50 – 2.00
Saucer, a.d.	$2.00 – 3.00
Shaker, ea.	$7.00 – 9.00
Sugar and cover	$12.00 – 14.00
Sugar, open a.d.	$8.00 – 10.00
Teapot, 6-cup	$55.00 – 65.00
Vase	$22.00 – 25.00
Vinegar bottle	$22.00 – 25.00

Row 1: Teapot; jug, 3 qt.; jug, 1¼ qt. Row 2: Vinegar bottle; bowl, oval, celery.
Row 3: Bowl, 8¾", sq.; bowl, 9".

TOMORROW'S CLASSIC FANTASY

Row 1: Candle, tall; coffee pot; ladle; gravy boat. Row 2: Egg cup; onion soup; butter; bowl, 9", soup.

Fantasy is a Hallcraft Tomorrow's Classic design expounding thin line intertwined parabolas to produce a modernistic effect. The design was created by Douglas Kelley, W. Katavolos, and Ross Littell who were Pratt Institute students of Eva Zeisel.

Fantasy	Price	Fantasy	Price
Ashtray	$4.50 – 6.00	Gravy boat	$18.00 – 22.00
Bowl, 5¾", fruit	$4.50 – 5.00	Jug, 1¼ qt.	$20.00 – 25.00
Bowl, 6", cereal	$5.00 – 6.00	Jug, 3 qt.	$22.00 – 27.00
Bowl, 9", coupe soup	$8.00 – 9.00	Ladle	$10.00 – 12.00
Bowl, 8¾", sq. open vegetable	$13.00 – 15.00	Marmite and cover	$20.00 – 25.00
Bowl, 14½", large salad	$17.00 – 19.00	Onion soup and cover	$22.00 – 27.00
Bowl, 11 oz., open baker	$12.00 – 14.00	Plate, 6"	$2.50 – 3.50
Bowl, oval, celery	$13.00 – 15.00	Plate, 8"	$4.50 – 6.50
Bowl, large, ftd. fruit	$22.00 – 27.00	Plate, 11"	$10.00 – 12.00
Butter dish	$45.00 – 55.00	Platter, 12¼"	$15.00 – 18.00
Candlestick, 4½"	$15.00 – 18.00	Platter, 15"	$18.00 – 22.00
Candlestick, 8"	$22.00 – 27.00	Platter, 17"	$22.00 – 27.00
Casserole, 1¼ qt.	$18.00 – 22.00	Saucer	$1.50 – 2.00
Casserole, 2 qt.	$22.00 – 27.00	Saucer, a.d.	$2.00 – 3.00
Coffee pot, 6-cup	$45.00 – 55.00	Shaker, ea.	$7.00 – 9.00
Creamer	$7.50 – 9.00	Sugar and cover	$12.00 – 14.00
Creamer, a.d.	$8.00 – 10.00	Sugar, open a.d.	$8.00 – 10.00
Cup	$4.50 – 6.00	Teapot, 6-cup	$55.00 – 65.00
Cup, a.d.	$5.00 – 7.50	Vase	$22.00 – 25.00
Egg cup	$18.00 – 22.00	Vinegar bottle	$22.00 – 25.00

TOMORROW'S CLASSIC FROST FLOWERS

Row 1: Gravy boat; teapot; bowl, 5¾", fruit. Row 2: Casserole; bowl, oval, celery.

The Tomorrow's Classic Frost Flowers pattern consists of a generous adornment of sprigs of blue flowers. The design was created by Eva Zeisel's assistant, Irene Haas.

Frost Flowers	Price	Frost Flowers	Price
Ashtray	$5.00 – 6.00	Gravy boat	$18.00 – 22.00
Bowl, 5¾", fruit	$4.50 – 5.00	Jug, 1¼ qt.	$20.00 – 25.00
Bowl, 6", cereal	$5.00 – 6.00	Jug, 3 qt.	$22.00 – 27.00
Bowl, 9", coupe soup	$8.00 – 10.00	Ladle	$10.00 – 12.00
Bowl, 8¾", sq. open vegetable	$14.00 – 16.00	Marmite and cover	$20.00 – 25.00
Bowl, 14½", large salad	$18.00 – 22.00	Onion soup and cover	$22.00 – 27.00
Bowl, 11 oz., open baker	$12.00 – 14.00	Plate, 6"	$2.50 – 3.50
Bowl, oval, celery	$13.00 – 15.00	Plate, 8"	$4.50 – 6.50
Bowl, large, ftd. fruit	$25.00 – 30.00	Plate, 11"	$10.00 – 12.00
Butter dish	$50.00 – 65.00	Platter, 12¼"	$15.00 – 18.00
Candlestick, 4½"	$15.00 – 18.00	Platter, 15"	$18.00 – 22.00
Candlestick, 8"	$25.00 – 30.00	Platter, 17"	$22.00 – 27.00
Casserole, 1¼ qt.	$18.00 – 22.00	Saucer	$1.50 – 2.00
Casserole, 2 qt.	$22.00 – 27.00	Saucer, a.d.	$2.00 – 3.00
Coffee pot, 6-cup	$55.00 – 65.00	Shaker, ea.	$7.00 – 9.00
Creamer	$7.50 – 9.00	Sugar and cover	$12.00 – 14.00
Creamer, a.d.	$8.00 – 10.00	Sugar, open a.d.	$8.00 – 10.00
Cup	$6.50 – 7.50	Teapot, 6-cup	$65.00 – 75.00
Cup, a.d.	$6.00 – 7.50	Vase	$22.00 – 25.00
Egg cup	$22.00 – 25.00	Vinegar bottle	$22.00 – 25.00

TOMORROW'S CLASSIC HARLEQUIN AND HOLIDAY

Row 1: Ball jug #3; cookie jar; ladle; teapot, Thorley design.

Row 2: Teapot; cup and saucer; candlestick, 4½"; jug, 1¼ qt.

    The Harlequin pattern shown on this page uses a series of abstract pink, gray, and black lines to produce a decoration. Notice in the photograph other shapes than those associated with Hallcraft will be found with this decoration.

    The Holiday pattern features an almost gaudy combination of red and black colors used to produce a leaf-like design.

Item	Harlequin	Holiday
Ashtray	$6.00 – 7.00	$5.00 – 6.50
Ball jug #3	$55.00 – 65.00	
Bowl, 5¾", fruit	$4.00 – 5.50	$4.00 – 5.50
Bowl, 6", cereal	$5.50 – 7.00	$5.00 – 6.00
Bowl, 9", coupe soup	$8.00 – 10.00	$7.00 – 9.00
Bowl, 8¾", sq. open vegetable	$14.00 – 16.00	$12.00 – 14.00
Bowl, 14½", large salad	$16.00 – 18.00	$15.00 – 17.00
Bowl, 11 oz., open baker	$12.00 – 14.00	$11.00 – 13.00
Bowl, oval, celery	$12.00 – 14.00	$11.00 – 13.00
Bowl, large, ftd. fruit	$27.00 – 32.00	$25.00 – 30.00
Butter dish	$55.00 – 65.00	$50.00 – 60.00
Candlestick, 4½"	$14.00 – 18.00	$14.00 – 18.00
Candlestick, 8"	$24.00 – 28.00	$22.00 – 27.00
Casserole, 1¼ qt.	$18.00 – 22.00	$18.00 – 20.00
Casserole, 2 qt.	$25.00 – 30.00	$22.00 – 27.00
Coffee pot, 6-cup	$45.00 – 55.00	$42.00 – 50.00
Cookie jar	$75.00 – 85.00	
Creamer	$8.00 – 10.00	$7.00 – 9.00
Creamer, a.d.	$8.00 – 10.00	$7.00 – 9.00
Cup	$6.00 – 7.00	$6.00 – 7.00
Cup, a.d.	$6.00 – 7.00	$6.00 – 7.00
Egg cup	$22.00 – 25.00	$22.00 – 25.00
Gravy boat	$18.00 – 22.00	$18.00 – 22.00
Jug, 1¼ qt.	$20.00 – 25.00	$18.00 – 22.00
Jug, 3 qt.	$25.00 – 30.00	$22.00 – 27.00
Ladle	$11.00 – 13.00	$11.00 – 13.00

Item	Harlequin	Holiday
Marmite and cover	$18.00 – 22.00	$18.00 – 22.00
Onion soup and cover	$18.00 – 22.00	$18.00 – 22.00
Plate, 6"	$2.50 – 3.50	$2.00 – 3.00
Plate, 8"	$4.50 – 6.00	$4.00 – 5.00
Plate, 11"	$10.00 – 12.00	$7.00 – 9.00
Platter, 12¼"	$14.00 – 18.00	$12.00 – 16.00
Platter, 15"	$18.00 – 22.00	$16.00 – 19.00
Platter, 17"	$22.00 – 27.00	$20.00 – 25.00
Saucer	$1.00 – 1.50	$1.00 – 1.50
Saucer, a.d.	$2.00 – 2.50	$2.00 – 2.50
Shaker, ea.	$8.00 – 9.00	$7.00 – 8.50
Sugar and cover	$12.00 – 15.00	$12.00 – 15.00
Sugar, open a.d.	$8.00 – 10.00	$7.00 – 9.00
Teapot, 6-cup	$55.00 – 65.00	$55.00 – 65.00
Teapot, Thorley	$85.00 – 95.00	
Vase	$22.00 – 24.00	$22.00 – 24.00
Vinegar bottle	$20.00 – 25.00	$20.00 – 22.00

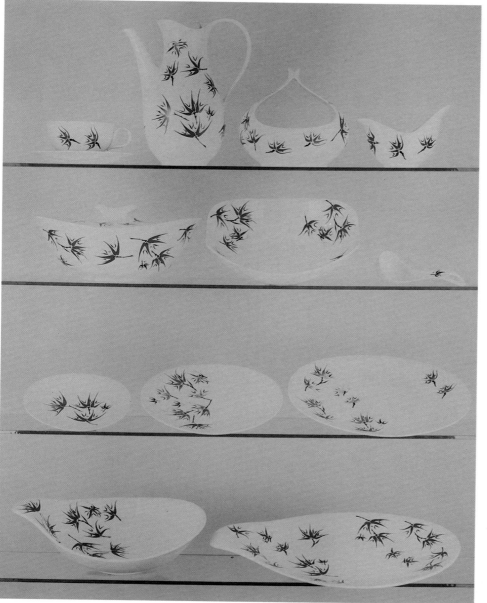

Row 1: Cup and saucer; coffee pot; gravy boat; creamer, a.d.

Row 2: Casserole; bowl, 8¾" sq.; ladle.

Row 3: Plate, 6"; Plate, 8"; Plate, 11".

Row 4: Bowl, 9"; platter, 12¼".

TOMORROW'S CLASSIC LYRIC, MULBERRY, AND PEACH BLOSSOM

Lyric

Bowl, 11 oz. open baker.

Lyric is a Hallcraft pattern which features an abstract chartreuse and black border design. It is proving to be one of the harder-to-find Hallcraft patterns.

The Hallcraft Mulberry pattern decal consists of a branch with green leaves laden with purple mulberries.

The Peach Blossom decal is a branch-like decal which has green leaves and pastel pink flowers and flower buds. Shapes other than Hallcraft have been found with this decal. An example is the E-style oval bowl shown in the picture.

Item	Lyric / Mulberry	Peach Blossom
Ashtray	$5.00 – 6.00	$7.00 – 8.00
Bowl, 5¾", fruit	$4.00 – 5.00	$5.00 – 6.50
Bowl, 6", cereal	$4.50 – 5.50	$6.50 – 7.50
Bowl, 9", coupe soup	$7.00 – 9.50	$9.00 – 11.00
Bowl, 8¾", sq. open vegetable	$10.00 – 12.00	$14.00 – 16.00
Bowl, 14½", large salad	$16.00 – 18.00	$25.00 – 30.00
Bowl, 11 oz., open baker	$9.00 – 11.00	$12.00 – 14.00
Bowl, oval, celery	$11.00 – 13.00	$14.00 – 16.00
Bowl, oval, E-shape		$18.00 – 22.00
Bowl, large, ftd. fruit	$22.00 – 27.00	$27.00 – 32.00
Butter dish	$45.00 – 55.00	$50.00 – 60.00
Candlestick, 4½"	$18.00 – 22.00	$22.00 – 25.00
Candlestick, 8"	$22.00 – 25.00	$27.00 – 32.00
Casserole, 1¼ qt.	$27.00 – 32.00	$30.00 – 35.00
Casserole, 2 qt.	$30.00 – 35.00	$32.00 – 37.00
Coffee pot, 6-cup	$50.00 – 60.00	$65.00 – 75.00
Creamer	$6.50 – 8.00	$9.00 – 12.00
Creamer, a.d.	$6.50 – 8.00	$9.00 – 12.00
Cup	$5.00 – 6.00	$6.00 – 7.00
Cup, a.d.	$8.00 – 10.00	$9.00 – 12.50

Item	Lyric / Mulberry	Peach Blossom
Egg cup	$20.00 – 25.00	$27.00 – 30.00
Gravy boat	$12.00 – 15.00	$22.00 – 25.00
Jug, 1¼ qt.	$18.00 – 22.00	$22.00 – 27.00
Jug, 3 qt.	$20.00 – 25.00	$25.00 – 30.00
Ladle	$14.00 – 16.00	$18.00 – 20.00
Marmite and cover	$18.00 – 22.00	$22.00 – 27.00
Onion soup and cover	$20.00 – 25.00	$25.00 – 30.00
Plate, 6"	$2.00 – 2.50	$3.50 – 5.00
Plate, 8"	$3.50 – 4.50	$4.50 – 6.50
Plate, 9", E-style		$5.00 – 6.00
Plate, 11"	$7.00 – 9.00	$10.00 – 12.00
Platter, 12¼"	$14.00 – 16.00	$18.00 – 22.00
Platter, 15"	$18.00 – 22.00	$22.00 – 27.00
Platter, 17"	$22.00 – 27.00	$27.00 – 32.00
Saucer	$1.00 – 1.50	$1.50 – 2.50
Saucer, a.d.	$2.00 – 2.50	$2.00 – 2.50
Shaker, ea.	$7.00 – 9.00	$9.00 – 11.00
Sugar and cover	$11.00 – 13.00	$12.00 – 15.00
Sugar, open a.d.	$6.50 – 8.00	$9.00 – 12.00
Teapot, 6-cup	$65.00 – 75.00	$75.00 – 85.00
Vase	$20.00 – 25.00	$27.00 – 32.00
Vinegar bottle	$20.00 – 25.00	$27.00 – 30.00

Mulberry

Row 1: Jug, 3 qt.; casserole, 1¼ qt.; cup and saucer.

Row 2: Shakers; ashtray; onion soup; ladle; gravy boat.

Row 3: Creamer and sugar; bowl, celery dish.

Peach Blossom

Row 1: Jug, 1¼ qt.; teapot; vinegar; shakers.

Row 2: Bowl, oval E-shape; creamer and sugar; cup and saucer.

TOMORROW'S CLASSIC PINECONE

Row 1: Teapot; casserole, 2 qt.; cup and saucer. Row 2: Gravy boat; bowl, coupe soup; marmite; mug.
Row 3: Bowl, 8¾" open vegetable; platter, 11".

Pinecone E-style dinnerware was produced for Grand Union during the fifties. In addition, the decal was also used on Hallcraft Classic shape pieces. It is not known whether all the items in the Hallcraft shape were produced. Therefore, the following listing will only include the Pinecone pieces which we have seen. The mug shown in the picture is an accessory piece which may be found in this pattern. Notice the gold trim around the top and at the base.

Pinecone — E-style Dinnerware	Price
Bowl, 5¼", fruit	$4.50 – 6.50
Bowl, 9", round	$18.00 – 22.00
Cup	$9.00 – 11.00
Plate, 6"	$2.50 – 4.00
Plate, 7¼"	$4.50 – 6.00
Plate, 9¼"	$6.50 – 8.50
Saucer	$1.00 – 1.50
Tidbit, 3-tier	$35.00 – 45.00

Pinecone — Tomorrow's Classic	Price
Ashtray	$5.00 – 6.00
Bowl, 5¾", fruit	$4.50 – 5.50
Bowl, 9", coupe soup	$9.00 – 11.00
Bowl, 8¾", sq. open vegetable	$14.00 – 16.00
Bowl, 14½", large salad	$18.00 – 22.00
Bowl, oval, celery	$12.00 – 15.00
Butter dish	$45.00 – 55.00
Casserole, 1¼ qt.	$20.00 – 25.00
Casserole, 2 qt.	$27.00 – 32.00

Pinecone — Tomorrow's Classic	Price
Creamer	$9.00 – 11.00
Cup	$7.00 – 9.00
Gravy boat	$18.00 – 22.00
Jug, 1¼ qt.	$18.00 – 22.00
Jug, 3 qt.	$20.00 – 25.00
Ladle	$14.00 – 16.00
Marmite and cover	$18.00 – 22.00
Mug	$20.00 – 25.00
Onion soup and cover	$20.00 – 25.00
Plate, 6"	$2.50 – 4.00
Plate, 8"	$4.50 – 6.50
Plate, 11"	$9.00 – 11.00
Platter, 12¼"	$16.00 – 18.00
Platter, 15"	$20.00 – 24.00
Saucer	$1.50 – 2.00
Shaker, ea.	$8.00 – 10.00
Sugar and cover	$16.00 – 18.00
Teapot, 6-cup	$75.00 – 85.00

TOMORROW'S CLASSIC SPRING

Row 1: Jug, 1¼ qt.; sugar, a.d.; creamer, a.d.; ashtray. Row 2: Butter dish; cup and saucer; plate, 6".
Row 3: Bowl, oval celery; bowl, 9", coupe soup.

Tomorrow's Classic Spring pattern features a pastel color floral arrangement. Pink, turquoise, and green are deftly interwoven to provide a soft pleasing pattern.

Spring	Price	Spring	Price
Ashtray	$4.50 – 6.00	Gravy boat	$18.00 – 22.00
Bowl, 5¾", fruit	$4.50 – 5.00	Jug, 1¼ qt.	$20.00 – 25.00
Bowl, 6", cereal	$5.00 – 6.00	Jug, 3 qt.	$22.00 – 27.00
Bowl, 9", coupe soup	$8.00 – 9.00	Ladle	$10.00 – 12.00
Bowl, 8¾", sq. open vegetable	$13.00 – 15.00	Marmite and cover	$20.00 – 25.00
Bowl, 14½", large salad	$17.00 – 19.00	Onion soup and cover	$22.00 – 27.00
Bowl, 11 oz., open baker	$11.00 – 13.00	Plate, 6"	$2.50 – 3.50
Bowl, oval, celery	$10.00 – 12.00	Plate, 8"	$4.50 – 6.50
Bowl, large, ftd. fruit	$22.00 – 27.00	Plate, 11"	$8.00 – 10.00
Butter dish	$45.00 – 55.00	Platter, 12¼"	$15.00 – 18.00
Candlestick, 4½"	$15.00 – 18.00	Platter, 15"	$18.00 – 22.00
Candlestick, 8"	$22.00 – 27.00	Platter, 17"	$22.00 – 27.00
Casserole, 1¼ qt.	$18.00 – 22.00	Saucer	$1.50 – 2.00
Casserole, 2 qt.	$22.00 – 27.00	Saucer, a.d.	$2.00 – 3.00
Coffee pot, 6-cup	$45.00 – 55.00	Shaker, ea.	$7.00 – 9.00
Creamer	$7.50 – 9.00	Sugar and cover	$12.00 – 14.00
Creamer, a.d.	$8.00 – 10.00	Sugar, open a.d.	$8.00 – 10.00
Cup	$5.00 – 6.00	Teapot, 6-cup	$55.00 – 65.00
Cup, a.d.	$5.00 – 7.50	Vase	$22.00 – 25.00
Egg cup	$18.00 – 22.00	Vinegar bottle	$22.00 – 25.00

PART II: KITCHENWARE SHAPES

Hall introduced its first modern era kitchenware line — "Medallion" — in 1932. The two initial colors were ivory and lettuce. Successful marketing in this venture soon led to the addition of other colors and the introduction of new shapes. Decals were also applied to both ivory and cobalt bodies and new patterns of kitchenware were developed. In addition to creating new kitchenware patterns, the kitchenware shapes were decorated with the appropriate decals and were incorporated into the dinnerware lines shown in Part I.

The collectibility of the solid color kitchenware has increased remarkably over the past few years since many collectors have learned that Hall kitchenware is very serviceable as well as attractive. The Chinese red and cobalt have been especially popular. Other interesting colors would probably also be popular with collectors if enough pieces could be found to put together meaningful sets.

The kitchenware section of this book is divided into two separate parts — kitchenware shapes and kitchenware decal designs. Patterns in each area will appear in alphabetical order.

These "Medallion" shape reamers are shown in the photo below. Although none is common, the one in the lettuce green color is seen most often. The other two are hard enough to find that they might be considered rare. For information on pricing see the "Medallion" and "Stonewall" sections in this kitchenware chapter. Collectors need to be aware that Hall China is currently producing a modified version of the "Medallion" reamer for a private distributor. The new reamer is being sold with the Autumn Leaf, Red Poppy, and Crocus decals. Look for it to be used with more decals in the future.

"Medallion" shape reamers.

Instructions and guarantee from Jewel pamphlet.

"FIVE BAND"

Row 1: Cookie jar; carafe; syrup; shakers. Row 2: Bowl, 6"; jug, 6¼"; jug, 5"; batter bowl.

The "Five Band" kitchenware line was introduced in 1936. Chinese red was the most popular color then and is still the most collectible color today. Other colors including cobalt, Indian red, marine, cadet, ivory, and canary are often found. Some items in the "Five Band" shape will also be found decorated with numerous decals in both dinnerware and kitchenware patterns. To date the carafe has not been found with a decal pattern. The casserole had two different types of lids — knob handle and loop-shaped handle.

Item	Red/Cobalt	Other Colors
Batter bowl	$40.00 – 55.00	$15.00 – 25.00
Bowl, 6"	$10.00 – 12.00	$7.00 – 10.00
Bowl, 7¼"	$15.00 – 18.00	$9.00 – 12.00
Bowl, 8¾"	$20.00 – 25.00	$10.00 – 15.00
Carafe	$100.00 – 135.00	$60.00 – 85.00
Casserole, 8"	$30.00 – 35.00	$15.00 – 25.00
Coffee pot		$16.00 – 18.00
Cookie jar	$65.00 – 85.00	$45.00 – 60.00
Jug, 6¼"	$22.00 – 25.00	$14.00 – 18.00
Jug, 5"	$30.00 – 35.00	$18.00 – 25.00
Shakers, ea.	$11.00 – 13.00	$9.00 – 11.00
Syrup	$50.00 – 65.00	$40.00 – 50.00

"MEDALLION"

"Medallion," which was introduced in 1932, was Hall's first kitchenware line. The original issue consisted of the square leftover, the teapot, the casserole, the four sizes of jugs, and the six piece bowl set. These were made initially in the ivory and lettuce colors. The #1 size bowl is the same as the custard and the #1 size jug is the same as the creamer. Later other colors and pieces were added, but the only other color appearing with any frequency is Chinese red. Unusual pieces include the all-china drip coffee pot, the stack set, the square leftover, and the juicer. The bowl pictured below is a scarcely found ruffled, tab-handled serving piece which has also been found in a few decal patterns.

"Medallion"	Lettuce	Ivory	Other Colors
Bowl, #2, 5¼"	$8.00 – 10.00	$3.50 – 5.00	$11.00 – 14.00
Bowl, #3, 6"	$7.00 – 9.00	$3.00 – 3.50	$10.00 – 12.00
Bowl, #4, 7¼"	$8.00 – 10.00	$4.00 – 5.00	$11.00 – 14.00
Bowl, #5, 8½"	$10.00 – 12.00	$6.00 – 7.00	$15.00 – 18.00
Bowl, #6, 10"	$18.00 – 22.00	$8.00 – 10.00	$25.00 – 30.00
Bowl, 9¼", ruffled	$35.00 – 45.00		
Casserole	$20.00 – 25.00	$9.00 – 11.00	$25.00 – 30.00
Creamer	$8.00 – 10.00	$3.00 – 4.00	$10.00 – 14.00
Custard	$5.00 – 6.50	$3.00 – 4.50	$6.00 – 9.00
Drip coffee pot	$85.00 – 110.00	$25.00 – 30.00	$100.00 – 145.00
Drip jar	$12.00 – 14.00	$7.00 – 9.00	$18.00 – 22.00
Jug, ice lip, 4 pt.	$18.00 – 22.00	$7.00 – 9.00	$27.00 – 32.00
Jug, ice lip, 5 pt.	$22.00 – 27.00	$8.00 – 10.00	$30.00 – 35.00
Jug, 4¼", 5", 5½"	$12.00 – 15.00	$6.00 – 9.00	$18.00 – 22.00
Jug, 6½", 7"	$18.00 – 22.00	$9.00 – 11.00	$20.00 – 28.00
Leftover, square	$35.00 – 45.00	$15.00 – 18.00	$45.00 – 55.00
Reamer	$350.00 – 400.00		$475.00 – 625.00
Shakers, ea.	$15.00 – 18.00	$10.00 – 12.00	$18.00 – 20.00
Stack set	$45.00 – 55.00	$22.00 – 27.00	$50.00 – 60.00
Sugar and lid	$14.00 – 16.00	$6.00 – 8.00	$14.00 – 16.00
Teapot, 40 oz.	$65.00 – 85.00	$30.00 – 40.00	$95.00 – 110.00
Teapot, 64 oz.	$70.00 – 90.00	$25.00 – 30.00	$100.00 – 125.00

Ruffled tab- handled "Medallion" bowl.

Row 1: Leftover, square; custard; teapot. Row 2: Juicer; casserole; juicer. Row 3: Drip coffee; bowl #3; jug #5.

"PERT," TAB-HANDLED, STRAIGHT-SIDED

The "Pert" kitchenware shape was introduced in 1941. It is most commonly found in the colors Chinese red/white and cadet/white. These pieces have solid colored bodies with contrasting Hi-white handles and knobs. Usually, the cadet/white colored items are found decorated with a floral decal such as Rose Parade. White bodied pieces in this shape also exist and they are usually decorated with a decal of one of the kitchenware patterns.

A lid to the sugar has appeared. The limited number of lids which have surfaced indicated that a lid was not a regular feature for this style sugar. The rounded oval shape of this lid is significantly different from that of the two sizes of teapot lids. For a comparison of the three lids see the photo below.

The tab-handled and straight-sided shapes are frequently found in Chinese red or cadet with contrasting Hi-white features, and are associated with the "Pert" line. Tab-handled items normally found are a casserole, drip jar, and bean pot. Straight-sided pieces which compliment "Pert" kitchenware are a custard cup and four sizes of mixing bowls.

Kitchenware	Chinese Red	Cadet
Bean pot, tab-handled	$40.00 – 50.00	$27.00 – 32.00
Bowl, 5¼", straight-sided	$8.00 – 10.00	$7.00 – 8.00
Bowl, 6", straight-sided	$10.00 – 12.00	$5.00 – 6.00
Bowl, 7½", straight-sided	$14.00 – 16.00	$8.00 – 10.00
Bowl, 9", straight-sided	$18.00 – 22.00	$12.00 – 14.00
Casserole, tab-handled	$25.00 – 30.00	$16.00 – 18.00
Creamer, "Pert"	$9.00 – 12.00	$7.00 – 9.00
Custard, straight-sided	$7.00 – 9.00	$4.00 – 5.00
Drip jar, tab-handled	$18.00 – 22.00	$10.00 – 12.00
Jug, 5", "Pert"	$14.00 – 18.00	$8.00 – 9.00
Jug, 6½", "Pert"	$18.00 – 22.00	$9.00 – 11.00
Jug, 7½", "Pert"	$25.00 – 30.00	$11.00 – 13.00
Shakers, "Pert", ea.	$7.00 – 9.00	$4.00 – 5.00
Sugar, "Pert"	$9.00 – 12.00	$6.00 – 7.00
Sugar lid, "Pert"	$175.00 – 225.00	UND
Teapot, 4-cup, "Pert"	$25.00 – 32.00	$14.00 – 16.00
Teapot, 6-cup, "Pert"	$32.00 – 37.00	$18.00 – 20.00

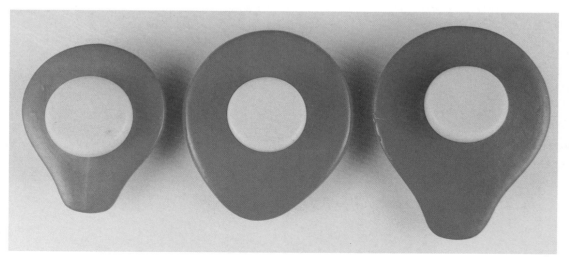

Left to Right: "Pert" 4-cup teapot lid; "Pert" sugar lid; "Pert" 6-cup teapot lid.

Row 1: Jug, 7½"; jug, 6½"; jug, 5".
Row 2: Teapot, 6-cup; teapot, 4-cup; sugar; creamer.
Row 3: Shakers; casserole, tab-handled; drip jar, tab-handled.
Row 4: Bean pot, tab-handled; bowl, 7½" straight-sided; bowl, 6" straight-sided.

"RADIANCE"

Following the success of the first kitchenware line, Hall introduced a second shape — "Radiance" — in 1933. "Radiance" will be found in a variety of colors, but Chinese red is the most common and the most desirable to today's collectors. The easiest pieces to find are the mixing bowls and the medium-size jugs. However, the lids to most sizes of the jugs are not easily found. Jugs without lids will generally bring about one-third of the prices listed below. The hardest items to locate are the condiment jar, the reamer, and the all-china drip coffee pot. The condiment jar is not turning up in the solid colors, although it is beginning to show up in several of the decal lines.

Although many cereal sets, which include four canisters and two matching shakers, have found their way into collectors hands, the demand for these sets has remained strong. The cereal set was introduced in 1938,

and was produced in numerous colors. Many "Radiance" shape kitchenware items will be found in the various decal lines.

A shape which is very similar to "Radiance" is the "Rayed" shape commonly associated with the Autumn Leaf pattern. "Rayed" shape pieces have a similar style and the same vertical line in their body. The most significant difference is in the ear-shaped handles which are present on such items as the "Rayed" jugs, teapots, and coffee pots.

The #2 mixing bowl and drip jar bottom are similar enough to cause some confusion among dealers and collectors. The following measurements should help to clarify the problem. The #2 bowl measures 5⅛" across the top and the base is about 2¼" in diameter. The drip jar bottom is 2⅝" in diameter at the top and has a 3¾" diameter base.

"Radiance"	Red/Cobalt	Ivory	Other Colors
Bowl, #1, 3½"	$8.00 – 10.00	$2.00 – 3.00	$6.00 – 7.00
Bowl, #2, 5¼"	$16.00 – 18.00	$3.50 – 5.00	$12.00 – 15.00
Bowl, #3, 6"	$9.00 – 11.00	$3.00 – 3.50	$7.00 – 9.00
Bowl, #4, 7¼"	$14.00 – 16.00	$5.00 – 6.00	$10.00 – 12.00
Bowl, #5, 8½"	$16.00 – 20.00	$7.00 – 9.00	$14.00 – 18.00
Bowl, #6, 10"	$22.00 – 27.00	$9.00 – 11.00	$20.00 – 25.00
Canister, 2 qt.	$85.00 – 100.00	$18.00 – 20.00	$85.00 – 100.00
Casserole	$30.00 – 35.00	$10.00 – 12.00	$20.00 – 30.00
Condiment jar	UND	UND	UND
Drip coffee pot	$150.00 – 200.00	$25.00 – 30.00	$150.00 – 200.00
Drip jar	$22.00 – 27.00	$7.00 – 9.00	$18.00 – 22.00
*Jug, 3¼" #1; 4¼" #2	$65.00 – 75.00	$10.00 – 14.00	$60.00 – 70.00
*Jug, 4¾" #3; 5¼" #4	$60.00 – 70.00	$12.00 – 14.00	$60.00 – 70.00
*Jug, 6¼" #5; 6¾ #6	$65.00 – 75.00	$12.00 – 14.00	$60.00 – 75.00
Reamer	UND	UND	UND
Shaker, canister style	$40.00 – 50.00	$10.00 – 20.00	$30.00 – 45.00
Stack set	$95.00 – 115.00	$30.00 – 42.00	$95.00 – 115.00
Teapot, 6-cup	$175.00 – 225.00	$50.00 – 65.00	$160.00 – 210.00

*With lid

Row 1: Cereal set canister set. Row 2: Cereal set shakers; bowl, 6"; teapot.

Row 1: Cereal set canisters: cadet blue, Indian red, cobalt, Chinese red.
Row 2: Cereal set shakers; jug and cover, 6¼"; jug and cover, 5¼"; jug and cover, 4¼".

"RIBBED"

"Ribbed" kitchenware was introduced in 1935 under the name Russetware. The line was originally named for its russet color. Later, Chinese red was produced and it became the predominate color in the line. Today, all colors of this shape, including Chinese red are hard-to-find. The bakers, ramekins, and custards were made in assorted sizes which are listed in the price guide below.

The 12 ounce covered onion soup (sometimes called a marmite) is listed in a 1935 Sears' catalog. Original prices included a set of six custard cups for $1.79; the bean pot for $1.15; and the individual onion soup for .49¢. According to the ad, the casserole was a truly multi-purpose item. It could be used as an open baker; a pie plate (the cover inverted); a two-unit baker (the casserole with the cover inverted); or as a covered baker. Russetware was heralded as "an inexpensive reproduction of expensive imported china" and was also listed by the Good Housekeeping Institute.

The "Rutherford" shape teapot will also be found in some of the decal lines without ribbing. The handled shakers will be found with black lettering and with raised letters. A four-piece set which includes salt, pepper, sugar, and flour is available. The two shapes of teapots and the side handled casserole are not often seen.

"Ribbed"	Russet/Red	Other Colors
Baker, 8, 10, & 12 oz., diag. rib	$4.00 – 6.00	$3.00 – 4.00
Baker, 1, 1½ & 2 pt., diag. rib	$6.00 – 9.00	$4.00 – 5.00
Baker, 2 & 3 qt. diag. rib	$14.00 – 16.00	$9.00 – 11.00
Baker, 2½ & 3 pt., vert. rib	$8.00 – 10.00	$4.00 – 6.00
Baker, 2 & 3 qt., vert. rib	$14.00 – 16.00	$9.00 – 11.00
Bowl, 9", salad	$16.00 – 18.00	$12.00 – 14.00
Bowl, 6¼"	$9.00 – 12.00	$5.00 – 6.00
Bowl, 8¼"	$14.00 – 16.00	$6.00 – 8.00
Bowl, 9½"	$16.00 – 18.00	$8.00 – 10.00
Casserole, 8"	$22.00 – 25.00	$14.00 – 16.00
Casserole, side handle	$45.00 – 50.00	$25.00 – 30.00
Custard, 3½, 5, & 7 oz.	$7.00 – 10.00	$3.00 – 5.00
Onion soup and cover	$25.00 – 30.00	$12.00 – 14.00
Ramekin, 2 & 2¾ oz.	$5.00 – 6.00	$3.00 – 3.50
Ramekin, 4 & 4½ oz.	$6.00 – 7.00	$4.00 – 5.00
Ramekin, 6 oz.	$6.50 – 7.50	$4.00 – 5.00
Ramekin, 4 oz., scalloped	$5.00 – 6.50	$4.00 – 5.00
Shaker, handled, ea.	$10.00 – 12.50	$6.00 – 8.00
Teapot, Globe shape	$195.00 – 225.00	
Teapot, "Rutherford"	$185.00 – 210.00	

Row 1: Teapot, "Rutherford" shape; teapot, Globe shape; shaker, handled with raised letters.
Row 2: Casserole, 9½"; shakers, handled with black letters. Row 3: Bowl, 6¼"; onion soup and cover; custard.

"Ribbed" side handle French casserole.

"SUNDIAL"

The "Sundial" kitchenware shape was introduced in 1938. The most commonly found color is Chinese red. The casseroles, sugars and creamers, individual teapots, and coffee pots will be found in a number of sizes and some of these pieces are still available. Look at the Hall backstamp on these pieces to help in determining age.

The hardest pieces to find are the coffee server and the cookie jar. The wholesale price of the cookie jar in 1940 was $2.00. Today, a cookie jar in cobalt or red will bring over $100.00.

"Sundial"	Red/Cobalt	Other Colors
Batter jug	$100.00 – 125.00	$65.00 – 75.00
*Casserole, #1, 4¾"	$18.00 – 22.00	$14.00 – 18.00
Casserole, #2, 5¼"	$25.00 – 30.00	$17.00 – 20.00
Casserole, #3, 6½"	$25.00 – 30.00	$17.00 – 20.00
Casserole, #4, 8"	$22.00 – 27.00	$22.00 – 27.00
Coffee pot, individual	$40.00 – 50.00	$35.00 – 40.00
*Creamer	$9.00 – 11.00	$7.00 – 10.00
Coffee server	$200.00 – 250.00	$150.00 – 200.00
Cookie jar	$150.00 – 175.00	$100.00 – 150.00
*Sugar	$10.00 – 12.00	$9.00 – 11.00
Syrup	$80.00 – 110.00	$60.00 – 80.00
Teapot, individual	$40.00 – 55.00	$30.00 – 40.00
Teapot, six cup	$85.00 – 125.00	$75.00 – 110.00

Row 1: Cookie jar; coffee server; teapot, six cup.
Row 2: Batter jug; coffee pot, individual; sugar and creamer.
Row 3: Syrup; casserole, 5¼"; casserole, 8".

KITCHENWARE PATTERNS
ACACIA AND BEAUTY

Acacia is a 1940s pattern which is not easy to find. Many of the pieces which have been turning up are in the "Radiance" shape. The appearance of the all-china drip coffee pot, the "Radiance" teapot, stack set, and covered jugs has generated renewed interest in this pattern among collectors. Dinnerware with this pattern has been found. However, all the dinnerware found to date had been made by Taylor, Smith, and Taylor. Hall purists may not find a mixture acceptable, but the two styles of pottery look nice together.

The name "Beauty" will usually have a color associated with it as collectors attempt to distinguish the color background upon which the decal has been placed. For example, if the decal is on an item with a totally white background, the piece is referred to as "White Beauty." Pieces of "Black Beauty" will have parts with a Hi-black glaze. However, the colorful orange and black decal will appear on a portion which has a Hi-white glaze. Very few kitchenware pieces with this decal are being found and no dinnerware is known. Among the items most frequently seen are the "Radiance" casserole and the handled shakers with a white background. The casserole shown on the left side of the middle shelf in the metal holder had the Foreman Brothers backstamp. The 12" round bowl on the left side of the bottom shelf is unusual. It has a light yellow glaze and is trimmed in platinum. The side handled French casserole and the #691 all-china drip coffee pot are new additions to the "Beauty" listing.

Kitchenware	Acacia	Beauty
Bean pot, New England, #4	$80.00 – 90.00	$90.00 – 110.00
Bowl, 9½", salad		$20.00 – 25.00
Bowl, 12", salad		$25.00 – 35.00
Bowl, 6", "Radiance"	$14.00 – 16.00	$16.00 – 18.00
Bowl, 7½", "Radiance"	$18.00 – 20.00	$20.00 – 22.00
Bowl, 9", "Radiance"	$18.00 – 22.00	$22.00 – 27.00
Bowl, 10", "Radiance"	$22.00 – 27.00	
Bowl, 8½", "Thin Rim"	$18.00 – 20.00	
Casserole, (Forman), 2-handled		$30.00 – 40.00
Casserole, "Medallion"	$32.00 – 35.00	
Casserole, "Radiance"	$30.00 – 35.00	$32.00 – 35.00
Casserole, round knob handle		$35.00 – 40.00
Casserole, side handled		$40.00 – 45.00
Casserole, "Thick Rim"		$32.00 – 37.00
Drip coffee pot, all-china, #691		$180.00 – 210.00
Drip coffee pot, all-china "Radiance"	$150.00 – 175.00	
Custard, "Radiance"	$7.00 – 9.00	
Drip jar and lid, "Radiance"	$20.00 – 25.00	
Drip jar and lid, "Thick Rim"		$22.00 – 27.00
*Jug, "Radiance", #1	$70.00 – 75.00	
*Jug, "Radiance", #2	$60.00 – 65.00	
*Jug, "Radiance", #3, #4	$45.00 – 55.00	
*Jug, "Radiance", #5, #6	$60.00 – 65.00	
Marmite and cover	$30.00 – 35.00	$32.00 – 37.00
Shakers, handled ea.	$14.00 – 16.00	$18.00 – 22.00
Stack set, "Radiance"	$80.00 – 95.00	$90.00 – 110.00
Teapot, "Radiance"	$135.00 – 165.00	
Teapot, "Rutherford"		$175.00 – 225.00
Tea set, Tea-for-Four	$225.00 – 250.00	

*With cover

Acacia

Row 1: Jug, #5, "Radiance"; Drip coffee pot, "Radiance"; teapot, "Radiance."

Row 2: Jug, #3, "Radiance"; tea set, Tea-for-Four; marmite.

Row 3: Bowl, 8½", "Thin Rim"; custard, "Radiance."

Beauty

Row 1: Drip coffee pot, #691; jug, #5, "Radiance"; casserole, round with knob handle.

Row 2: Casserole, 2-handled, Forman Brothers; casserole, side handled, French; shakers, handled.

Row 3: Salad bowl, 12", Lemon Beauty; bowl, 9½", salad.

BLUE BLOSSOM

Blue Blossom is a blue-body decal kitchenware line which was introduced in 1939. The decal consists of an elongated green leaf tipped with a colorful red, yellow, and white iris-like flower. A Blue Blossom morning set tea service has been found advertised in a 1940s Blackwell-Wieland Company wholesale catalog. It is referred to in that catalog as an "Apple Blossom" pattern. The wholesale price for the entire set — teapot, sugar, creamer, and lids — was $2.60. Notice the teapot and creamer are the same shape as the No. 1 tea set teapot and creamer. However, the sugar to the Blue Blossom set has handles and a lid. The sugar to the No. 1 tea set is handleless and has no lid. Also, no cups, saucers, or plates have been found with the Blue Blossom set.

New shapes with this decal continue to be uncovered. Perhaps the crown jewel of the new additions to this pattern is the #691 all-china drip coffee pot. Other pieces new to the listing are the Hook Cover teapot, the Donut jug, the "Zephyr" water bottle, and the New York teapot. Significant additions to any collection include canisters and matching shakers, the Airflow teapot, and the "Zephyr" style butter and leftover. Other interesting pieces which are difficult to find are the Streamline teapot, and the "Sundial" coffee server, batter bowl, and cookie jar. Notice the decal on the shirred egg dish is on the white interior area.

Considering the relatively high price of the more desirable pieces of this pattern, collector interest is almost unbelievable. New collectors are aggressively competing with seasoned veterans for the limited supply and the prices are gradually rising.

Rare New York shape teapot in Blue Blossom pattern.

Kitchenware	Price
Ball jug, #1	$100.00 – 125.00
Ball jug, #2	$100.00 – 125.00
Ball jug, #3	$95.00 – 110.00
Ball jug, #4	$100.00 – 125.00
Batter jug, "Sundial"	$200.00 – 250.00
Bean pot, New England, #4	$140.00 – 165.00
Bowl, 6", "Thick Rim"	$27.00 – 30.00
Bowl, 7½", "Thick Rim"	$27.00 – 32.00
Bowl, 8½", "Thick Rim"	$30.00 – 40.00
Butter, 1 lb., "Zephyr"-style	$400.00 – 500.00
Canister, "Radiance"	$140.00 – 160.00
Casserole, #76, round	$40.00 – 55.00
Casserole, #77, round	$45.00 – 60.00
Casserole, #100, oval	$55.00 – 65.00
Casserole, "Five Band"	$50.00 – 60.00
Casserole, "Sundial", #1	$50.00 – 60.00
Casserole, "Sundial", #4	$40.00 – 55.00
Casserole, "Thick Rim"	$50.00 – 60.00

Kitchenware	Price
Coffee server, "Sundial"	$300.00 – 340.00
Cookie jar, "Five Band"	$150.00 – 175.00
Cookie jar, "Sundial"	$250.00 – 290.00
Creamer, morning set	$35.00 – 45.00
Creamer, New York	$30.00 – 40.00
Custard, "Thick Rim"	$14.00 – 16.00
Drip coffee pot, #691	$325.00 – 375.00
Drip jar, #1188, open	$40.00 – 50.00
Drip jar and cover, "Thick Rim"	$45.00 – 55.00
Jug, Donut	$195.00 – 225.00
Jug, 1½ pt., "Five Band"	$50.00 – 60.00
Jug, 2 qt., "Five Band"	$65.00 – 75.00
Jug, loop handle	$90.00 – 110.00
Leftover, loop handle	$85.00 – 100.00
Leftover, "Zephyr"-style	$110.00 – 135.00
Shakers, "Five Band", ea	$20.00 – 25.00
Shakers, handled, ea. (4)	$20.00 – 27.00
Shakers, "Radiance", canister style, ea.	$45.00 – 55.00

Kitchenware	Price		Kitchenware	Price
Shirred egg dish	$55.00 – 65.00		Teapot, morning set	$195.00 – 220.00
Sugar and lid, morning set	$50.00 – 60.00		Teapot, New York	$200.00 – 235.00
Sugar and lid, New York	$40.00 – 50.00		Teapot, "Sundial"	$240.00 – 260.00
Syrup, "Sundial"	$120.00 – 145.00		Teapot, Streamline	$245.00 – 285.00
Teapot, Airflow	$200.00 – 250.00		Water bottle, "Zephyr"	$225.00 – 250.00
Teapot, Hook Cove	$200.00 – 250.00			

Row 1: Cookie jar, "Sundial"; coffee server, "Sundial"; teapot, "Sundial."

Row 2: Batter jug, "Sundial"; syrup, "Sundial"; casserole, #1, "Sundial."

Row 3: Leftover, loop handle; casserole #77, round; custard, "Thick Rim."

Row 1: Jug, loop-handled; drip coffee pot, #691; jug, Donut.

Row 2: Ball jug, #4; Ball jug, #3; Ball jug, #2.

Row 3: Ball jug, #1; teapot, morning set; creamer and sugar, morning set.

Row 1: Canisters, "Radiance"; shakers, canister style, "Radiance."
Row 2: Teapot, Hook Cover; teapot, Streamline.
Row 3: Leftover, "Zephyr" style; butter, "Zephyr" style; shirred egg dish.

Row 1: Cookie jar, "Five Band"; jug, 2 qt., "Five Band"; jug, 1½ pt., "Five Band."
Row 2: Bean pot, New England, #4; shakers, handled; shakers, "Five Band."

"BLUE CROCUS" AND "BLUE FLORAL"

"Blue Crocus" is a kitchenware pattern which uses the crocus decal with pieces having a cadet blue body. Currently, only a few bowls, a casserole, and the handled shakers have been found in this pattern

"Blue Crocus" handled shakers.

WILL HAVE THESE ITEMS AVAILABLE HIS NEXT TRIP!

2 - QUART CASSEROLE
Covered casserole for simplified cooking and serving. Guaranteed against heat breakage. Cooks evenly. Makes an attractive help-yourself serving dish. Hall Ovenware . . . Cadet Blue pattern.

$350

3 - PIECE BOWL SET
A nest of one, two, and three-quart bowls. Ideal for mixing, baking, serving, storing. Guaranteed against heat breakage. Cadet Blue pattern — blue on the outside with dainty floral pattern on the inside rim.

$200

Jewel Company ad showing "Blue Floral."

The "Blue Floral" pattern consists of a set of three mixing bowls and a casserole. The bowls have cadet blue exteriors and white interiors with a tiny floral sprig decoration. The casserole has a cadet blue base and a white lid with a large blue knob. The floral decoration of the casserole is on the white part of the lid. This pattern was made for the Jewel Tea Company during the mid 1940s. The casserole retailed for $2.00 and the three piece bowl set was $3.50.

Kitchenware	"Blue Floral"	"Blue Crocus"
Bowl, 6¼"	$10.00 – 12.00	
Bowl, 7¾"	$12.00 – 14.00	
Bowl, 9"	$16.00 – 18.00	
Bowl, 6", straight-sided		$16.00 – 18.00
Bowl, 7½", straight-sided		$18.00 – 22.00
Bowl, 9", straight-sided		$25.00 – 27.00
Bowl, 6", "Thick Rim"		$16.00 – 18.00
Bowl, 7½", "Thick Rim"		$18.00 – 22.00
Bowl, 8½", "Thick Rim"		$25.00 – 27.00
Casserole	$25.00 – 30.00	
Casserole, "Thick Rim"		$40.00 – 50.00
Shakers, handled, ea.		$25.00 – 30.00

BLUE GARDEN

Blue Garden is a kitchenware pattern employing a floral decal on a cobalt body. The delicate white flowers and green leaves are not as colorful as the decoration of the Blue Blossom pattern, but they are still attractive enough to perk collector interest. Also, prize pieces such as the "Sundial" coffee server, "Zephyr" style water bottle, butter, or leftover are bound to attract a lot of attention in any collection. Some veteran Hall collectors, who had previously thought Blue Garden contained an insignificant number of pieces, are now looking at this pattern again. Both old and new collectors are finding the search for these pieces is not effortless. The only item anyone is finding in abundance is the "Sundial" #4 casserole. Most other pieces are scarce, but the list of known items continues to grow and so does the number of collectors.

New additions to the list of known pieces are both sizes of "Five Band" jug, the canister style shakers, the "Five Band" casserole, and the Donut jug.

Row 1: Donut jug; bean pot, New England, #4; jug, 1½ pt., "Five Band."
Row 2: Water bottle, "Zephyr"; leftover, "Zephyr"; butter, "Zephyr."
Row 3: Casserole, "Five Band"; shakers, handled; custard, "Thick Rim."

Kitchenware	Price
Ball jug, #1	$70.00 – 85.00
Ball jug, #2	$70.00 – 85.00
Ball jug, #3	$60.00 – 70.00
Ball jug, #4	$65.00 – 75.00
Batter jug, "Sundial"	$185.00 – 210.00
Bean pot, New England, #4	$125.00 – 145.00
Bowl, 6", "Radiance"	$20.00 – 22.00
Bowl, 7½", "Radiance"	$22.00 – 27.00
Bowl, 9", "Radiance"	$30.00 – 35.00
Bowl, 6", "Thick Rim"	$18.00 – 20.00
Bowl, 7½", "Thick Rim"	$22.00 – 25.00
Bowl, 8½", "Thick Rim"	$27.00 – 30.00
Butter, 1 lb., "Zephyr"	$350.00 – 400.00
Canister, "Radiance"	$110.00 – 130.00
Casserole, "Sundial", #1	$35.00 – 45.00
Casserole, "Sundial", #4	$20.00 – 25.00
Coffee server, "Sundial"	$260.00 – 295.00
Cookie jar, "Five Band"	$140.00 – 160.00
Cookie jar, "Sundial"	$220.00 – 225.00
Creamer, morning set	$25.00 – 35.00
Creamer, New York	$20.00 – 25.00
Custard, "Thick Rim"	$10.00 – 13.00
Drip jar, #1188, open	$35.00 – 40.00
Drip jar and cover, "Thick Rim"	$35.00 – 45.00
Jug, Donut	$150.00 – 175.00
Jug, 1½ pt., "Five Band"	$40.00 – 50.00
Jug, 2 qt., "Five Band"	$50.00 – 60.00
Jug, loop handle	$90.00 – 110.00
Leftover, loop handle	$85.00 – 95.00
Leftover, "Zephyr"	$110.00 – 130.00
Shakers, canister style, ea.	$35.00 – 45.00
Shakers, handled, ea. (4)	$15.00 – 20.00
Sugar and lid, morning set	$40.00 – 50.00
Sugar and lid, New York	$30.00 – 35.00
Syrup, "Sundial"	$120.00 – 140.00
Teapot, Airflow	$185.00 – 210.00
Teapot, Aladdin	$175.00 – 200.00
Teapot, morning set	$175.00 – 200.00
Teapot, New York	$190.00 – 210.00
Teapot, "Sundial"	$175.00 – 200.00
Teapot, Streamline	$225.00 – 265.00
Water bottle, "Zephyr"	$175.00 – 225.00

Row 1: Canister set, "Radiance."
Row 2: Teapot, Streamline; Ball jug, #4; Ball jug, #2.
Row 3: Casserole, round; drip jar, "Thick Rim"; bowl, 6", "Thick Rim."

Row 1: Cookie jar, "Sundial"; coffee server, "Sundial"; teapot, "Sundial."
Row 2: Batter jug, "Sundial"; syrup, "Sundial"; jug, loop handle.
Row 3: Leftover, loop handle; teapot, morning set;
creamer and sugar, morning set.

BLUE WILLOW

Row 1: Teapot, 4-cup, Boston; teapot, 4-cup, Boston; teapot, 2-cup, Boston.
Row 2: Shallow 4" finger bowl; bowl, shallow 6"; shallow 4" finger bowl.
Row 3: Casserole, 5"; casserole, 7½"; Chinese tea cup.

The Blue Willow decal is only being found on a few pieces and the reports of collectors finding these pieces are infrequent. Perhaps the most exciting news to teapot collectors is the existence of this decoration on three different size Boston teapots. Notice in the photo that two different oriental scenes may be found. The first two teapots on the top row and the two bowls on the center shelf are examples.

The casserole will be found in two sizes. Both sizes are pictured on the bottom row of the photo. The lid features the Blue Willow pattern, is gently domed, and has a knob handle.

Although most of Hall's Blue Willow which collectors have been finding appears to date to the twenties, an ashtray has been made recently. It has the new back-stamp which would place it in the post 1970 era. Also, the decal lacks the quality and fine detail of the decals on the earlier pieces.

Blue Willow Kitchenware	Price
Ashtray	$7.00 – 10.00
Bowl, 4", finger	$22.00 – 27.00
Bowl, 6", plum pudding	$27.00 – 32.00
Casserole, 5"	$35.00 – 45.00
Casserole, 7½"	$55.00 – 65.00
Teacup, Chinese, (2-styles)	$18.00 – 22.00
Teapot, 2-cup, Boston	$175.00 – 200.00
Teapot, 4-cup, Boston	$150.00 – 200.00
Teapot, 6-cup, Boston	$195.00 – 235.00

CACTUS

According to an article in the trade magazine *China, Glass and Lamps*, Hall introduced the Cactus pattern to retailers at trade shows in January, 1937. The article described the pattern as "blending shades of green, yellow, red, orange, blue, brown, and gray." The decal appeared on a new Hall kitchenware shape which was also being introduced in various solid colors. The new shape was not named in the article but the illustration pictures the shape we are calling "Five Band." Items with the Cactus decal originally introduced on the "Five Band" shape were as follows: cookie jar, covered syrup,

shakers, two sizes of jugs, three sizes of mixing bowls, a casserole, and a batter bowl.

Hall also used the Cactus decal on other shapes. One of the most commonly found items is the "Viking" Drip-O-lator coffee pot which was made for the Enterprise Aluminum Company of Massilon, Ohio. Enterprise supplied the aluminum dripper and marketed the finished product under its Drip-O-lator trademark. A covered sugar and creamer in this shape may also be found with diligent searching.

Kitchenware	Price	Kitchenware	Price
Ball jug, #3	$85.00 – 95.00	Creamer, New York	$18.00 – 22.00
Batter bowl, "Five Band"	$35.00 – 45.00	Creamer, "Viking"	$18.00 – 22.00
Bowl, 6", "Five Band"	$16.00 – 18.00	Custard, "Radiance"	$12.00 – 14.00
Bowl, 7¼", "Five Band"	$18.00 – 22.00	Jug, 1½ pt., "Five Band"	$40.00 – 50.00
Bowl, 8¾", "Five Band"	$22.00 – 27.00	Jug, 2 qt., "Five Band"	$50.00 – 60.00
Bowl, 6", "Radiance"	$18.00 – 20.00	Onion soup, individual	$45.00 – 55.00
Bowl, 7½", "Radiance"	$20.00 – 25.00	Shakers, "Five Band", ea.	$15.00 – 20.00
Bowl, 9", "Radiance"	$27.00 – 32.00	Shakers, handled, ea.	$15.00 – 20.00
Bowl, 10", "Radiance"	$35.00 – 40.00	Stack set, "Radiance"	$95.00 – 110.00
Casserole, "Five Band"	$40.00 – 50.00	Sugar and lid, New York	$22.00 – 27.00
Casserole, "Radiance"	$40.00 – 50.00	Sugar and lid, "Viking"	$22.00 – 27.00
Coffee pot, "Five Band"	$60.00 – 70.00	Syrup, "Five Band"	$80.00 – 95.00
Coffee pot, "Viking" Drip-O-lator	$28.00 – 35.00	Teapot, French	$125.00 – 155.00
Cookie jar, "Five Band"	$125.00 – 150.00		

Row 1: Teapot, French; stack set, "Radiance"; Ball jug #3. Row 2: Creamer and sugar, New York; shakers, handled; shakers, "Five Band." Row 3: Bowl, 9", "Radiance"; bowl, 8¾", "Five Band"; onion soup, individual.

Row 1: Coffee pot, "Viking"; batter bowl, "Five Band"; cookie jar, "Five Band." Row 2: Jug, 2 qt., "Five Band"; jug, 1½ pt., "Five Band"; syrup, "Five Band." Row 3: Casserole, "Five Band"; creamer and sugar, "Viking."

CARROT AND GOLDEN CARROT

Although it is possible to assemble a collection of Hall's Carrot pattern, much diligent searching will be required to find many of the pieces. The Carrot/Golden Carrot kitchenware listing has turned out to be more extensive than many collectors originally anticipated. However, the number of items with gold decoration is still quite limited. Only the Windshield teapot, the Zeisel cookie jar, the #65, #68, #70, #95¾ casseroles, the 12½" Welsh rarebit, and the three-piece "Thick Rim" bowl set have been reported with gold trim. Of these pieces, the teapot is found most frequently, but it is also the most desirable item, which keeps the price relatively high.

The handled shakers are new to this listing. Only the salt and pepper have been reported. Also a smaller size New England bean pot has been found. It is shown in the photo at the bottom left. Notice there are two different styles of custard cups in this pattern. Both shapes are shown in the photo at the bottom left.

Kitchenware	Price
Ball jug, #3	$90.00 – 100.00
Batter bowl, "Five Band"	$50.00 – 65.00
Bean pot, New England, #4	$90.00 – 100.00
Bean pot, New England, #2	$110.00 – 130.00
Bowl, 6", "Five Band"	$16.00 – 18.00
Bowl, 7¼", "Five Band"	$18.00 – 22.00
Bowl, 8¾", "Five Band"	$22.00 – 28.00
Bowl, 6", "Radiance"	$18.00 – 20.00
Bowl, 7½", "Radiance"	$20.00 – 25.00
Bowl, 9", "Radiance"	$27.00 – 32.00
Bowl, 10", "Radiance"	$35.00 – 40.00
Bowl, 6", "Thick Rim"	$16.00 – 18.00
Bowl, 7½", "Thick Rim"	$18.00 – 22.00
Bowl, 8½", "Thick Rim"	$22.00 – 27.00
Casserole, 5¾", #65 rnd.	$30.00 – 37.00
Casserole, 8¼", #68 rnd.	$37.00 – 47.00

Kitchenware	Price
Casserole, 10", #70 rnd.	$50.00 – 55.00
Casserole, 11½", oval	$65.00 – 75.00
Casserole, "Radiance"	$40.00 – 50.00
Cookie jar, "Five Band"	$140.00 – 165.00
Cookie jar, Zeisel	$135.00 – 155.00
Custard, #351½	$13.00 – 15.00
Custard, "Radiance"	$14.00 – 16.00
Dish, 12½", Welsh Rarebit	$30.00 – 40.00
Jug, #5, "Radiance"	$35.00 – 40.00
Shaker, "Five Band", ea.	$18.00 – 22.00
Shaker, handled, ea.	$18.00 – 22.00
Shaker, "Novelty Radiance," ea.	$30.00 – 35.00
Stack set, "Radiance"	$110.00 – 135.00
Syrup, "Five Band"	$90.00 – 110.00
Teapot, "Radiance"	$200.00 – 250.00
Teapot, Windshield	$150.00 – 175.00

Row 1: Ball jug, #3; bean pot, New England, #4; bean pot, New England, #2. Row 2: Custard, "Radiance"; custard, #351 ½; shakers, "Novelty Radiance." Row 3: Shakers, handled; casserole, "Radiance."

Row 1: Teapot, Windshield; cookie jar, Zeisel-style. Row 2: Dish, 12½", Welsh rarebit; casserole, #70 round. Row 3: Casserole, 11½", oval; casserole, #68 round; casserole, #65 round.

CLOVER AND GOLDEN CLOVER

The Clover decal is a very stylized and colorful red, blue, and green decal. Items with this decal will be found both with and without gold decoration. Pieces which are gold encrusted are called Golden Clover. According to Hall ads, the Golden Clover line consists of the Windshield teapot, the #68 round casserole, the "big-eared" Zeisel cookie jar, and the three-piece "Thick Rim" mixing bowl set. However, as may be seen from the photo, other pieces with gold decoration may be found. Other sizes of round casseroles, the "Five Band" jug, and the stack set may be found with gold decoration.

The handled shakers may be found as a four-piece set. Other new items in the listing include the "Five Band" cookie jar, "Novelty Radiance" shakers, the "Five Band" jug, "Radiance" #1 jug and cover, the covered onion soup, and the "Thick Rim" casserole.

Row 1: Cookie jar, "Five Band"; cookie jar, Zeisel-style. Row 2: Jug and cover, #1 "Radiance"; teapot, Windshield; jug, 1½ pint, "Five Band." Row 3: Stack set; shakers, handled.

Kitchenware	Price
Ball jug, #3	$90.00 – 100.00
Batter bowl, "Five Band"	$45.00 – 55.00
Bowl, 6", "Radiance"	$16.00 – 18.00
Bowl, 7½", "Radiance"	$18.00 – 22.00
Bowl, 9", "Radiance"	$22.00 – 28.00
Bowl, 10", "Radiance"	$32.00 – 37.00
Bowl, 6", "Thick Rim"	$16.00 – 18.00
Bowl, 7½", "Thick Rim"	$18.00 – 22.00
Bowl, 8½", "Thick Rim"	$20.00 – 25.00
Casserole, 5¾", #65 rnd.	$32.00 – 37.00
Casserole, 8¼", #68 rnd.	$35.00 – 45.00
Casserole, 10", #70 rnd.	$45.00 – 55.00

Kitchenware	Price
Casserole, "Radiance"	$37.00 – 42.00
Casserole, "Thick Rim"	$35.00 – 45.00
Cookie jar, "Five Band"	$140.00 – 160.00
Cookie jar, Zeisel-style	$125.00 – 145.00
Jug, 1½ pt., "Five Band"	$45.00 – 55.00
Jug/cover, #1, "Radiance"	$65.00 – 75.00
Jug, #5, "Radiance"	$32.00 – 37.00
Shaker, handled, ea. (4)	$18.00 – 22.00
Shaker, "Novelty Radiance," ea.	$27.00 – 32.00
Stack set	$100.00 – 125.00
Teapot, Windshield	$150.00 – 165.00

CLOVER (PINK)

Very few pieces of this Pink Clover design are showing up. A "Medallion" jug was shown in the last book. Since then, "Radiance" canisters, "Thick Rim" bowls, "Radiance" casseroles, an oval casserole, and a round baker have been found.

Left to Right: Casserole, #761, oval; baker, #503, round.

Kitchenware	Price
Baker, 6", #503, round	$18.00 – 20.00
Bowl, 6", "Thick Rim"	$10.00 – 12.00
Bowl, 7½", "Thick Rim"	$14.00 – 16.00
Bowl, 8½", "Thick Rim"	$18.00 – 22.00
Canister, "Radiance"	$100.00 – 125.00
Casserole, "Radiance"	$45.00 – 55.00
Casserole, 10", #761, oval	$45.00 – 55.00
Jug, "Medallion"	$50.00 – 60.00

EGGSHELL BUFFET SERVICE

Hall's Eggshell Buffet Service with the Dot design is a line with a large number of pieces. The most frequently found color of Dot is red, but other color dots such as green, blue, and orange will also be seen. Generally, the dots are found on an eggshell body, but some pieces with an ivory body are also available. An example of the ivory body with red dots is the pair of handled shakers on the bottom row of the top photo on page 154. Two pieces — a pretzel jar and a "Radiance" casserole — with Half-Dot designs on an ivory body compliment the handled shakers with an ivory body. When the lids and bottoms of these two pieces are lined up correctly a whole dot pattern is created.

As may be seen from the listing, the Dot design appears on some kitchenware shapes which are not usually found in other decorated patterns. Examples of these are the handled cocotte, the #691 Drip coffee, and the buffet style round and oval casseroles. The "Thin Rim" bowls and the custard may be found either smooth or with vertical ribs. The 13½" fish-shaped salad is part of the set even though it only has matching trim and does not have any dots. This platter is still being made in numerous colors and now comes in two different sizes.

The pieces appearing most often are the handled shakers. Many teapot collectors are still eagerly waiting to acquire the "Rutherford" teapot. Another hard-to-find piece is the Tom and Jerry bowl.

In addition to the Dot pattern illustrated on page 154, some pieces of the Buffet Service will be found in other patterns. One example is the "Swag" pattern as seen on the pieces on the bottom row of the photo below. Another pattern which is illustrated on the fish platter below is called "Plaid."

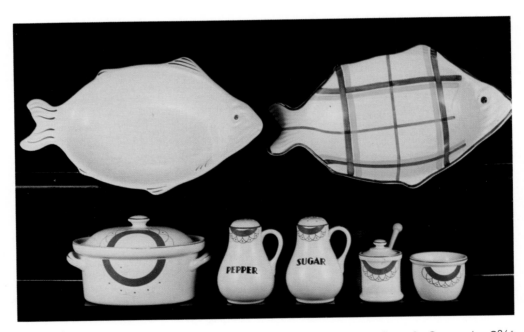

Row 1: Baker, fish-shape; baker, fish-shape with "Plaid" pattern. Row 2: Casserole, 9¾", oval, "Swag" pattern; shakers, handled, "Swag" pattern; mustard, "Swag" pattern; custard, "Swag" pattern.

Kitchenware	Dot	"Plaid" or "Swag" Patterns
Baker, 13½", fish-shape	$30.00 – 40.00	$40.00 – 50.00
Bean pot, New England, #3	$85.00 – 95.00	
Bean pot, New England, #4	$85.00 – 95.00	
Bowl, 8¾", salad	$18.00 – 22.00	
Bowl, 9¾", salad	$22.00 – 25.00	
Bowl, 6", "Ribbed"	$11.00 – 13.00	$14.00 – 16.00
Bowl, 7¼", "Ribbed"	$16.00 – 18.00	$18.00 – 20.00
Bowl, 8½", "Ribbed"	$18.00 – 22.00	$20.00 – 25.00
Bowl, 6", "Thin Rim"	$11.00 – 13.00	
Bowl, 7¼", "Thin Rim"	$16.00 – 18.00	
Bowl, 8½", "Thin Rim"	$18.00 – 22.00	
Bowl, ftd., Tom & Jerry	$90.00 – 110.00	
Casserole, 9¾, oval	$42.00 – 47.00	$40.00 – 50.00
Casserole, 8½", 9¼", round	$45.00 – 50.00	$45.00 – 55.00
Cocotte, 4", handled	$16.00 – 18.00	$20.00 – 22.00
Custard	$7.00 – 9.00	$8.00 – 10.00
Custard, "Ribbed"	$6.00 – 8.00	
Drip, #188, open	$25.00 – 30.00	$27.00 – 32.00
Drip coffee, #691	$185.00 – 210.00	
Jug and cover, "Radiance," #1	$55.00 – 60.00	
Jug and cover, "Radiance," #2	$55.00 – 60.00	
Jug and cover, "Radiance," #3	$55.00 – 65.00	
Jug and cover, "Radiance," #5	$60.00 – 70.00	
Jug, room service	$70.00 – 80.00	
Mug, Tom & Jerry	$9.00 – 11.00	
Mustard	$30.00 – 35.00	$32.00 – 37.00
Onion soup	$27.00 – 32.00	
Shakers, handled (4), ea.	$17.00 – 20.00	$18.00 – 22.00
Shirred egg dish	$20.00 – 25.00	
Teapot, "Rutherford"	$150.00 – 195.00	

Kitchenware	Dot with Ivory Body
Casserole, "Radiance"	$25.00 – 35.00
Pretzel jar	$95.00 – 110.00
Shakers, handled, ea.	$17.00 – 20.00

Row 1: Teapot, "Rutherford", jug and cover, #5, "Radiance", jug and cover, #3, "Radiance." Row 2: Jug, room service; bean pot, New England, #3; dish, shirred egg. Row 3: Onion soup and cover; shakers, handled, Red Dot on ivory body.

Row 1: Punch bowl, Tom & Jerry; mug, Tom & Jerry; bowl, 7¼", "Thin Rim"; custard, "Ribbed." Row 2: Casserole, round buffet; casserole, oval buffet; mustard; cocette, handled. Row 3: Bowl, 9¾", salad; shakers, handled, Green Dot on ivory body.

FANTASY

Fantasy is a very colorful — almost gaudy — floral decal which is found infrequently. Most pieces are also neatly trimmed with a narrow red band. The only commonly found pieces are the handled shakers and all styles of casseroles. Special finds would include the "Sundial" coffee server, loop handle leftover, and the morning tea set. Finding a Streamline teapot in Fantasy would send most any teapot collector to dreamland.

New finds since the last book include the "Five Band" cookie jar, "Five Band" syrup, "Five Band" jug, "Sundial" teapot, "Sundial" cookie jar, and a rectangular baker.

Kitchenware	Price
Baker, rectangular	$80.00 – 90.00
Ball jug, #1	$100.00 – 125.00
Ball jug, #2	$100.00 – 125.00
Ball jug, #3	$90.00 – 100.00
Ball jug, #4	$100.00 – 125.00
Batter jug, "Sundial"	$200.00 – 250.00
Bean pot, New England, #4	$100.00 – 125.00
Bowl, 6", "Thick Rim"	$18.00 – 22.00
Bowl, 7½", "Thick Rim"	$22.00 – 27.00
Bowl, 8½", "Thick Rim"	$32.00 – 37.00
Casserole, "Radiance"	$32.00 – 37.00
Casserole, "Sundial," #1	$50.00 – 60.00
Casserole, "Sundial," #4	$32.00 – 37.00
Casserole, "Thick Rim"	$40.00 – 45.00
Coffee server, "Sundial"	$240.00 – 280.00
Cookie jar, "Five Band"	$175.00 – 195.00

Kitchenware	Price
Cookie jar, "Sundial"	$240.00 – 280.00
Creamer, morning set	$22.00 – 28.00
Creamer, New York	$20.00 – 25.00
Custard, "Thick Rim"	$16.00 – 18.00
Drip jar, #1188, open	$32.00 – 37.00
Drip jar and cover, "Thick Rim"	$30.00 – 35.00
Jug, 1½ pt., "Five Band"	$40.00 – 50.00
Jug, Donut	$150.00 – 195.00
Leftover, loop handle	$90.00 – 110.00
Shakers, handled, ea.	$17.00 – 20.00
Sugar and lid, morning set	$30.00 – 37.00
Syrup, "Five Band"	$90.00 – 100.00
Syrup, "Sundial"	$130.00 – 150.00
Teapot, morning set	$200.00 – 250.00
Teapot, Streamline	$225.00 – 275.00
Teapot, "Sundial"	$250.00 – 295.00

Teapot, Streamline.

Row 1: Ball jug, #1; Ball jug, #3; cookie jar, "Five Band."
Row 2: Jug, 1½ pint, "Five Band"; bean pot, New England, #4;
leftover, loop handled.
Row 3: Batter jug, "Sundial"; baker, rectangular.

Row 1: Teapot, "Sundial"; jug Donut; shakers, handled.
Row 2: Creamer, sugar, and lid, morning set; casserole, "Sundial," #4;
casserole, "Thick Rim."

FLAMINGO

The Flamingo listing as a kitchenware pattern was shown in the last book for the first time. Previously the decal had been listed as appearing on the "Viking" Drip-O-lator which Hall made for the Enterprise Aluminum Company. Other pieces with this decal have been found in the last few years. Items new to this edition are the "Five Band" shakers and the "Radiance" casserole.

Collectors will find this decal more commonly on the "Five Band" batter bowl and the "Viking" Drip-O-lator coffee pot. Interesting, but hard-to-find pieces, are the #691 drip coffee pot, the Streamline teapot, and the "Five Band" cookie jar. Any Streamline teapots appearing on the market are eagerly snatched by teapot collectors.

Kitchenware	Price
Batter bowl, "Five Band"	$85.00 – 95.00
Casserole, "Five Band"	$45.00 – 55.00
Casserole, "Radiance"	$37.00 – 42.00
Coffee pot, "Viking" Drip-O-lator	$30.00 – 40.00
Cookie jar, "Five Band"	$160.00 – 180.00
Creamer, "Viking"	$20.00 – 28.00
Drip coffee pot, #691	$175.00 – 195.00
Shaker, "Five Band", ea.	$18.00 – 22.00
Shaker, handled, ea.	$18.00 – 22.00
Sugar and lid, "Viking"	$27.00 – 32.00
Syrup, "Five Band"	$100.00 – 125.00
Teapot, Streamline	$250.00 – 295.00

Row 1: Cookie jar, "Five Band"; drip coffee pot, #691; coffee pot, "Viking."

Row 2: Batter bowl, "Five Band"; syrup, "Five Band"; casserole, "Five Band."

Row 3: Sugar and creamer, "Viking"; shaker, handled; shakers, "Five Band."

FLORAL LATTICE

The Floral Lattice kitchenware has a decal which consists of a vine-like potted flower that is intertwined in a lattice framework. This mini-floral decal may be frequently spotted on the "Five Band" batter bowl and syrup. Other pieces in this pattern are not easily found. Notice some pieces are trimmed in red while others are trimmed with platinum bands.

New additions to the list include the "Kadota" all-china drip coffee pot and the tea tile.

Kitchenware	Price
Ball jug, #3	$90.00 – 110.00
Batter bowl, "Five Band"	$25.00 – 35.00
Bowl, 6", "Five Band"	$12.00 – 14.00
Bowl, 7¼", "Five Band"	$18.00 – 22.00
Bowl, 8¾", "Five Band"	$20.00 – 27.00
Canister, "Radiance"	$90.00 – 110.00
Casserole, #99, oval	$35.00 – 45.00
Casserole, #76, round	$30.00 – 37.00
Casserole, #101, round	$30.00 – 40.00
Coffee pot, "Viking", Drip-O-lator	$30.00 – 40.00
Cookie jar, "Five Band"	$110.00 – 135.00
Drip coffee pot, "Kadota"	$125.00 – 150.00
Onion soup, individual	$27.00 – 32.00
Shaker, canister style, ea.	$35.00 – 40.00
Shaker, handled, ea.	$16.00 – 18.00
Syrup, "Five Band"	$35.00 – 45.00
Tea tile, 6", round	$27.00 – 32.00

Row 1: Cookie jar, "Five Band; canister, "Radiance"; shaker, canister style.

Row 2: Batter bowl, "Five Band"; syrup, "Five Band"; coffee pot bottom, "Kadota."

Row 3: Casserole, #99 oval; onion soup.

FLAREWARE

Row 1: Cookie jar with Heather Rose decal; cookie jar with Autumn Leaf decal; teapot with Gold Lace design.

Row 2: Casserole, 2 qt. with Gold Lace design; bowl with Heather Rose decal; coffee server, Gold Lace design with brass and wooden candle warmer.

Flareware is essentially a serving type kitchenware line which was offered by Hall in the early sixties. Basic decorations were Autumn Leaf, Gold Lace, Chestnut, and Radial. Today the only decoration found in any quantity is Gold Lace. A common variation of the Gold Lace decoration includes pieces found with the Heather Rose decal used in combination with the star-like Gold Lace design. The Flareware Autumn Leaf has nothing in common with the Autumn Leaf dinnerware pattern shown earlier in this book which was distributed by Jewel Tea. An example of the pattern may be seen on the cookie jar in the center of the picture. The Radial design has thin black vertical lines over a white base. Pieces of the Chestnut pattern have an all-over brown glaze.

The coffee server was designed to be used with the brass and wooden three-legged candle warmer. Another multi-purpose three-legged warmer, made of china, was used with the teapot, coffee urn, and casserole. The coffee urn is shaped like the cookie jar and has a spigot to dispense the coffee instead of a pour spout. The brass warmer has no design and was used with all the patterns. Therefore, it will only be listed once in the price guide below.

Kitchenware	Gold Lace	Autumn Leaf	Heather Rose	Radial
Bowl, 6"	$6.00 – 7.00	$5.00 – 6.00	$7.00 – 9.00	$4.00 – 5.00
Bowl, 7"	$7.00 – 8.00	$6.00 – 7.00	$8.00 – 10.00	$5.00 – 6.00
Bowl, 8"	$9.00 – 10.00	$7.00 – 9.00	$10.00 – 12.00	$6.00 – 7.00
Bowl, 5", salad	$8.00 – 10.00	$7.00 – 9.00	$10.00 – 12.00	$5.00 – 6.00
Casserole, 3 pt.	$12.00 – 15.00	$8.00 – 10.00		$6.00 – 8.00
Casserole, 2 qt.	$20.00 – 25.00	$15.00 – 18.00	$22.00 – 27.00	$12.00 – 14.00
Coffee server, 15-cup	$30.00 – 35.00	$22.00 – 25.00		$16.00 – 20.00
Coffee urn, 15-cup	$40.00 – 45.00	$22.00 – 28.00		$18.00 – 22.00
Cookie jar	$22.00 – 25.00	$16.00 – 19.00	$25.00 – 30.00	$15.00 – 18.00
Teapot, 6-cup	$30.00 – 35.00	$22.00 – 25.00		$18.00 – 22.00
Trivet, china	$11.00 – 13.00			
Warmer, brass	$8.00 – 10.00			

FRENCH FLOWER

Although the French Flower design is most often found on the French shape teapot, it was also used on other kitchenware shapes. Therefore, the design has been added to the kitchenware section of this book. Several other teapots such as the Aladdin, Boston, New York, Cube, and McCormick have been found with this gold decoration.

Kitchenware	Price
Ball jug, #3	$60.00 – 75.00
Coffee pot, Washington	$55.00 – 65.00
Creamer, Bellevue	$16.00 – 18.00
Creamer, Boston	$18.00 – 22.00
Jug, Donut	$75.00 – 85.00
Jug, loop handle	$60.00 – 75.00
Jug, room service	$55.00 – 65.00
Sugar and lid, Boston	$25.00 – 30.00
Teapot, Aladdin	$70.00 – 90.00
Teapot, Boston	$70.00 – 90.00
Teapot, buffet service	$45.00 – 55.00
Teapot, Cube	$90.00 – 110.00
Teapot, French	$25.00 – 45.00
Teapot, McCormick	$90.00 – 110.00
Teapot, New York	$70.00 – 80.00

Row 1: Jug, loop handle; coffee pot, Washington; jug, Donut.
Row 2: Teapot, French; teapot, Cube; teapot, buffet service; creamer, Bellevue.

GOLD LABEL KITCHENWARE

Hall selected twelve teapot shapes from the Gold Decorated line in the mid fifties and added additional gold decoration to produce the Gold Label line. Teapots in this new line exhibit a singular new gold decoration and may be identified through a gold code number on the bottom followed by the letters "GL." The handles, spouts, and knobs of the lids to these teapots are covered with gold.

In addition to the teapots, eight kitchenware shapes were also selected for use in the Gold Label line. Included were the 9" salad bowl, "Terrace" coffee pot, Zeisel cookie jar, "Rayed" jug, the #101 round casserole, and the three-piece "Thick Rim" bowl set. As may be seen in the photograph, a French baker also exists in the squiggle design, but we have not seen this piece in the other gold designs.

The following listing provides the names of the teapots and the names associated with the design as assigned by researchers.

Teapot	Design	Price
Aladdin	Swag	$40.00 – 55.00
Albany	Reflection	$50.00 – 65.00
Baltimore	Nova	$40.00 – 50.00
Boston, 2 or 3 cup	Fleur-de-lis	$45.00 – 55.00
Boston, 4, 6, or 8 cup	Fleur-de-lis	$35.00 – 40.00
French, 1, 2, or 3 cup	Daisy	$45.00 – 55.00
French, 4 or 6 cup	Daisy	$32.00 – 37.00
French, 8 – 12 cup	Daisy	$45.00 – 55.00
Hollywood	Grid	$30.00 – 40.00
Hook Cover	Star	$32.00 – 37.00
Los Angeles	Medallion	$35.00 – 40.00
New York, 2 or 4 cup	Flower	$35.00 – 45.00
New York, 6 or 8 cup	Flower	$27.00 – 32.00
New York, 10 or 12 cup	Flower	$40.00 – 50.00
Parade	Squiggle	$25.00 – 30.00
Philadelphia	Basket	$32.00 – 40.00
Windshield	Dot	$30.00 – 40.00

Kitchenware Accessories	Price
Baker, French	$11.00 – 14.00
Bowl, 6", "Thick Rim"	$8.00 – 10.00
Bowl, 7½", "Thick Rim"	$11.00 – 13.00
Bowl, 9", "Thick Rim"	$14.00 – 16.00
Bowl, 9", salad	$15.00 – 18.00
Casserole, #101, round	$20.00 – 27.00
Coffee pot, "Terrace"	$30.00 – 37.00
Cookie jar, Zeisel	$40.00 – 50.00
Jug, "Rayed"	$11.00 – 14.00

Row 1: Cookie jar, Zeisel, Medallion design; teapot, Windshield, Dot design; cookie jar, Zeisel, Dot design. Row 2: Teapot, New York, Flower design; teapot, Hook Cover, Star design; teapot, Aladdin, Swag design. Row 3: Casserole, #101 round, Basket design; Cookie jar, Zeisel, Squiggle design; jug, "Rayed", Squiggle design. Row 4: Casserole, #101 round, Squiggle design; bowl, 9" salad, Squiggle design; baker, French, Squiggle design.

GOLDEN GLO

Row 1: Coffee pot, coffee set shape; jug, "Five Band"; bean pot, New England, #4.
Row 2: Casserole, oval with basketweave pattern; casserole, #100, 8½", oval.

Golden Glo is a Hall kitchenware line which dates back to the 1940s and is still in production today. As a result of this long period of production, many different pieces have been subjected to this gold treatment. The gold color top glaze is normally applied over a Hi-white base. An example of the gold color backstamp used on older Golden Glo pieces is shown below. Pieces made after 1970 will have the new square backstamp. According to information contained in its backstamp, the oval casserole with the basketweave pattern was made for Bump's of San Francisco.

Golden Glo Kitchenware	Price
Ashtray, shell shape	$5.00 – 6.00
Baking shell, 4"	$5.00 – 6.00
Baker, French, 7¼"	$10.00 – 12.00
Baker, French, 8½"	$10.00 – 12.00
Bean pot, New England, #4	$40.00 – 50.00
Bowl, Medallion, #3, #4, #5	$14.00 – 16.00
Bowl, salad, 9¾"	$12.00 – 14.00
Casserole, duck knob	$25.00 – 35.00
Casserole, French side handle, 4¼", 8¼", 10¼"	$18.00 – 27.00
Casserole, oval, #100, #101, #103	$25.00 – 30.00
Casserole, round, #75, #76, #78	$25.00 – 30.00
Coffee pot, demi coffee set	$80.00 – 95.00
Creamer, Boston	$10.00 – 12.00
Creamer, demi coffee set	$16.00 – 20.00
Creamer, morning set	$16.00 – 20.00
Jug, "Five Band"	$18.00 – 22.00

Golden Glo Kitchenware	Price
Mug, Irish coffee	$16.00 – 20.00
Mug, #343	$10.00 – 12.00
Sugar and lid, Boston	$16.00 – 20.00
Sugar, demi coffee set	$16.00 – 20.00
Sugar and lid, morning set	$22.00 – 27.00
Teapot, Airflow	$55.00 – 65.00
Teapot, Aladdin	$75.00 – 85.00
Teapot, Boston	$55.00 – 65.00
Teapot, morning set	$90.00 – 110.00

Golden Glo backstamp.

GOLDEN GLO
HALL
MADE IN U.S.A.
WARRANTED 22 CARAT GOLD
783

HAND-PAINTED KITCHENWARE

Many, but not all, hand decorated pieces were decorated by artists at Hall. Pictured below are some artist decorated pieces and a child's New York creamer with an animal decal.

		Price
Row 1:	Carafe, signed "Jean Alpert"	$95.00 – 120.00
	Cookie jar, signed "Kay '79"	$95.00 – 110.00
	Syrup, "Sundial," signed "Eita"	$55.00 – 65.00
	Creamer, New York with children's decal	$25.00 – 35.00
Row 2:	Teapot, Aladdin, signed "E. L. Cross"	$145.00 – 175.00
	Shakers, handled, signed "Edith Payment"	$35.00 – 40.00
	Teapot, Boston, signed "Edith Payment"	$100.00 – 125.00

Row 1:
    Zeisel cookie jar with cherries signed, "Wood."

Price
$110.00 – 140.00

    Drip-O-lator coffee pot with floral painting and gold trim signed,
        "Nan '54."

$75.00 – 85.00

Row 2:
    "Rayed" creamer, sugar, and lid with floral painting unsigned.

$45.00 – 55.00

    "Pert" creamer and sugar with painted leaves, unsigned.

$35.00 – 40.00

Top:
    Tomorrow's Classic gravy boat with hand-painted flowers.

Price
$30.00 – 35.00

Bottom:
    Aladdin teapot with painted floral design and gold trim.

$95.00 – 110.00

    "Five Band" coffee pot with hand-painted flowers and gold trim.

$65.00 – 75.00

MEADOW FLOWER

Row 1: Ball jug, #3; canisters, "Radiance"; custard, "Thick Rim."
Row 2: Jug, "Five Band"; shakers, handled; teapot, Streamline.

Hall's use of the Meadow Flower decal dates to the late 1930s. Many collectors find these red-trimmed pieces with their colorful variegated floral decals quite attractive. Although the list of known shapes with this decal is gradually increasing, none of the pieces is easy to find. The most significant discoveries have been a canister set and the Streamline teapot. The existence of the canisters means the canister-style shakers should exist, but to date no one has reported finding them.

Kitchenware	Price
Ball jug, #1	$90.00 – 100.00
Ball jug, #2	$90.00 – 100.00
Ball jug, #3	$70.00 – 90.00
Ball jug, #4	$85.00 – 95.00
Bean pot, New England, #4	$95.00 – 110.00
Bowl, 6", "Thick Rim"	$16.00 – 18.00
Bowl, 7½", "Thick Rim"	$18.00 – 22.00
Bowl, 8½", "Thick Rim"	$22.00 – 27.00
Canister, "Radiance"	$100.00 – 125.00
Casserole, "Radiance"	$30.00 – 40.00

Kitchenware	Price
Casserole, "Sundial", #4	$45.00 – 55.00
Casserole, "Thick Rim"	$40.00 – 50.00
Cookie jar, "Five Band"	$140.00 – 160.00
Custard, "Thick Rim"	$12.00 – 14.00
Drip jar, #1188, open	$27.00 – 32.00
Drip jar and cover, "Thick Rim"	$25.00 – 30.00
Jug, "Five Band"	$40.00 – 50.00
Shakers, handled, ea.	$16.00 – 20.00
Teapot, Streamline	$250.00 – 300.00

MORNING GLORY

The Morning Glory kitchen-ware line was produced by Hall during the 1940s to coordinate with the Wildwood dinnerware pattern of the Jewel Company. Morning Glory, like Autumn Leaf, was a decal which was reserved exclusively for use on pieces produced for the Jewel Tea Company of Barrington, Illinois. The pieces have a cadet body with contrasting Hi-white areas which contain the Morning Glory decal.

Since the number of available pieces in this decal is limited, many collectors mix these items with other cadet-colored patterns such as Rose Parade and Royal Rose. All the patterns with cadet bodies go well together to create an interesting and useful collection.

"Thick Rim" bowls and casseroles have been found. This shape bowl is not as plentiful as the straight-sided bowl. The casseroles have a white lid which contains the pattern and a blue bottom which has no pattern.

Description of Morning Glory coffee maker and Aladdin teapot from a Jewel Premium booklet.

Row 1: Drip coffee pot, all-china; teapot, Aladdin.
Row 2: Casserole, "Thick Rim"; bowl, 7½", "Thick Rim."

Morning Glory Kitchenware	Price		Morning Glory Kitchenware	Price	
Bowl, 4⅜", straight-sided	$14.00 —	16.00	Bowl, 7½", "Thick Rim"	$14.00 —	16.00
Bowl, 5", straight-sided	$18.00 —	20.00	Bowl, 8½", "Thick Rim"	$16.00 —	18.00
Bowl, 6", straight-sided	$12.00 —	14.00	Casserole, "Thick Rim"	$27.00 —	32.00
Bowl, 7½", straight-sided	$18.00 —	22.00	Custard, 3½", straight-sided	$9.00 —	11.00
Bowl, 9", straight-sided	$20.00 —	25.00	Drip coffee pot, all-china	$175.00 —	225.00
Bowl, 6", "Thick Rim"	$11.00 —	13.00	Teapot, Aladdin	$100.00 —	125.00

Morning Glory 5-piece bowl set as shown in a Jewel premium booklet.

Description of Morning Glory bowl set and a recipe from a Jewel premium booklet.

MORNING GLORY 5-PIECE BOWL SET . . .
ITEM NO. 550

New!   Beautiful!   Useful!

Five stunning bowls, graceful in shape, exquisite — exterior color is cadet blue, inside is shell white graced with a vine of Morning Glories in blue, pink, and green. *Five Sizes* . . . enough for every need. The largest — average casserole size and just the thing for big, leafy salads, too. Two medium sizes for smaller salads and casserole recipes. Two others for gravy, relishes, preserves, left-overs, or for baking individual casseroles or custards.

The brim capacities are 1½ cups, ¾ quart, 1¼ quarts, 2¼ quarts, and 4 quarts — use capacities 1 cup, 2 cups, 1 quart, 2 quarts, and 3½ quarts. They measure 4⅜, 5 1/16, 6⅛,

7½, and 9 inches across, respectively. All five bowls nest conveniently, and add a decorative touch to the kitchen. Try a Mary Dunbar Mountaineer Salad in the 2¼ quart size bowl.

MOUNTAINEER SALAD

3 cups shredded cabbage
½ cup shredded cocoanut
1 cup diced pineapple (4 slices)
6 marshmallows, cut
¾ teaspoon salt
Jewel Mayonnaise

Mix together in medium size bowl. Serve on lettuce leaf. Dust with paprika. Serves six.

See Page 10 for
HOW TO CARE FOR HALL CHINA OVENWARE

26

RAINBOW BOWL SET

Photo of Jewel Rainbow bowl set from Jewel premium catalog.

Hall produced a set of four bowls for the Jewel Tea Company in the forties. The brightly colored bowls are know as the Rainbow bowl set and have the following backstamp: "Hall Radiant Ware." Each bowl will be found in a single color.

Bowl	Price
Red	$18.00 – 22.00
Blue	$15.00 – 18.00
Yellow	$11.00 – 13.00
Green	$10.00 – 12.00

Description of Rainbow bowl set from Jewel premium catalog.

JEWEL RAINBOW BOWL SET . . . ITEM NO. 320

A set of gayly colored bowls that are truly delightful and a real household aid. The shades are deep orange, blue, green, and yellow — each a different color and a different size. They nest together conveniently and furnish a size for every need. 2, 3½, 6, and 9 cup brim capacities — use capacities 1½, 3, 5, and 8 cup. They measure 5½, 6½, 7½, and 9 inches across, respectively. Just the thing for serving or mixing, and because of their variety, they go well with any color scheme.

24

HOW TO CARE FOR HALL CHINA TEAPOTS AND COFFEE SERVERS

China will break if used improperly. Your Hall China Coffee Server or Teapot will give you pleasure and satisfaction if you follow these few precautions:

1. *Never place directly over open flame or electric stove unit.*
2. *Scald with boiling water before dripping coffee into server.*
3. *Never use over high heat — flame or electricity — high heat will break china even when asbestos pad is used.*
4. *When warming coffee, use asbestos pad and low heat.*

ROSE PARADE

Rose Parade kitchenware has a cadet blue body with contrasting white trim. The areas of white trim are accented by a petite pastel floral decal. The most commonly found color of flower is pink. However, other colors including blue and yellow may also be found. This line dates to the 1940s and has become very popular with collectors again today.

Generally, sets of Rose Parade are fairly easy to assemble. Collectors seem to be having problems finding the fluted baker, salad bowl, custard, sugar, and creamer. A lid to the sugar, which would be like the red lid shown in the "Pert" section has been reported. We have only seen the blue sugar lid in the photo. More are sure to exist, but it is certainly the scarcest piece of Rose Parade.

Some collectors have trouble distinguishing between this pattern and another pattern with a similar pink flower on a blue body with white trim called Royal Rose. Identification has been made somewhat easier by Hall, since the majority of Rose Parade pieces contain the backstamp with the identifying words Rose Parade. For pieces which may have escaped the backstamp, the Royal Rose line has silver trim and the Rose Parade pieces do not.

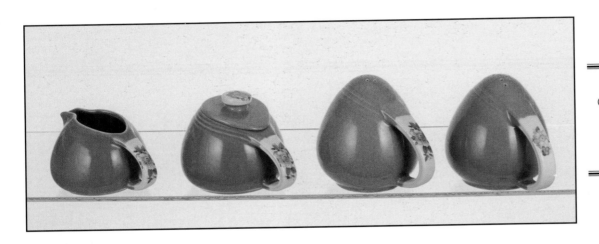

Left to Right: Creamer, "Pert"; sugar and lid, "Pert"; shakers, "Pert."

Kitchenware	Price
Baker, French, fluted	$28.00 – 32.00
Bean pot, tab-handled	$55.00 – 65.00
Bowl, 9", salad	$27.00 – 32.00
Bowl, 6", straight-sided	$12.00 – 15.00
Bowl, 7½", straight-sided	$16.00 – 18.00
Bowl, 9", straight-sided	$18.00 – 22.00
Casserole, tab-handled	$27.00 – 32.00
Creamer, "Pert"	$14.00 – 16.00
Custard, straight-sided	$14.00 – 16.00

Kitchenware	Price
Drip jar and cover, tab-handled	$22.00 – 27.00
Jug, 5", "Pert"	$20.00 – 25.00
Jug, 6½", "Pert"	$25.00 – 30.00
Jug, 7½", "Pert"	$35.00 – 40.00
Shaker, "Pert", ea.	$12.00 – 15.00
Sugar, "Pert"	$12.00 – 15.00
Sugar lid, "Pert"	UND
Teapot, 4-cup, "Pert"	$30.00 – 35.00
Teapot, 6-cup, "Pert"	$35.00 – 40.00

Row 1: Jug, 6½", "Pert"; jug, 5", "Pert"; drip jar, tab-handled.
Row 2: Bean pot, tab-handled; custard; casserole, tab-handled.
Row 3: Teapot, 3-cup, "Pert"; sugar, "Pert"; creamer, "Pert." Row 4: Baker, French, fluted; bowl, 9", salad.

ROSE WHITE

The Rose White kitchenware pattern features a pink rose decal on a Hi-white body with silver trim. This rose decal is the same as the decal used on blue-bodied Royal Rose pieces. However the shape of the body of the Rose White items is the same as that in Rose Parade. The listing of Rose White pieces is not extensive, and with few exceptions, a complete set is not difficult to obtain.

The hardest pieces to find are the "Medallion" bowl, the fluted baker, the small custard, and the sugar and creamer. Items easiest to get appear to be the teapots, shakers, drip jar, and casserole.

In addition to the normal straight-sided bowl set, a set of bowls in the "Medallion" shape has appeared with the Rose White decal. The bottom of the bean pot will be found both with and without the rose decal. There have been no reports of a sugar lid in this pattern, but if one exists in Rose Parade, then one might also be found for this pattern.

Rose White backstamp.

Kitchenware	Price
Baker, French, fluted	$27.00 – 30.00
Bean pot, tab-handled	$45.00 – 55.00
Bowl, 6", "Medallion"	$14.00 – 16.00
Bowl, 7¼", "Medallion"	$16.00 – 18.00
Bowl, 8½", "Medallion"	$20.00 – 22.00
Bowl, 6", straight-sided	$10.00 – 12.00
Bowl, 7½", straight-sided	$12.00 – 14.00
Bowl, 9", straight-sided	$18.00 – 20.00
Bowl, 9", salad	$20.00 – 25.00
Casserole, tab-handled	$22.00 – 27.00
Creamer, "Pert"	$12.00 – 14.00
Custard, straight-sided	$12.00 – 15.00
Drip jar and cover, tab-handled	$18.00 – 22.00
Jug, 5", "Pert"	$18.00 – 22.00
Jug, 6½", "Pert"	$22.00 – 27.00
Jug, 7½", "Pert"	$27.00 – 32.00
Shaker, "Pert", ea.	$12.00 – 14.00
Sugar, "Pert"	$12.00 – 14.00
Teapot, 3-cup, "Pert"	$30.00 – 35.00
Teapot, 6-cup, "Pert"	$35.00 – 40.00

Row 1: Teapot, "Pert," 6-cup; teapot, "Pert," 3-cup; mixing bowl, "Medallion."
Row 2: Bean pot, tab-handled; jug, "Pert," 6½"; jug, "Pert," 5".
Row 3: Casserole, tab-handled; shaker, "Pert"; drip jar, tab-handled; shaker, "Pert."

ROYAL ROSE

Row 1: Teapot, French; Ball jug, #3; teapot, Aladdin.
Row 2: Casserole, "Thick Rim"; shaker, handled; drip jar, "Thick Rim"; shaker, handled.
Row 3: Bowl, 9", salad; bowl, 6", "Thick Rim"; bowl, 7½", "Thick Rim."

Royal Rose kitchenware has a cadet body with contrasting Hi-white features. The decoration consists of a pink rose decal and silver trim. Many people confuse this pattern with the similar blue bodied pattern — Rose Parade. However, Royal Rose pieces are accented with silver trim and the shapes are different from those used in the Rose Parade pattern.

The Aladdin teapot is the most difficult item to find in Royal Rose. Also, the 9" salad bowl is not easily found.

Kitchenware	Price
Ball jug, #3	$45.00 – 55.00
Bowl, 9", salad	$25.00 – 30.00
Bowl, 6", straight-sided	$14.00 – 16.00
Bowl, 7½", straight-sided	$16.00 – 18.00
Bowl, 9", straight-sided	$18.00 – 22.00
Bowl, 6", "Thick Rim"	$14.00 – 16.00
Bowl, 7½", "Thick Rim"	$16.00 – 18.00
Bowl, 8½", "Thick Rim"	$18.00 – 22.00
Casserole, "Thick Rim"	$27.00 – 32.00
Custard, straight-sided	$11.00 – 13.00
Drip jar and cover, "Thick Rim"	$20.00 – 25.00
Shaker, handled, ea.	$14.00 – 16.00
Teapot, Aladdin	$140.00 – 180.00
Teapot, French	$60.00 – 85.00

Rx

Hall pieces with the Rx decoration were used as a premium for pharmacists by the Owens-Illinois Corporation. The piece most often seen is the electric percolator. Other Hall items are listed below. Dinnerware made by Taylor, Smith, and Taylor may be found with this decoration.

Row 1: Gravy boat and underplate; electric percolator; cup and saucer.
Row 2: Shaker; casserole; butter, ¼ pound.

Rx Kitchenware	*Price*
Butter, ¼ pound	$45.00 – 55.00
Casserole	$20.00 – 25.00
Cup	$6.00 – 8.00
Gravy boat & underplate	$18.00 – 20.00
Mug, Irish coffee	$12.00 – 15.00
Percolator, electric	$45.00 – 55.00
Saucer	$2.00 – 3.00

"SHAGGY TULIP"

Row 1: Coffee pot, bottom, "Radiance", all-china; condiment jar, "Radiance"; stack set part, "Radiance." Row 2: Shaker, handled; shirred egg dish, 6½"; shirred egg dish, 5¼".

"Shaggy Tulip" is a colorful floral decal line dating from the mid-thirties. Not much new information concerning "Shaggy Tulip" has been uncovered in the past few years. However, the discovery of the "Radiance" all-china coffee pot and the "Radiance" condiment jar have perked interest in this pattern. Add these pieces to the canisters and the "Radiance" teapot and you have a very exciting collection. Collectors should be aware that the "Kadota" all-china drip coffee pot is one of the most common pieces of this pattern. The "Radiance" shape jug will be found with or without a cover. Keep in mind the covers are scarce and those jugs having covers are worth about double the value of those without.

Remember, the rolling pin, pie lifter, spoon, fork, and dinnerware which are sometimes found with this decal are not Hall items, but were made by Harker. However many enthusiasts find these are also very attractive items to display.

Kitchenware	Price	Kitchenware	Price
Bean pot, New England, #4	$80.00 – 95.00	Drip jar and cover, "Radiance"	$20.00 – 25.00
Bowl, 6", "Radiance"	$14.00 – 16.00	Jug and cover, "Radiance," (#2, #3)	$50.00 – 60.00
Bowl, 7½", "Radiance"	$17.00 – 19.00	Jug and cover, "Radiance," (#4, #5, #6)	$65.00 – 80.00
Bowl, 9", "Radiance"	$20.00 – 25.00	Pretzel jar	$100.00 – 125.00
Canister, "Radiance"	$100.00 – 125.00	Shakers, handled ea. (4)	$16.00 – 20.00
Casserole, "Radiance"	$28.00 – 32.00	Shakers, "Radiance Novelty," ea.	$27.00 – 32.00
Coffee pot, "Perk"	$55.00 – 65.00	Shirred egg dish, 5¼"	$22.00 – 27.00
Condiment jar, "Radiance"	$300.00 – 350.00	Shirred egg dish, 6½"	$20.00 – 25.00
Custard, "Radiance"	$9.00 – 11.00	Stack set, "Radiance"	$90.00 – 110.00
Drip coffee pot, "Kadota," all-china	$65.00 – 75.00	Teapot, "Radiance"	$190.00 – 225.00
Drip coffee pot, "Radiance," all-china	$250.00 – 300.00		

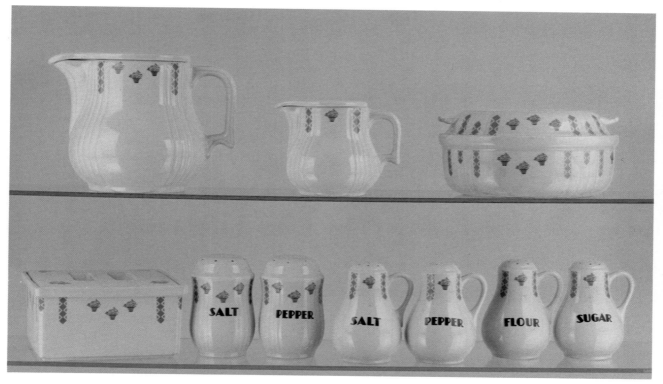

Row 1: Jug and cover, "Radiance," #5; jug and cover, "Radiance," #2; casserole, "Radiance."
Row 2: Leftover, square; shakers, "Novelty Radiance"; shakers, handled.

The "Stonewall" decal consists of green vertical bars which look like an inverted wooden fence slat. These green bars have a white zigzag line running along each side. Positioned between the bars will be one or more green baskets of pink and orange flowers. Although most of the items in this pattern are being found with an ivory body, a few pieces have been found with an eggshell body.

The number of pieces in this listing has expanded phenomenally since the last book. However, none of these pieces is easy to find and anyone who chooses to collect this pattern is undertaking a considerable challenge.

The "Radiance" jugs are sometimes found without covers. Consider the bottoms worth about half to two-thirds less than the indicated values.

Kitchenware	Price
Bowl, 6", "Radiance"	$14.00 – 16.00
Bowl, 7½", "Radiance"	$17.00 – 19.00
Bowl, 9", "Radiance"	$20.00 – 25.00
Casserole, "Radiance"	$27.00 – 32.00
Custard, "Radiance"	$10.00 – 12.00
Drip jar, #1188, open	$22.00 – 27.00
Drip coffee pot, "Kadota," all-china	$145.00 – 165.00
Jug and cover, #1, #2, "Radiance"	$60.00 – 75.00
Jug and cover, #4, #5, "Radiance"	$55.00 – 65.00
Jug and cover, #6, "Radiance"	$75.00 – 85.00
Juicer, "Medallion"	$450.00 – 550.00
Leftover, rectangular	$40.00 – 50.00
Leftover, square	$50.00 – 60.00
Shakers, handled, ea. (4)	$17.00 – 20.00
Shakers, "Novelty Radiance," ea.	$27.00 – 32.00
Stack set, "Radiance"	$85.00 – 95.00
Teapot, "Radiance"	$195.00 – 225.00

"WILD POPPY"

Unusual "Wild Poppy" mustard with spoon lid.

The "Wild Poppy" decal first appeared in the late 1930s. It combines a rust-colored poppy-like flower with a sprig of wheat. This pattern was sold by Macy's, which probably explains why many of the more unusual pieces are being found in the New York area. Many items have been added to the list of known pieces in the last few years. Some of the more interesting are a number of all-china coffee pots. These may be seen in the photographs.

Items of significant rarity new to the listing since the last book include the "Radiance" condiment jar, mustard with spoon lid, "Zephyr" leftover, rectangular baker, and Ball jug #3.

"Radiance" mixing bowls with colored interiors also exist. Some have been found with maroon interiors and others have green glaze on the inside. An abundance of casseroles and other ovenware items were also produced in this pattern. The French drip coffee biggin has been found in two, four, six, and eight cup sizes. Notice the French teapot in the photo with the infusor. A French teapot with an infusor is unusual in a decal pattern. The "Radiance" custard will be found with and without the wheat sprig.

Row 1: Canister set, "Radiance."

Row 2: Shakers, handled; shakers, "Novelty Radiance"; shaker, "Radiance" canister-style.

Row 3: Bean pot, New England, #4, bean pot, New England, #3; leftover, "Medallion," square.

Row 1: Jug and cover, "Radiance," #6; jug and cover, "Radiance," #5; jug and cover, "Radiance," #4.

Row 2: Jug "Radiance," #3; jug and cover, "Radiance," #2; jug and cover, "Radiance," #1; mustard, spoon lid.

Row 3: Butter, 1 lb. "Zephyr"; onion soup; shirred egg dish, 5¼".

Row 1: Coffee pot, small-size "Terrace," all-china; coffee pot, 12-cup, Washington; teapot, "Radiance."

Row 2: Teapot, 6-cup, New York; teapot, 4-cup, New York; creamer, sugar, and lid, New York.

Row 3: Casserole, "Radiance"; casserole, 10½" round; casserole, "Sundial," #1.

"Wild Poppy"

Kitchenware	Price		Kitchenware	Price
Baker, oval	$45.00 – 55.00		Custard, "Radiance"	$14.00 – 16.00
Baker, rectangular	$85.00 – 95.00		Drip coffee pot, #691, all-china	$295.00 – 320.00
Ball jug, #3	$140.00 – 165.00		Drip coffee pot, "Radiance," all-china	$300.00 – 340.00
Bean pot, New England, #3	$170.00 – 190.00		Drip coffee pot, sm., "Terrace"	$150.00 – 175.00
Bean pot, New England, #4	$140.00 – 165.00		Drip jar, #1188, open	$35.00 – 40.00
Bowl, 5¼", "Radiance"	$22.00 – 27.00		Jug and cover, #1, #2, "Radiance"	$100.00 – 125.00
Bowl, 6", "Radiance"	$18.00 – 22.00		Jug and cover, #3, #4, #5, "Radiance"	$90.00 – 110.00
Bowl, 7½", "Radiance"	$20.00 – 25.00		Jug and cover, #6, "Radiance"	$100.00 – 135.00
Bowl, 9", "Radiance"	$22.00 – 27.00		Leftover, sq.	$75.00 – 85.00
Bowl, 10", "Radiance"	$35.00 – 40.00		Leftover, "Zephyr"	$185.00 – 210.00
Butter dish, 1 lb., "Zephyr"	$450.00 – 550.00		Mustard, spoon lid	$250.00 – 295.00
Canister, "Radiance"	$120.00 – 145.00		Onion soup, individual	$40.00 – 55.00
Casserole, #101, oval	$70.00 – 90.00		Shakers, handled, ea. (4)	$20.00 – 25.00
Casserole, #103, oval	$95.00 – 110.00		Shakers, "Novelty Radiance," ea.	$40.00 – 50.00
Casserole, 8", round, 2-H	$40.00 – 50.00		Shakers, "Radiance," canister style, ea.	$45.00 – 55.00
Casserole, 10½", round, #76	$50.00 – 60.00		Shirred egg dish, 5¼"	$30.00 – 40.00
Casserole, "Radiance"	$30.00 – 37.00		Shirred egg dish, 6½"	$30.00 – 40.00
Casserole, "Sundial," #1	$45.00 – 55.00		Stack set, "Radiance"	$140.00 – 160.00
Casserole, "Sundial," #4	$35.00 – 40.00		Sugar and lid, Hollywood	$45.00 – 55.00
Casserole, "Thick Rim"	$45.00 – 55.00		Sugar and lid, New York	$40.00 – 50.00
Coccette, handled	$45.00 – 55.00		Teapot, French	$285.00 – 325.00
Coffee pot, French drip coffee biggin	$295.00 – 345.00		Teapot, New York, 2 or 4-cup	$250.00 – 295.00
Coffee pot, 2-cup, Washington	$90.00 – 110.00		Teapot, New York, 6-cup	$185.00 – 225.00
Coffee pot, 12-cup, Washington	$175.00 – 225.00		Teapot, New York, 8-cup	$280.00 – 310.00
Cookie jar, "Five Band"	$185.00 – 225.00		Teapot, "Radiance"	$195.00 – 225.00
Condiment jar, "Radiance"	$400.00 – 500.00		Teapot, Tea for Two set	UND
Creamer, Hollywood	$25.00 – 30.00		Teapot, Tea for Four set	UND
Creamer, New York	$25.00 – 30.00		Tea tile, 6"	$40.00 – 50.00

Row 1: Coffee pot, 6-cup French drip coffee biggin; drip coffee pot, #691; drip coffee pot, "Radiance."

Row 2: Coffee pot bottom, 2-cup French drip coffee biggin; coffee pot bottom, 4-cup French drip coffee biggin; teapot with infusor, French.

Row 3: Casserole, #101, 9½", oval, casserole, #103, 11¼", oval.

ZEISEL KITCHENWARE

In addition to the dinnerware lines which have been discussed previously, Eva Zeisel designed a kitchenware shape for Hall during the 1950s. Two patterns — Casual Living and Tri-Tone — are available.

Casual Living pieces are Seal brown and white with a decoration of pastel brushstrokes and dots in the white area.

Tri-Tone pieces have a three-color decoration — pink, turquoise, and gray over a white body. The pink and turquoise areas overlap to form gray triangles and the knobs of lids are also gray.

The cookie jar and the bean pot are similar in shape. The cookie jar has a flared collar into which the lid fits and the bottom is a little fatter than the bean pot bottom. The bean pot has no collar.

Tri-Tone
Row 1: Cookie jar; bean pot; jug, refrigerator.

Row 2: Teapot, 6-cup; teapot, side handled; mug.

Row 3: Shakers; jam jar; sugar and lid; creamer.

Tri-Tone
Row 1: Jug, 5 pint; casserole, oval, 3 pint; bowl, covered, 2-H soup.

Row 2: Bowl, 5", mixing; bowl, individual salad; bowl, large salad.

Row 3: Casserole, 3 pint; casserole, individual; relish, 1 handle.

Casual Living
Row 1: Relish, 1-handle; jug, 5 pint; teapot, 6-cup.

Row 2: Tureen, 8 pint; sugar and lid; creamer; jam jar.

Kitchenware	Casual Living	Tri-Tone
Bean pot	$42.00 – 55.00	$75.00 – 95.00
Bowl, covered, 2-H soup	$14.00 – 18.00	$35.00 – 40.00
Bowl, individual salad	$6.00 – 7.00	$13.00 – 15.00
Bowl, large salad	$14.00 – 17.00	$22.00 – 27.00
Bowl, 5"		$9.00 – 11.00
Bowl, 6"		$12.00 – 14.00
Bowl, 7"		$15.00 – 17.00
Bowl, 8"		$18.00 – 22.00
Bowl, 9"		$25.00 – 30.00
Casserole, individual	$14.00 – 18.00	$27.00 – 32.00
Casserole, oval, 3 pt.	$18.00 – 20.00	$32.00 – 37.00
Casserole, oval, 6 pt.	$22.00 – 25.00	$35.00 – 45.00
Cookie jar	$50.00 – 65.00	$85.00 – 110.00
Creamer	$8.00 – 10.00	$15.00 – 18.00
Jam jar	$18.00 – 22.00	$37.00 – 45.00
Jug, 5 pt.	$40.00 – 50.00	$80.00 – 95.00
Jug, refrigerator	$50.00 – 60.00	$75.00 – 85.00
Leftover and cover	$14.00 – 16.00	$27.00 – 32.00
Mug	$16.00 – 18.00	$30.00 – 35.00
Relish, 1-handle	$9.00 – 11.00	$18.00 – 22.00
Shakers, ea.	$10.00 – 12.50	$18.00 – 20.00
Sugar and lid	$14.00 – 16.00	$25.00 – 30.00
Teapot, 6-cup	$65.00 – 75.00	$90.00 – 110.00
Teapot, side-handled	$75.00 – 85.00	$95.00 – 120.00
Tureen, 5 pt.	$20.00 – 25.00	$45.00 – 55.00
Tureen, 8 pt.	$30.00 – 40.00	$75.00 – 85.00

HALL KITCHENWARE

The pieces shown in these photos represent patterns about which very little is known at this time. In all of these patterns we have seen less than a half dozen pieces, and in most, fewer. Some patterns have been named by researchers or collectors. We will use those names whenever possible and continue to search for answers to questions about the history of these patterns.

Row 1: The pieces on this row all have the same daisy-like floral design. From left to right are a "Cathedral" Drip-O-lator coffee pot; a "Five Band" cookie jar; and a pair of handled shakers. In addition a "Five Band" batter bowl and "Radiance" canisters exist in this pattern.

Row 2: The teapot on the left is unusual. It is an 8-cup "Radiance" teapot with a bright orange shaggy floral decal. The Art Deco sugar and Boston teapot share the same orange and yellow floral decal. The flowers are attached to a vine-like branch with gray and brown leaves. A large "Terrace" coffee pot may also be found with this pattern.

The Ball jug and 4-cup Boston teapot in this photo are decorated with
multicolored floral sprigs.

Row 1: The large-size coffee pot on the left is decorated with bouquets of pink, yellow, and blue flowers. The handled shakers are decorated with pink and yellow flowers on an eggshell background. The Zeisel-style bean pot with the bird shield has the letters "Elena" below the decal.

Row 2: The pretzel jar and the buffet casserole have a decal collectors are calling "Autumn Flowers." The pretzel jar has an ivory body and the casserole has an eggshell body. There is also a "Radiance" mixing bowl set in this pattern. The handled shakers have a bright red floral decal with dark green leaves. Both the top and bottom edges are trimmed with platinum.

RED KITCHENWARE

		Price
Row 1:	Covered Tom & Jerry bowl	$95.00 – 125.00
	Tom & Jerry #2044 mug	$8.00 – 10.00
	Terrace coffee pot, small size	$100.00 – 125.00
Row 2:	Creamer, Bellvue	$12.00 – 15.00
	Salad bowl, 9"	$18.00 – 22.00
	Chocolate tumbler, #342	$8.00 – 10.00
	French casserole, side handled	$40.00 – 50.00
Row 3:	Baker, rectangular	$25.00 – 30.00
	Casserole, "Sundial," #1	$18.00 – 22.00
	Drip jar, #1188, open	$25.00 – 30.00

		Price			*Price*
Row 1:	Pretzel jar	$70.00 – 80.00	Row 3:	Sugar and creamer, "Norse"	$32.00 – 37.00
	Coffee pot, "Baron"	$42.00 – 47.00		Petite Marmite	$12.00 – 15.00
	Tea for Two set	$90.00 – 125.00		Ashtray	$10.00 – 2.00
	Vase, #641	$18.00 – 22.00		Bean pot, New England	$55.00 – 65.00
Row 2:	Water server, #628	$75.00 – 85.00	Row 4:	Teapot, morning set	$95.00 – 125.00
	Water server, Plaza	$90.00 – 110.00		Covered sugar, morning set	$30.00 – 35.00
	Shakers, handled with			Creamer, morning set	$18.00 – 22.00
	embossed letters, ea.	$18.00 – 22.00		Trivet	$15.00 – 18.00

PART III: REFRIGERATOR WARE

The popularity of the modern electric refrigerator in the late 1930s resulted in the production of numerous types of cold storage units from glass and china. Hall China made items for retail sale as well as exclusive designs for Westinghouse, General Electric, Sears, Hotpoint, and Montgomery Ward. Premium type refrigerator items were also an important part of the production of the era. The accompanying McCormick ad reprint illustrates an example of one such premium.

Three basic items are included in the Hall refrigerator line. They are water bottles or water servers, leftovers or refrigerator boxes, and covered butters.

The water containers are covered pieces intended to be placed in the refrigerator for water storage. Closure is achieved with either a cork-encased china stopper or with a china lid. Leftovers are deep dishes with a shallow or flat china lid. The butter dishes have a flat bottom and a deep lid.

Today the popularity of Hall refrigerator ware is astounding. Many people are again using these items in their refrigerators and the water servers are especially popular. The renewed interest in Hall water servers may have been partly responsible for Hall's re-introduction of the Streamline and "Nora" shapes for the retail market a few years ago.

Genuine Hall china. Choice of 3 colors. At your grocer's. Supply limited. Hurry!

Get this beautiful

ICED TEA PITCHER

ONLY **89¢** (*2.00 VALUE)
with purchase of
McCormick Tea or Tea Bags
(This offer not available in certain areas.)

McCORMICK TEA

It's the *Magic Blend* of the choicest tea leaves grown ...created by the world's foremost flavor experts.

Mc TEA BAGS McCORMICK

For years, the wonderful flavor of McCormick Tea has been protected in *foil-lined* tea bag cartons.

Mc
McCORMICK
ONE FAMOUS EMBLEM—TWO GREAT BRANDS
McCORMICK and
Schilling

THE HOUSE OF McCORMICK

WESTINGHOUSE

The "Hercules" shape was offered as "Peasant Ware" by Westinghouse in 1940 and 1941. A set consisted of a rectangular butter, a water server, and two leftovers. Cobalt is the most common color of the water server, but it may also be found in tan with the Westinghouse backstamp. Later, this mold was used to produce water servers for Toucan Enterprises of Chicago. The colors of these water servers were cobalt, tan, brown, and ivory. Most of these will have the "TOUCAN ENTERPRISES, CHICAGO" backstamp. Beginning in 1984, Hall began producing this covered water server in several colors as part of the Hall American line. To identify the new pieces look for the new square backstamp. In addition to the regular split-lid shape water server another style has been found. The second shape, which has a full-length, detached, semi-hinged lid is shown in the photo below.

The "General" design was offered in 1939, as an accessory to Westinghouse refrigerators. Sets were comprised of a water server, two leftovers, and a butter. The water server is found frequently in delphinium, and has been showing up with some regularity in garden green. The butter and leftovers are usually seen in garden, sunset, delphinium, and yellow.

"Phoenix" was the earliest line of Hall refrigerator ware used by Westinghouse. This line was introduced in 1938, and consisted of a water server, a leftover, and a butter. The most commonly found color is delphinium, but all three pieces are also found occasionally in lettuce green. There have also been reports of a cobalt water server.

The "Adonis" line in blue and daffodil was offered by Westinghouse in 1952. A set consisted of a water server, four small round leftovers, and two rectangular leftovers. Two styles of ovenware sets were offered at the same time. These pieces are shown on page 191. Each set was comprised of three pieces — two covered casseroles and one open baker. The "Ridged" line came in canary and the "Plain" line was made in delphinium.

Refrigerator Ware	"Hercules"	"General"	"Phoenix"	"Adonis"
Butter	$22.00 – 27.00	$20.00 – 25.00	$18.00 – 22.00	
Leftover, rect.	$18.00 – 22.00	$15.00 – 18.00	$15.00 – 18.00	$16.00 – 20.00
Leftover, round		$6.00 – 8.00		
Water server	$85.00 – 95.00*	$45.00 – 55.00	$40.00 – 50.00	$40.00 – 50.00
Water server, hinged lid	$115.00 – 125.00			

* Re-issued as part of the Hall American line.

Bakeware	"Ridged"	"Plain"
Casserole, covered	$16.00 – 18.00	$16.00 – 18.00
Baker, open	$10.00 – 12.00	$10.00 – 12.00

Hinged-lid "Hercules" water server.

Black and white Sears' leftover.

Row 1: Water server, "Hercules"; water server, "Hercules"; leftover, "Hercules"; butter, "Hercules."
Row 2: Leftover, "General"; butter, "General"; water server, "General."
Row 3: Water server, "Phoenix"; leftover, "Phoenix"; butter, "Phoenix."
Row 4: Leftover, rectangular, "Adonis"; water server, "Adonis"; leftover, small round, "Adonis."

MONTGOMERY WARD, HOTPOINT, SEARS, GENERAL ELECTRIC

Hall produced a line of refrigerator ware for Montgomery Ward in the early forties. The color usually seen is delphinium, but pieces can also be found in the mid-white color. There are two styles of rectangular leftovers. The larger one with the V-shape lid is not easy to find. Also included in the set are three sizes of round covered bowls with raised elongated handles, a rectangular butter, and a water server.

Refrigerator Ware	Price	Refrigerator Ware	Price
Bowl, sm., covered	$15.00 – 18.00	Butter	$22.00 – 27.00
Bowl, med., covered	$16.00 – 20.00	Leftover, rect.	$14.00 – 16.00
Bowl, lg., covered	$18.00 – 22.00	Leftover, lg., rect.	$25.00 – 30.00
Bowl, knob handle	$16.00 – 18.00	Water server	$40.00 – 50.00

Bright colored leftovers were included in a refrigerator ware line which Hall produced for Hotpoint. The line consisted of a water server, three round leftovers, five square leftovers, and a rectangular leftover. The water servers with the cork encased china stoppers are not easy to find. Some sizes of the square leftovers and the rectangular leftover are also proving hard-to-find. For some reason, many dealers think the presence of the Hotpoint insignia on these pieces automatically makes them a rare advertising collectible. Some leftovers we have seen have been priced as museum pieces rather than as a common collectible.

Refrigerator Ware	Price	Refrigerator Ware	Price
Leftover, rect.	$18.00 – 22.00	Leftover, 4¾", sq.	$20.00 – 25.00
Leftover, 6¾", round	$18.00 – 20.00	Leftover, 5¾", sq.	$20.00 – 25.00
Leftover, 7¾", round	$20.00 – 22.00	Leftover, 6¾", sq.	$22.00 – 27.00
Leftover, 8¾", round	$22.00 – 28.00	Leftover, 8½", sq.	$28.00 – 32.00
Leftover, 4", sq.	$18.00 – 22.00	Water server	$55.00 – 65.00

Hall made one piece of refrigerator ware for Sears. It is a three-part leftover which is normally found in the cadet and Hi-white colors. The center piece is solid cadet and the end pieces have cadet bases and Hi-white lids. There have been several reports of another color combination being found. This set has a solid Hi-black center piece and Hi-white end pieces which have Hi-black lids. An example of the end section is shown in the photo on page 188.

Refrigerator Ware	Price
Sears' leftover, 3-part	$55.00 – 67.00

Hall modified its Westinghouse "Adonis" line for use with General Electric refrigerators. The GE logo was used on the lids and the new colors were addison and daffodil. Two new pieces were added — a handled casserole and a large round leftover.

Refrigerator Ware	Price	Refrigerator Ware	Price
Casserole	$22.00 – 27.00	Leftover, lg. round	$16.00 – 20.00
Leftover, rect.	$16.00 – 18.00	Water server	$40.00 – 50.00
Leftover, sm. round	$7.00 – 9.00		

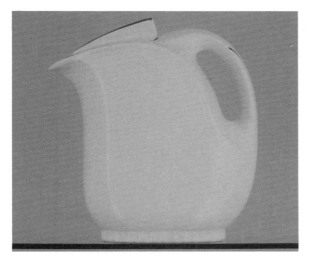

Montgomery Ward water server,
white with red trim.

Row 1: Casserole, covered, "Ridged," Westinghouse; baker, open "Ridged," Westinghouse; casserole, covered, "Plain," Westinghouse (Priced on page 188).

Row 2: Leftover, rectangular, Montgomery Ward; bowl, covered, Montgomery Ward; water server, Montgomery Ward; leftover, large rectangular, Montgomery Ward.

Row 3: Water server, Hotpoint; leftover, 8½", square, Hotpoint; leftover 6¾", round, Hotpoint.

Row 4: Leftover, 3-section, Sears.

Row 5: Water server, General Electric; casserole, General Electric; leftover rectangular, General Electric.

MISCELLANEOUS REFRIGERATOR WARE

Hall made numerous shapes of refrigerator ware for the retail market. Some of these shapes are still in the current line and are being sold at department stores and specialty shops around the country.

The Ball jug was introduced in 1938, and quickly became a best seller for Hall. It may be found in numerous solid colors and is in virtually all the decal lines. It is available in four different sizes — 1½ pt., 2⅓ pt., 2 qt., and 5¼ pt. The #3 size, 2 quart, is the most commonly found size. Although this shape was not chosen for re-issue in the Hall American line, new Ball jugs in stock green and stock brown are available in the institutional line.

The "Nora" water servers came with and without china lids. They were a covered water server available in Hall's general line and also a premium item for McCormick Tea in their lidless form. See the reprint from a 1955 magazine at the front of this section. New covered jugs in this shape were produced as part of the Hall American line beginning in 1984.

The Donut jug was introduced in the late thirties and is still in the institutional line. This jug was also re-issued in 1984, as a part of Hall's re-entry into the retail market. The old Donut jug may be found in two sizes and a variety of solid colors. It has also been found in a few of the decal lines and some have been appearing with gold decoration. The green one in the picture has the gold "French Flower" decoration along with a gold encrusted handle and gold around the lip.

The loop handle jug was introduced in the thirties and is still available in the general line. It was made in two sizes and is found in many different solid colors and a few of the decal lines. The smaller size appears to be harder to find than the larger size.

The Plaza water server may be found with a cork encased china stopper, but so many of these jugs have been found without stoppers that they were probably issued without them in some promotion. Although the jug was produced from the thirties to the sixties, not many are found today.

The Streamline jug was selected for re-issue in the Hall American line. The older jugs are not easy to find and date to the thirties. New pieces will bear the square backstamp.

The #628 water server has been found in numerous colors. It was introduced in the late thirties, but is no longer in production.

The "Zephyr" line consists of two sizes of stoppered water bottles, a covered one-pound butter, and a covered rectangular leftover. The line dates to the late thirties and will be found predominantly in the Chinese red color. However, pieces do exist in a few of the decal lines, and recently, a blue water bottle was discovered. Pictured below are the two sizes of water bottles. The smaller bottle is 7" tall and holds 27 ounces. The larger bottle is 7½" tall and holds 48 ounces.

Refrigerator Ware	Green/Brown/Light Blues	Red/Cobalt
Ball jug, #1, 5¼"	$20.00 – 35.00	$45.00 – 55.00
Ball jug, #2, 5¾"	$18.00 – 30.00	$45.00 – 55.00
Ball jug, #3, 7"	$15.00 – 28.00	$40.00 – 50.00
Ball jug, #4, 7½"	$22.00 – 32.00	$50.00 – 60.00
Butter, "Zephyr"	$95.00 – 110.00	$110.00 – 135.00
Jug, Donut, large	$30.00 – 45.00	$60.00 – 70.00
Jug, Donut, small	$30.00 – 45.00	$55.00 – 65.00
Jug, loop handle, large	$40.00 – 55.00	$60.00 – 75.00
Jug, loop handle, small	$40.00 – 55.00	$60.00 – 75.00
Jug, Streamline	$45.00 – 55.00	$65.00 – 75.00
Leftover, "Zephyr"	$65.00 – 85.00	$85.00 – 95.00
Water bottle, "Zephyr," (2 sizes)	$90.00 – 110.00	$115.00 – 145.00
Water server, #628	$40.00 – 55.00	$75.00 – 85.00
Water server, "Nora"	$18.00 – 22.00	
Water server, Plaza	$55.00 – 65.00	$90.00 – 110.00

Water bottles, "Zephyr."

Row 1: Ball jug, #3; Ball jug, #3; Water server, "Nora." Row 2: Jug, Donut; Jug, Donut with gold "French Flower" decoration; Jug, loop handle. Row 3: Water server, Plaza; Jug, Streamline; Water server, #628. Row 4: Water bottle, "Zephyr"; Butter "Zephyr"; Leftover, "Zephyr."

Decorated With Gold!

The lovely Airflow brewer, an exclusive Hall China design, is beautifully shaped, richly colored, and decorated with gleaming gold! Like all genuine Hall Teapots, it will not stain or absorb because it is made of secret process china that keeps sweet and clean. If your dealer does not have the exact shape or color you prefer please remember that much of our production of chinaware is for our fighting forces.

THE HALL CHINA COMPANY....World's Largest Manufacturer of Decorated Teapots and Cooking China

BUY MORE WAR BONDS

Hall Teapots
OF SUPERIOR QUALITY CHINA

Beauty and Utility United!

The Aladdin Teapot brings pleasure to all who love the golden beverage. It is a lovely, traditional design, enriched with genuine gold decoration. And, its use assures perfect tea every time, for it is made of secret process china that will never craze, stain, or absorb.

The Hall China Company—World's Largest Manufacturer of Decorated Teapots and Cooking China.

Hall Teapots
OF SUPERIOR QUALITY CHINA

Sold by All Leading Dealers

PREFERRED for Perfect Tea

This lovely French shape is decorated with gleaming gold that glistens on a colorful glaze that will never craze. Like all genuine Hall Teapots, it is made of secret process china that will not stain or absorb. Use it ... for perfect tea, graciously served. That's why Hall Teapots are preferred!

The Hall China Company
World's Largest Manufacturer of Decorated Teapots and Cooking China

Hall Teapots
OF SUPERIOR QUALITY CHINA

Sold by All Leading Dealers

Charming TEA SERVICE

Hall China Gold Decorated Teapots appeal irresistibly to all who know good tea, and appreciate lovely chinaware. Made of secret process china .... they brew tea that is deliciously delicate and fresh in flavor. If you cannot obtain the Hall teapot design you prefer, please remember that the needs of our fighting forces have first call. The Hall China Company ... World's Largest Manufacturer of Decorated Teapots and Cooking China.

BUY WAR BONDS FIRST

Hall Teapots
OF SUPERIOR QUALITY CHINA

SOLD BY ALL LEADING DEALERS

PART IV: TEAPOTS AND COFFEE POTS

The first Hall teapots were part of the institutional line. The early colors were stock brown, stock green, and white. In 1920, the Boston, New York, and French shapes were selected for a store promotion. These teapots were decorated with gold and Hall's Gold Decorated Teapot line was born. The new line was very successful and many new shapes were added over the next few decades. These new shapes were combined with a rainbow of new colors to catapult Hall China into prominence as the leading producer of teapots in the world.

Many of Hall's teapots, which are collectible today, are part of the Gold Decorated line. The backstamp on these teapots will usually include a gold code number which was used for reordering purposes. Each shape teapot will have a standard gold design, although some experimentation in the early years has resulted in different gold designs on some of the older teapots. Also, on some shapes there is a gold decoration which collectors refer to as "special." "Specials" have the standard gold design for their shape. In addition, they also will have gold encrusted handles, spouts, and knobs. The gold mark on the backstamp will usually be followed by an "S."

Undecorated teapots will usually have the #3 backstamp, red teapots have the #4 kitchenware backstamp, and teapots made in the twenties or early thirties have the #2 backstamp.

In the thirties, six teapots were selected for decal decoration. The shapes chosen were the Baltimore, French, Los Angeles, Newport, New York, and Philadelphia. Sales of these teapots with the decal decorations were not very good. Therefore, most of them are difficult for collectors to find.

In the early forties Hall introduced a series of six teapots which has become known as the Victorian line. Although several of these teapots have been found in two colors, they were essentially only offered in one basic color. Later, gold decoration was added in an attempt to increase sales. However, this line was never very popular, and it was discontinued by the end of the decade.

Also in the forties, another series of six teapots, called the Brilliant Series, was designed by J. Palin Thorley. These teapots were made in several colors, but each style has a single color in which it will be found most often. Decorations included rhinestones, decals, and gold, but many of these teapots will also be found undecorated. This line was offered sporadically through the late sixties.

In the late fifties, Hall brought out a new line of teapots call Gold Label. These teapots were very gaudy — almost covered with gold decoration. The shapes of the teapots were selected from among those used earlier. No new shapes were introduced. This new line of teapots was sold along with several other matching kitchenware accessories. Gold Label decorated teapots may be identified through the letters "GL" which follow the gold code number on the bottom of the teapots.

In the 1960s another attempt was made to revive the interest in teapots through the use of decals. The six teapots chosen and their decorations are as follows:

Teapot	Decoration
Boston	gold fruit decal
French	gold rose decal
Hollywood	gold leaf decal
Los Angeles	green and yellow leaf decal
Philadelphia	black hearth scene decal
Windshield	green, white, and brown floral band

In 1984, Hall began offering teapots to the public again through retail outlets via their Hall American line. The Airflow, Rhythm, and square T-Ball teapots were marketed through major department stores and specialty shops across the country. Today, many of these later teapots may be found at flea markets, resale shops, and antique malls throughout the country. To identify these new issues look for the square backstamp.

Hall produced many different coffee pots. Many of these pots were used in the decal lines and will be identified there. However, some were sold to other companies such as Enterprise, Tricolator, and Westinghouse. These companies then added the metal parts and marketed the finished product. Some, but not all of the coffee pots will bear a Hall backstamp.

To help with identification, the coffee pots and teapots in the following photographs will have both their shape name and color name. In some cases recognition of the colors may still be difficult, since some colors do not print the exact shade. Since color is such an important factor in the price of the teapots, an attempt will be made to note the hard-to-find colors for each shape. The price guide has been divided into as many categories as practical to aid collectors in their attempt to distinguish between common and unusual teapots.

NOVELTY TEAPOTS

The automobile is a six-cup novelty teapot which was introduced in 1938. The unique styling of this teapot continuously amazes spectators at glass and pottery shows today. Even unenlightened browsers are impressed by the lines of this unusual teapot, and that is even before they find out the price. The automobile may be found in a number of solid colors. Red, cobalt, maroon, canary, and turquoise appear to be most common. Also, it may be found in many of these same colors with either gold or platinum trim. The decorated teapots usually have an encrusted spout, solid decoration on the raised areas of the lid, and highlighted wheels, fenders, and door hinges and handles. However, some teapots will be found with a decoration which consists of merely a few simple gold or platinum lines. Collectors need to be aware this teapot was re-issued in 1993, as a limited edition collectible. For more detailed information see the Re-issues in the back of this book.

The basket is a six-cup teapot which was first made in 1938. It is the easiest to find of all the novelty teapots. Baskets are usually found in canary and will be commonly decorated with a few platinum lines. The most easily found undecorated colors are Chinese red and canary. The basket will also be found in other colors, but these are rather unusual.

The basketball has consistently proven to be the hardest to find of the novelty teapots. It is a six-cup teapot which first made its appearance in 1938. However, it has not surpassed the football or automobile in desirability or price. The most commonly found colors are undecorated Chinese red and decorated turquoise. The decorated basketball in the picture is what collectors call a "special" since it has a gold encrusted handle and spout in addition to the standard decoration.

The birdcage is a hard-to-find novelty teapot which was introduced in 1938. It will be found in solid colors and with gold decoration. Gold decoration consists of highlighting lines on the cage and gold decoration on the embossed birds. The most commonly found undecorated color is Chinese red. Decorated birdcages are turning up most often in maroon, blue, and emerald green.

The donut, which first appeared in 1938, is one of the easiest to find of all the novelty teapots. However, phenomenal collector demand has kept the price high and the supply low. Gold decoration consists of a few simple lines accenting the handle, spout, and lid. The donut is found in a variety of solid colors and is the only novelty teapot which has been found in the dinnerware decal patterns. It is found most often with the Orange Poppy decal and is also know to exist in the Crocus pattern.

The football seems to be appearing more frequently lately than it has in the past. Maybe its high price is forcing some out of attics. However, collector enthusiasm for these teapots is keeping the price high and the supply of all mint condition teapots is being quickly absorbed into collections. The football has been found in numerous solid colors. Of these red, cobalt, maroon, and turquoise are probably the most common. Gold decoration normally consists of a few simple lines on the handle, lid, and side of the teapot. However, a variation dubbed a "special" will be found having a gold encrusted handle and spout in addition to the standard gold lines. Beginning in 1993, Hall re-introduced the football teapot as part of a limited edition series for a private company. See the Re-issues section of this book for details.

Teapot	Introduced	Red/Cobalt*	Other Colors*
Automobile	1938	$500.00 – 650.00	$400.00 – 500.00
Basket	1938	$175.00 – 245.00	$85.00 – 125.00
Basketball	1938	$550.00 – 650.00	$500.00 – 600.00
Birdcage	1938	$350.00 – 400.00	$225.00 – 350.00
Donut	1938	$295.00 – 350.00	$200.00 – 250.00
Football	1938	$550.00 – 650.00	$450.00 – 550.00

*Gold or silver decoration, add 10%.

Row 1: Automobile, cobalt; automobile, canary/gold; automobile, maroon/platinum.
Row 2: Basket, canary/platinum; basketball, turquoise/gold; basketball, Chinese red.
Row 3: Birdcage, maroon/gold; birdcage, cadet; donut, cobalt.
Row 4: Donut, ivory; football, cobalt; football, cobalt/gold.

AIRFLOW TEAPOT

Row 1: Airflow, 8-cup, emerald/standard gold; Airflow, 8-cup, maroon/standard gold; Airflow, 6-cup, cobalt/gold "special." Row 2: Airflow, 6-cup, cadet/standard gold; Airflow, 6-cup, Chinese red; Airflow, 6-cup, marine/standard gold.

The Airflow teapot was introduced in 1940, and was produced in eight-cup and six-cup sizes. Today, the larger eight-cup size is much harder to find than the smaller version. The Airflow will be found in a variety of solid colors. The most commonly found colors are cobalt, canary, and Chinese red. In addition, a standard gold decoration and several variations of the standard decoration will be found. The standard decoration consists of a large single rose on the center of each side of the teapot and multiple gold leaf sprigs around the opening. The foot, handle, and lid are accented with gold lines. All the teapots in the picture except the cobalt and red have the standard decoration. A variation of the gold decoration includes a "special" which may be seen on the cobalt teapot shown on the top row. This consists of a gold encrusted handle and spout used in combination with the standard decoration. Other variations are achieved by deleting a part of the standard decoration. One version omits the large center rose on the sides of the teapot. Another style omits both the flowers and leaves, leaving only the thin gold highlighting lines. The only reports of any Airflow teapots appearing with decals have been in the blue Blossom and Blue Garden patterns.

The Airflow teapot was one of the items Hall chose to re-introduce in 1985, when the retail business was re-established. New Airflow teapots will be found, but all should have the square backstamp which has been in use since the seventies. Also, at this writing, new gold decorated teapots have not been produced.

Teapot	Red	Canary/ Turquoise	Other Solid Colors	Gold Decorated "Special"
Airflow, 6-cup	$85.00 – 110.00	$37.00 – 42.00	$50.00 – 65.00	$45.00 – 55.00
Airflow, 8-cup	$85.00 – 125.00	$40.00 – 50.00	$55.00 – 75.00	$50.00 – 60.00

Standard gold decorated prices are the same as for solid colors.

ALADDIN TEAPOTS

Row 1: Aladdin, matte black and white with satin gold; Aladdin, chartreuse/gold; Aladdin, turquoise blue/gold. Row 2: Aladdin, daffodil, Gold Label, Squiggle design; Aladdin, pink, Gold Label, Swag design; Aladdin, maroon, Gold Label, Swag design.

The original thin style Aladdin teapot with the round opening was introduced in 1939. In 1940, an optional infuser was offered. A few years later Hall experimented with an Aladdin teapot with an oval opening and an oval lid and infuser. However, by the end of World War II, the teapot with the round opening was re-instated. In 1942, a modified wide-bodied version of the Aladdin teapot was introduced to be used with Jewel's Autumn and Morning Glory patterns. For the most part, very few other patterns or decorations will be found on this style of teapot, however, there are some exceptions as can be seen in the photo on the next page. The hand-painted teapot and the one with the floral basket decal feature the wide-body Aladdin.

Undecorated Aladdin teapots may be found in almost any Hall color. There are several variations of gold decorated Aladdin teapots. The simplest decoration consists of thin gold lines highlighting the handle, spout, lid opening, lid base, and knob. This may be seen on the blue and chartreuse teapots in the top row. The yellow teapot on the second row is an example of a Gold Label decoration called Squiggle. Colors available in this pattern are daffodil and ivory. For other matching pieces in this pattern see page 162. The heavily gold encrusted pink and maroon teapots are also part of the Gold Label line. The design on these teapots is called Swag. Other colors which are sometimes found with this design include ivory and marine.

The yellow teapot with gold splatter, shown in the photo on the next page, appears to have been decorated with a sponge. This is one of the more gaudy and unusually decorated Aladdin teapots. The turquoise teapot on the bottom row with the gold handle and the gold knob on the lid is what is referred to as a "special." A variation of these "specials" will be found with a gold encrusted spout. This teapot also features the much scarcer oval opening. Notice the accompanying sugar and creamer in the Boston shape which completes this set.

A multitude of regular-style Aladdin teapots will be found with decals. Some of the more common ones are in the Blue Bouquet, Red Poppy, and Wildfire patterns. Other patterns where the Aladdin teapot is a rarity include Crocus, Blue Blossom, Blue Garden, and Brown-eyed Susan. For more information on the availability and prices of Aladdin teapots with decals, see the individual dinnerware and kitchenware listings.

Aladdin & French Teapots

Teapot	Red / Cobalt*	Other Solid Colors	Gold Label
Aladdin, oval opening	$95.00 – 125.00	$35.00 – 45.00	
Aladdin, round opening	$95.00 – 125.00	$30.00 – 40.00	$40.00 – 55.00

*Gold decorated, add 20%.
Hand-painted, or very unusual gold decoration, $95.00 – 125.00.

Row 1: Aladdin, ivory with Floral Basket decal; Aladdin, canary with gold spatter; Aladdin, ivory, hand-painted, artist signed. Row 2: Aladdin, turquoise, "special" gold decoration with matching Boston sugar and creamer.

Left to Right: French, 6-cup, ivory, Gold Label, "daisy" decoration; French, 4-cup cadet, Gold Label, "daisy" decoration; French, 3-cup, cobalt with gold band; French, 2-cup, stock brown, French Flower decoration; French, 2-cup, canary.

BELLVUE AND FRENCH TEAPOTS

Row 1: Bellvue, 2-cup, cobalt/gold; French, 6-cup, ivory with embossed gold band decoration; French 4-cup with infuser and standard New York gold decoration; French, 4-cup, ivory with hand-painted Nouveau decoration. Row 2: French, 6-cup, matte black with Sears gold rose decal; French 8-cup, cobalt with gold palm leaf decoration and matching Boston shape sugar and creamer.

Interest in the Bellvue teapot among many collectors has been minimal. The teapot introduced in the 1920s will be found in at least six different sizes and is still being made in some colors. It is most commonly found in stock brown and stock green, but as can be seen in the photo, it will occasionally be found in attractive colors and with gold decoration. It has been found in one decal dinnerware line in the 2-cup size — Orange Poppy — and attracts great collector interest among those interested in that pattern.

The French teapot was one of the earliest to be added to the Gold Decorated line. This style teapot is a perfect example of Hall's decorating diversity. The gold decorations on some of the early teapots exhibit excellent craftsmanship. A prime example is the cobalt teapot with the gold palm leaf decoration which is shown in the photograph. Some of the early teapots dating from the 1920s, such as the two cobalt ones pictured, will be found with infusors. Later French teapots do not have infusors. The two most frequently found gold decorations are the "daisy" from the Gold Label line and the gold flower decoration like the one shown on the 2-cup stock brown teapot. These two decorations are found on all sizes of French teapots ranging from the 1-cup size to the 12-cup size. The various sizes of the French teapot which have been found are 1, 1½, 2, 3, 4, 6, 8, 10, and 12-cups. The 6 and 8-cup sizes of French teapots are the most common. The 6-cup teapot will also be found in numerous colors with Lipton Tea embossed in the bottom. Boston shape sugars and creamers will also be found to match these teapots in most colors. The matte black 6-cup teapot with the gold rose decal to the left on the second shelf was sold by Sears during the sixties.

Teapot	Common Solid Colors*	Red	Old Gold Decorated	Gold Label
Bellvue, 2, 4-cup	$12.00 – 15.00	$45.00 – 60.00		
Bellvue, 6, 10-cup	$22.00 – 30.00	$50.00 – 65.00		
French, 1, 3-cup	$25.00 – 35.00	$90.00 – 125.00	$55.00 – 75.00	$45.00 – 55.00
French, 4, 6-cup	$22.00 – 32.00	$85.00 – 100.00	$50.00 – 65.00	$32.00 – 37.00
French, 8, 12-cup	$25.00 – 35.00	$90.00 – 125.00	$55.00 – 65.00	$45.00 – 55.00

*Stock Brown or Stock Green, $15.00 – 20.00.
Bellvue, gold decorated, $35.00 – 45.00.
French, gold palm leaf decoration, $125.00 – 150.00.

GLOBE, HOOK COVER, MANHATTAN, WORLD'S FAIR, MELODY

The six-cup Globe teapot was made with two different shapes of spouts. The No-Drip spout Globe shown on the top row has a different standard gold decoration than the regular Globe pictured on the second row. Both teapots are found more often with gold decoration than without. Both styles are hard-to-find, but the No-Drip version appears to be a little more available than the other style.

The Hook Cover is a six-cup teapot which was introduced in 1940. It derives its name from the small hook on the body over which an opening in the lid fits to lock it into place. Colors usually found are cadet and delphinium. The standard gold decoration consists of a large gold flower along with four gold sprigs on each side of the body and gold trim on the foot, spout, handle, and around the lid and lid opening. The Gold Label version of the Hook Cover is covered with gold stars and sports a gold encrusted handle and spout.

The side-handled Manhattan teapot is usually found in the small two-cup size. It is most frequently seen in stock brown, maroon, and cobalt and we have not seen this teapot decorated.

The World's Fair teapot was a promotional item for the 1940 New York World's Fair. It incorporates a gold trylon and perisphere on a cobalt body of the Star shape. Most have the following backstamp: "A GENUINE HALL TEAPOT — MADE IN U.S.A. — SOLD EXCLUSIVELY AT THE NEW YORK WORLD'S FAIR — 1940." A few teapots have been found with a 1939 date in the backstamp.

The Melody teapot was first produced in 1939. It is a six-cup teapot which may be found with gold decoration; although it is probably found more frequently without decoration. The standard gold design on the body is three rings close to the base and three more rings inside the white collar in addition to trim on the handle and around the top edge. The lid is also decorated with a gold ring. The Melody is also sometimes found decorated with the Orange Poppy decal.

Star-shaped teapot with World's Fair decoration.

Teapot	Red	Other Colors*	Gold Label
Globe	$120.00 – 140.00	$70.00 – 85.00	
Globe, No-Drip		$65.00 – 75.00	
Hook Cover	$90.00 – 100.00	$20.00 – 30.00	$32.00 – 37.00
Manhattan	$75.00 – 95.00	$45.00 – 55.00	
World's Fair		$500.00 – 600.00	
Melody	$200.00 – 245.00	$150.00 – 200.00	

*Gold decorated price the same as solid colors.

Row 1: Globe No-Drip, marine with standard gold decoration; Globe No-Drip, Monterrey with standard gold decoration; Globe No-Drip, Addison with standard gold decoration. Row 2: Globe, cobalt with standard gold decoration; Globe, emerald; Hook Cover, cobalt. Row 3: Side-handle Manhattan, cobalt; side-handle Manhattan, stock brown; World's Fair, Star, cobalt. Row 4: Melody, cobalt with standard gold decoration; Melody, Chinese red.

MODERNE, NAUTILUS, PARADE, RHYTHM AND "SUNDIAL"

The Moderne teapot has a six-cup capacity. It is commonly found in ivory, canary, and cadet, and is usually seen without gold decoration. The standard gold application is limited to the knob of the lid, the very inside tip of the spout, and the foot. The plain design of this teapot has caused many common color Moderne teapots to be left on dealer's tables begging for homes.

The Nautilus is a sea shell-shaped six-cup teapot which first appeared in 1939. This teapot is hard-to-find and commands a respectable price. Normal gold decoration is limited to a few simple lines as may be seen on the turquoise teapot in the photo.

The Parade is a common six-cup teapot which is usually found in canary. The standard gold decoration is illustrated in the photograph. Finding colors such as red, maroon, or cobalt is a challenge, but not an impossible task. The Parade teapot is also part of the Gold Label line. The most commonly found color of the Gold Label teapot is also canary and the gold design is Squiggle.

The Rhythm is a six-cup teapot which was introduced in 1939. Due to the design of the teapot, it is very difficult to find this piece with a good lid. The standard gold decoration is pictured and the easiest color to find is canary.

The "Sundial" teapot is usually seen in canary. The standard gold decoration is shown on the canary teapot in the picture. This shape teapot is a basic part of one of Hall's major kitchenware shapes and will also be found with several decal decorations. The "Sundial" teapot was also made in the 8 oz. and 10 oz. individual sizes. These sizes are still being made in stock green and stock brown.

Teapot	Red	Common Colors	Unusual Colors	Gold Label
Moderne	$140.00 – 175.00	$18.00 – 22.00	$30.00 – 40.00	
Nautilus	$175.00 – 225.00	$95.00 – 125.00	$150.00 – 175.00	
Parade	$95.00 – 115.00	$22.00 – 30.00	$45.00 – 65.00	$25.00 – 30.00
Rhythm	$150.00 – 175.00	$60.00 – 75.00	$95.00 – 125.00	
"Sundial"	$150.00 – 175.00	$45.00 – 60.00	$85.00 – 125.00	

Row 1: Moderne, ivory/gold; Nautilus, Chinese red; Nautilus, cobalt/gold.

Row 2: Parade, canary/gold; Parade, cobalt/gold; Rhythm, Monterrey/gold.

Row 3: "Sundial," cobalt; "Sundial," canary/gold; "Sundial," Blue Blossom decal; "Sundial," 2-cup marine.

STAR AND STREAMLINE TEAPOTS

Row 1: Star, turquoise/gold; Star, cobalt/gold; Streamline, emerald.
Row 2: Streamline, canary with "special" gold decoration; Streamline, delphinium/gold; Streamline, Chinese red.

The Star teapot has been named for its style of decoration. It was introduced in 1939, and is only available in the six-cup size. Turquoise and cobalt are the only common colors. Other decorated colors will be found with diligent searching. Also, undecorated versions of this teapot were made. Again, the most abundant undecorated colors are turquoise and cobalt. The 1939 and 1940 New York World's Fair logo will appear on the bottom of some cobalt Star teapots. Either date may be found and the World's Fair trylon and perisphere will be found on the side of these cobalt teapots. The 1939 date is the hardest to find, but both of these teapots are unusual.

The Streamline is a six-cup teapot which first appeared in 1937. It is commonly found in canary, delphinium, and Chinese red. Gold decoration most often consists of a few narrow lines outlining the lid opening, handle, spout, lid, and knob. However, a "special" gold decoration exists which features a gold encrusted handle, spout, and knob. This may be seen on the yellow teapot in the photo. A platinum decoration has also been found on some canary teapots. The platinum bands are much wider and more gaudy than the standard gold lines. The Streamline shape is also used in a number of the decal lines.

Teapot	Red	Common Colors	Unusual Colors
Star	$195.00 – 225.00	$25.00 – 35.00	$65.00 – 85.00
World's Fair		$500.00 – 600.00	
Streamline	$95.00 – 110.00	$35.00 – 50.00	$60.00 – 75.00*

* With "special" gold decoration, $55.00 – 65.00.

SURFSIDE AND WINDSHIELD TEAPOTS

Row 1: Surfside, canary/gold; Surfside, emerald with "special" gold decoration. Row 2: Windshield, ivory with pheasant decal; Windshield, yellow with brown, green, and white floral band; Windshield, ivory Gold Label polka dot; Windshield, maroon/gold.

The Surfside teapot has a six-cup capacity and was introduced in 1937. It is usually found with the standard gold decoration shown on the canary teapot in the picture. However, it may also be found in various solid colors without decoration or with the "special" gold decoration as seen on the emerald green teapot in the photo. "Special" teapots such as this were often sold in sets with an accompanying sugar and creamer. In this case the matching sugar and creamer set is the Boston shape. The most readily found colors are emerald and canary. Unusual colors include black, all blues, pink, rose, and orchid. The Surfside has not been found in any of the decal patterns.

The six-cup Windshield teapot was first offered in 1941. The colors easiest to find are camellia, maroon, and the ivory Gold Label with polka dots. Hard-to-find colors include black, all blues, all greens, pink, and rose. This style teapot is available both with and without gold decoration and will also be found in some of the decal patterns. The standard Windshield gold floral decoration is shown on the maroon teapot. The Gold Label teapot also has matching kitchenware accessories which include a cookie jar, casserole, and three-piece bowl set. The yellow teapot is from a decal line Hall experimented with in the 1960s. Several game bird decals will be found on ivory Windshield teapots. These include scenes with ducks, pheasants, and grouse.

Teapot	Common Color	Unusual Color	Gold Label	Gold Special
Surfside	$85.00 – 100.00	$125.00 – 150.00		$110.00 – 145.00
*Windshield	$25.00 – 35.00	$65.00 – 95.00	$30.00 – 40.00	

*With game bird decal, $145.00 – 165.00.
 With Carrot or Clover decal, $150.00 – 175.00.

ALBANY TEAPOTS

Row 1: Albany, turquoise blue/standard gold; Albany, emerald/standard gold; Albany, cobalt with "special" gold decoration. Row 2: Albany, mahogany Gold Label; Albany, pink Gold Label.

The six-cup Albany teapot was introduced in the early 1930s. It will be found undecorated and with three different gold decorations. the color seen most frequently with the standard decoration is turquoise.

The three different styles of gold decorations are shown in the photograph. The turquoise blue and emerald teapots depict the standard Albany gold decoration. The "special" variation is illustrated by the cobalt teapot. This includes the standard decoration and a gold encrusted handle, spout, and knob on the lid. The teapots in the second row are examples of the two colors associated with the Gold Label Line.

The more common and less collectible colors are all greens, all browns, pink, black, ivory, turquoise, and most lighter blues.

Unusual and more collectible colors include cobalt, rose, warm yellow, canary, maroon, orchid, and gray.

Teapot	Common Color	Unusual Color	Gold Label	Gold Special
Albany	$35.00 – 45.00	$65.00 – 95.00	$50.00 – 65.00	$50.00 – 60.00

BALTIMORE AND BOSTON TEAPOTS

Row 1: Baltimore, maroon Gold Label; Baltimore, ivory with pink rose decal; Baltimore, cadet/standard gold. Row 2: Boston, pink with Gold Label Fleur-de-lis; Boston, Dresden/standard gold sugar and creamer with matching teapot.

The Baltimore teapot holds six cups and first appeared in the early 1930s. It may be found undecorated, with several styles of gold decorations, or with different decals. Colors which are easiest to find include maroon, emerald, and marine. The cadet teapot in the picture is an example of the standard gold decoration. The maroon teapot is from the Gold Label Line. Although the Baltimore teapot has not been found as a part of the regular decal dinnerware or kitchenware lines, this teapot has been found with several interesting decals. One decal, shown in the picture, features multiple pink roses on an ivory body. Another decal, Minuet, is usually found on a warm yellow teapot. An example of this decal may be seen on a Philadelphia teapot, pictured on page 217.

The Boston shape teapot was one of the original four teapots selected for Hall's venture into the retail markets in 1920. During the 1920s several different styles of gold decoration were used. These early decorations are not easy to find today, but are seen most often on teapots with a cobalt body. Look for the embossed HALL mark used in combination with the #2 backstamp to help identify these early teapots.

The decoration shown on the blue teapot above is the one normally found on this shape teapot produced for the Gold Decorated Line. These teapots will be found in sizes ranging from one cup to eight cups. Also, notice the sugar and creamer of the same shape with a matching decoration.

The pink teapot above is from the Gold Label Line. These teapots are decorated with an all-over Fleur-de-lis pattern and have golden handles, spouts, and knobs. The usual color found with this decoration is Dresden, but other colors will also be found.

Baltimore

Prices of standard gold decorated teapots are about the same as the same color undecorated teapots.

Common and less collectible colors: most greens, most lighter blues, yellows, black, maroon, pink, and ivory.

Unusual and more collectible colors: rose, orchid, red, and cobalt.

Teapot	Common Color	Unusual Color*	Gold Label	Decal Decoration
Baltimore	$35.00 – 45.00	$50.00 – 75.00	$40.00 – 50.00	$60.00 – 75.00

*Red, $95.00 – 125.00.

BOSTON TEAPOTS

The rose teapot and the black teapot are examples of early gold decorations. The design on the rose teapot is referred to as "Trailing Astor." The black teapot utilizes the same gold floral decoration which is normally found on the French shape teapots. This design is usually called "French Flower." Notice the handle and spout of this teapot are gold encrusted. Boston shape teapots "in blue, green, and brown glaze with gold stamped decoration" were advertised in the 5-cup size in a 1925 Butler Brothers catalog at $1.50 each.

The silver teapot is from a short-lived Hall experiment to develop a chip-proof teapot. This regular china teapot has been coated with a nickel alloy by an outside company. Production during the 1950s was limited as attempts to perfect this idea were unsuccessful. Several other shapes of metal-clad teapots and coffee pots will also be found.

The gold coated set is from Hall's Golden Glo line. The bright gold glaze has been applied over a Hi-white base. The Golden Glo line is quite extensive and many of these pieces were made as early as the forties. However, some pieces are still in production. For more information about the items available in this line, see the Golden Glo listing under kitchenware.

The Boston shape has been subjected to various decal applications. Hall developed a retail teapot line during the 1960s, in which a Boston teapot with a decal was used. The body of this teapot was green and it contained a golden fruit decal in a band around the center. This shape teapot has also been used in some of the regular decal dinnerware and kitchenware lines.

Prices of teapots with the standard gold decoration are about the same as undecorated teapots of the same color.

Common and less collectible colors: all greens, all browns, most lighter blues, yellows, black, maroon, pink, ivory, and gray.

Unusual and more collectible colors: red, cobalt, rose, orchid, and turquoise.

Row 1: Boston, rose color with gold "Trailing Astor" design; Boston, black with gold "French Flower" decoration; Boston, Hi-white. Row 2: Boston, metal-clad; Boston, Golden Glo sugar, creamer, and matching teapot.

Teapot	Common Color	Unusual Color*	Early Gold Design	Gold Label
Boston 1, 1½, 2-cup	$40.00 – 55.00	$60.00 – 70.00	$65.00 – 75.00	$45.00 – 55.00
Boston, 3, 4, 5-cup	$35.00 – 45.00	$55.00 – 65.00	$55.00 – 65.00	$35.00 – 40.00
Boston 6-cup	$25.00 – 30.00	$50.00 – 60.00	$40.00 – 50.00	$35.00 – 40.00
Boston 8-cup	$30.00 – 40.00	$55.00 – 65.00	$45.00 – 55.00	$35.00 – 40.00

*Red, $95.00 – 125.00.

CLEVELAND TEAPOTS

Left to Right: Cleveland, turquoise; Cleveland, warm yellow with standard gold; Cleveland, emerald with standard gold.

The Cleveland is a six-cup teapot which was introduced in the late thirties. It is most commonly found in emerald with gold decoration, but is also available in other colors with and without gold decoration. The standard gold decoration is shown on the two gold decorated teapots in the picture. Those collectors who are seeking undecorated teapots will have to be more patient than those looking for gold decorated ones. However, prices for both types are currently about the same for equivalent colors.

Common and less collectible colors: turquoise, all yellows, all greens.

Unusual and more collectible colors: most blues, red, gray, orchid, rose, and maroon.

Teapot	Red	Common Colors	Unusual Colors
Cleveland	$110.00 – 135.00	$55.00 – 65.00	$70.00 – 90.00

HOLLYWOOD TEAPOTS

Hollywood teapots with unusual decals.

Top Row:
1. Noel
2. Christmas Holly

Bottom Row:
1. Floral design
2. Floral

HOLLYWOOD TEAPOTS

Row 1: Hollywood, 8-cup, stock green/gold; Hollywood, 6-cup, Hi-black/Gold Label; Hollywood, 4-cup, emerald/gold. Row 2: Hollywood, pearl-color/"special" gold; Hollywood-shape creamer and sugar.

The Hollywood teapot first appeared in the late 1920s. It may be found in a 5-cup size in addition to the three sizes illustrated here — 4-cup, 6-cup, and 8-cup. There is also a matching sugar and creamer available for some decorations. The standard decoration is shown on the two teapots at each end of the top row. The black teapot in the center is an example of the Gold Label decoration. A more commonly found color with this decoration is pink.

The pearlized-color teapot shown on the second row is uncommon. The "special" gold treatment of the handle and spout add to the appeal of this teapot. Several other shapes of teapots with this unusual color glaze have been found. These are highly desirable additions to the collections of teapot lovers.

The Hollywood teapot is often found in maroon and in a variety of greens and the lighter blue colors. Also, the six-cup size is the most common of the four sizes.

Common or less collectible colors: all greens, all browns, black, maroon, all lighter blues, all yellows, pink, and ivory.

Unusual or more collectible colors: red, cobalt, rose, orchid, gray, and Dresden.

The standard gold decorated teapots will be priced about the same as undecorated teapots of the same color.

Teapot	Red	Common Colors*	Unusual Colors**	Gold Label
Hollywood, 4 or 5-cup	$100.00 – 125.00	$35.00 – 45.00	$55.00 – 70.00	
Hollywood, 6-cup	$95.00 – 110.00	$30.00 – 40.00	$50.00 – 65.00	$30.00 – 40.00
Hollywood, 8-cup	$100.00 – 125.00	$35.00 – 45.00	$50.00 – 65.00	
Sugar/creamer	$50.00 – 65.00	$25.00 – 30.00	$40.00 – 50.00	

*With Christmas decals, $150.00 – 175.00.
**With floral decals, $110.00 – 125.00.
**Pearl-color glaze, $125.00 – 150.00.

ILLINOIS, LOS ANGELES, AND NEWPORT TEAPOTS

The Illinois is a very hard-to-find six-cup teapot which dates to the 1930s. The standard gold decoration is pictured, and we are aware of another gold decoration for this teapot. This decoration consists of gold spirals which form a series of circles near the top of the teapot. The colors found most readily appear to be cobalt and maroon.

The Los Angeles teapot may be found in three sizes — 8-cup, 6-cup, and 4-cup. Of the three sizes, the 6-cup is the most common. This teapot first appeared in the mid-twenties and was subjected to a number of different decorations during its many years of production. The standard gold decoration may be seen on the emerald 4-cup teapot to the right and the Gold Label version is illustrated by the pink teapot in the center. In addition to gold decoration, decals were also applied to this shape teapot. A 1930s floral band decal is shown circling the upper body on the 8-cup teapot pictured on the left side of the bottom row. A band of green leaves is often found in this same position on a mustard color teapot which was produced during the 1960s.

The Newport teapot was introduced in the 1930s. It will be found in both seven-cup and five-cup sizes. This teapot was used in the Autumn Leaf pattern and is most commonly found with that decal in the seven-cup size. In addition, the Newport will be found in a variety of solid colors and with gold and decal decorations. The standard gold decoration consists of a narrow gold floral band on the lid. The handle and spout are also trimmed with gold lines. A decal decoration for the Newport is pictured. This decoration is from the 1930s and features a bouquet of multicolored flowers in a black urn. The handle, spout, and lid are also accented with black trim.

Illinois common colors: maroon, canary, and cobalt.

Illinois unusual colors: any other colors.

Los Angeles common colors: all greens, pink, cobalt, maroon, and brown.

Los Angeles unusual colors: red, most blues, orchid, and rose.

Newport common colors: pink, stock green, stock brown, and ivory.

Newport unusual colors: all other colors.

Teapot	Red	Common Colors**	Unusual Colors**	Decal Decorated
Illinois	$250.00 – 300.00	$125.00 – 150.00	$150.00 – 175.00	
Los Angeles, 8-cup	$100.00 – 125.00	$35.00 – 40.00	$45.00 – 60.00	$100.00 – 125.00
Los Angeles*, 6-cup	$95.00 – 110.00	$27.00 – 35.00	$40.00 – 55.00	$95.00 – 110.00
Los Angeles, 4-cup	$100.00 – 125.00	$35.00 – 40.00	$50.00 – 60.00	
Newport**	$95.00 – 110.00	$25.00 – 30.00	$50.00 – 65.00	$75.00 – 85.00

*Gold Label, $35.00 – 40.00.
**Gold decorated, add 20%.

Row 1: Illinois, maroon/standard gold; Illinois, stock brown/standard gold; Newport, pink/flower pot decal. Row 2: Los Angeles, 8-cup with milky blue glaze and flower band decoration; Los Angeles, 6-cup pink/Gold Label; Los Angeles, 4-cup emerald/standard gold.

NEW YORK TEAPOTS

The New York teapot was added to the Gold Decorated line from the institutional line in 1920. In the ensuing years it was to become one of the most successful of all Hall teapots. It will be found in more colors, sizes, and decorations than any other Hall teapot. The New York shape was also used in many of the decal lines and was the teapot shape selected by the National Autumn Leaf Collectors Club for their first limited edition piece produced by Hall. The New York teapot is still being produced for the institutional line. To identify the newer teapots, look for the square Hall backstamp.

Nine different sizes — 1, 1½, 2, 3, 4, 6, 8, 10 and 12-cup — of the New York teapot have been produced. Today collectors are finding the four, six, and eight-cup sizes most often. The other larger and smaller sizes appear less frequently. The standard gold decoration is best seen on the Dresden teapot with the matching sugar and creamer.

The older New York teapots are appearing primarily in the cobalt color. These teapots are generally identified by their non-standard gold decorations and their early backstamp. The early backstamp used on the teapots during the 1920s is like the #2 backstamp shown in the identification section or may be a slight variation. In the variations, the "Made in U.S.A." is missing or is outside the circle.

The green teapot on the right side of the top row is referred to as a "special." It has the standard gold decoration along with a gold encrusted handle and spout. The teapot shown on the left side of the top row is very unusual. The decoration consists of an all-over floral pattern and extensive gold embellishment. Hand-painted gold and enamel decorations also consist of a palm leaf design similar to the one seen on the French teapot (shown on page 201) and the Burbick design pictured on the left side of the third row. This teapot has been found advertised in a 1928 Sears catalog with a matching sugar and creamer. The set sold for $3.75.

Three different combinations of game bird decals consisting of ducks, pheasants, or grouse have been found by collectors. These decals are usually found on 4-cup and 6-cup teapots, but are also known to exist in the 2-cup size. The silver teapot shown on the right side of the third row is an example of a metal clad teapot. These teapots were coated with a special metal alloy to resist chipping.

The teapots in the bottom photograph represent various sizes and colors of the New York teapot with the Gold Label decoration.

In addition, the New York shape has been found with the same multi-colored floral and black urn decal which is pictured on the Newport teapot shown on page 213. This decal dates to the 1930s, and is not commonly found today.

Common or less collectible colors: lighter blues, all greens, all browns, all yellows, ivory, pink, and black.

Unusual or more collectible colors: red, cobalt, blue turquoise, rose, and orchid.

The standard gold decorated teapots are priced the same as the undecorated teapots of the same color.

Teapot	Common Color	Unusual Colors*	Old Gold Decoration**	Gold Label	Decal Decorated
New York, 1, 1½, 2-cup	$35.00 – 40.00	$45.00 – 55.00	$55.00 – 65.00	$35.00 – 45.00	$125.00 – 150.00
New York, 3, 4-cup	$32.00 – 37.00	$40.00 – 50.00	$50.00 – 60.00	$35.00 – 45.00	$110.00 – 130.00
New York, 6, 8-cup	$25.00 – 30.00	$35.00 – 45.00	$50.00 – 60.00	$27.00 – 32.00	$100.00 – 125.00
New York, 10, 12-cup	$32.00 – 37.00	$40.00 – 50.00	$55.00 – 65.00	$40.00 – 50.00	
New York sugar and creamer	$25.00 – 30.00	$40.00 – 55.00	UND		

*Paisley decoration, $85.00 – 95.00.
**Burbick decoration, $95.00 – 110.00.

Row 1: New York, paisley decoration/gold; New York, canary/gold band; New York, stock green/gold "special." Row 2: New York, Dresden/standard gold with matching sugar and creamer; New York, stock green/standard gold. Row 3: New York, cobalt with enameled Burbick decoration; New York, game bird decal; New York, metal clad.

New York Teapots with Gold Label Decoration.

Row 1: New York, 12-cup, blue turquoise; New York, 10-cup, black; New York, 8-cup, pink.
Row 2: New York, 6-cup, matte pink; New York, 4-cup, ivory; New York, 2-cup, cadet.

PHILADELPHIA

The Philadelphia teapot was produced in the 10, 7, 6, 5, 4, 3, and 1½-cup sizes. The Philadelphia shape was one of the first to be added to the Gold Decorated line in the early 1920s. Due to this early introduction, and as a result of its success, this shape was treated to a number of different gold and decal decorations.

One of the earlier gold designs is illustrated by the rose color teapot in the center of the top row. The teapot has an all-over "Gold Loop" design and the handle, spout, and lid opening are trimmed with gold. This design teapot along with a matching sugar and creamer was advertised in a 1928 Sears catalog. Other early gold designs are shown on the two stock brown teapots in the center of the second row. The decoration on the larger teapot is being called "Nouveau" and the smaller teapot is an example of the "Tiny Bubble" design.

The blue turquoise teapot on the top row is from the Gold Label line of the mid fifties. The basket design is commonly found on a pink body and less often in this color. Matching kitchenware accessories will also be found with this decoration. For more information see the Gold Label pattern in the kitchenware section.

The pink teapot in the top photo illustrates the Minuet decal. This decal is also commonly found on the Baltimore teapot and a Drip-O-lator coffee pot. Other decals will also be found on Philadelphia teapots. In the 1930s, a large colorful floral decal was used. Decal decoration in the 1960s featured a black hearth scene, usually on a teapot with a blue body.

The two teapots on the top row of the bottom picture are an example of the standard gold decoration for the Philadelphia. The teapot on the bottom row with the matching sugar and creamer has a mother-of-pearl glaze. The beauty of this set is further enhanced through extensive gold decoration.

Common or less collectible colors: stock green, stock brown, canary, pink, ivory, turquoise, and lighter blues.

Unusual or more collectible colors: red, cobalt, blue turquoise, rose, and orchid.

Teapots with the standard gold decoration are priced the same as undecorated teapots of the same color.

Teapot	Common Color	Unusual Color**	Old Gold Decoration	Decal Decoration
Philadelphia, 1½ to 5-cup	$27.00 – 35.00	$40.00 – 50.00	$45.00 – 55.00	
Philadelphia, 6-cup*	$25.00 – 30.00	$35.00 – 45.00	$35.00 – 45.00	$55.00 – 65.00
Philadelphia, 7 & 10-cup	$28.00 – 35.00	$40.00 – 50.00	$40.00 – 50.00	
Creamer and sugar	$27.00 – 32.00	$40.00 – 45.00	$40.00 – 50.00	

*Gold Label, $32.00 – 40.00.
**Red, $95.00 – 115.00; irridized colors, $85.00 – 95.00.

Row 1: Philadelphia, blue turquoise/Gold Label; Philadelphia, old rose/"Gold Loop" design; Philadelphia, pink/Minuet decal. Row 2: Philadelphia, silver luster; Philadelphia, stock brown/Gold "Nouveau" design; Philadelphia, stock brown/Gold "Tiny Bubble" design; Philadelphia, stock green.

Row 1: Philadelphia, turquoise/standard gold; Philadelphia, warm yellow/standard gold. Row 2: Philadelphia, mother-of-pearl glaze and matching sugar and creamer.

TEAPOT MISCELLANY

The "Bowling Ball", a teapot from the late thirties, was very successful at disguising its existence until a few years ago. After its initial confirmation as a Hall teapot, a virtual avalanche of "Bowling Balls" appeared. Recently, it seems as if this teapot has gone back into hiding again and really may be as scarce as was once thought. The usual color it is found in is turquoise. We have seen one in cobalt and have not heard of the "Bowling Ball" being found in any other color or with any gold decoration.

The "Philbe" is illustrated by the canary teapot on the top row. This teapot has proven to be very scarce. Another example, a cobalt one with a "special" style gold decoration was pictured in the first book. The original source for this teapot could confirm this is a Hall teapot, but could not contribute any other details on its history.

The Tip-Pot was made by Hall for the Forman family. It has two spouts, but only one internal chamber and is designed to fit into the candle warmer style holder shown in the picture. The Tip-Pot backstamp reads: "TIP-POT — The ultimate in serving hot tea or coffee. 10-cup — FIREPROOF — HALL CHINA — ANOTHER FORMAN FAMILY PRODUCT." The most frequently found colors are ivory and black satin with gold decoration. For more information on Forman Family products see the coffee pot section.

The round T-Ball was introduced in 1948. It was made by Hall for Bacharach of New York and has the following backstamp: "T-BALL TEAPOT — MADE FOR BACHARACH BY HALL CHINA COMPANY." A number of undecorated colors may be found, and a black teapot with gold decoration also exists. The black does not have the Bacharach backstamp. Instead it has a "HALL" mark and gold number (0850GL), with the letters "GL" possibly indicating this teapot was a part of the Gold Label line.

The square T-Ball was also made for Bacharach in the late 1940s. This teapot was re-introduced as part of the Hall American line in 1984. The old teapots will have the Bacharach backstamp. Both the round and square versions of the T-Ball have a side pocket on each side in which a tea bag may be placed.

The "Rutherford" teapot is the same shape as the "Ribbed" teapot shown in the kitchenware section. This smooth version is shown here with green trim. It will also be found with decals in some of the dinnerware lines and in the Buffet Service in matte white decorated with dots.

The cobalt Ohio teapot with the gold decoration in the center of the third row is one of the older gold decorated teapots. This teapot is usually found in pink or black with a gold dot decoration.

The Kansas and Indiana are two teapots which are still lacking from many collections. Both will be found with gold decoration more often than without. The usual gold decorations and most common colors may be seen in the photograph.

The French drip coffee biggin is actually a coffee pot with its dripper in place. However, it can also be used as a teapot with the dripper removed. It may be found in numerous colors and in sizes ranging from two-cup to eight-cup. We have not seen it with gold decoration. Common colors are stock brown, stock green, and canary. This teapot has also been found in a few of the decal lines.

Teapot	Common Color	Unusual Color
"Bowling Ball"	$300.00 – 350.00	
French drip coffee biggin	$60.00 – 70.00	$80.00 – 95.00
Indiana	$150.00 – 195.00	$250.00 – 295.00
Kansas	$225.00 – 250.00	$275.00 – 325.00
Ohio	$175.00 – 200.00	$200.00 – 250.00
"Philbe"	UND	UND
"Rutherford"	$75.00 – 85.00	$95.00 – 125.00
T-Ball round	$70.00 – 80.00	$125.00 – 150.00
T-Ball square	$50.00 – 60.00	$65.00 – 80.00
Tip-Pot/Holder	$80.00 – 95.00	$95.00 – 125.00

Row 1: "Bowling Ball," cobalt; "Philbe," canary; Tip-Pot, ivory. Row 2: T-Ball, round, black/gold; T-Ball, round, emerald; T-Ball, square, cobalt. Row 3: "Rutherford," with green trim; Ohio, cobalt/gold; Kansas, emerald/gold. Row 4: Indiana, warm yellow/gold; French drip coffee biggin, canary; French drip coffee biggin, blue.

VICTORIAN STYLE TEAPOTS

Six Victorian style six-cup teapots were introduced in the early forties. This was not a dramatically successful line and gold decoration was later added to help stimulate sales. However, success was not attained and the line was dropped by the end of the decade. As a result, although undecorated teapots are available in sufficient quantity, collectors are finding great difficulty in obtaining decorated teapots.

An ad from a 1947 catalog illustrates that two of these teapots — the "Plume" and "Birch" — were sold by Jewel for $1.75 each.

For the most part, each teapot is only available in a single color. However, an occasional one may be found in an odd color. An example is the "Benjamin," which has been found in a gold color as well as the usual green.

The amount of gold decoration varies considerably among the different shapes. The "Benjamin," "Birch," and "Connie" feature generous gold decoration. They each have gold encrusted handles, and spouts along with liberal gold use on the teapot body. The "Plume," "Bowknot," and "Murphy" display a conservative use of gold.

Teapot	Common Color	Unusual Color	Gold Decorated
"Benjamin"	$27.00 – 32.00	$55.00 – 65.00	$90.00 – 110.00
"Birch"	$30.00 – 35.00		$100.00 – 125.00
"Bowknot"	$30.00 – 37.00	$55.00 – 65.00	$70.00 – 85.00
"Connie"	$25.00 – 30.00	$50.00 – 60.00	$85.00 – 90.00
"Murphy"	$30.00 – 35.00		$70.00 – 85.00
"Plume"	$22.00 – 28.00		$60.00 – 70.00

"Plume," pink with gold floral decoration.

Row 1: "Murphy," blue; "Benjamin," gold; "Bowknot," pink.
Row 2: "Plume," pink; "Birch," blue/gold; "Connie," green.

Left to Right: "Benjamin," green/gold; "Plume," pink/gold.

THORLEY TEAPOTS

A series of six new teapots which collectors call "Thorley Teapots" was introduced in the early 1950s. These teapots were designed by the noted J. Palin Thorley and were probably intended to replace the Victorian series teapots which had been discontinued due to lackluster sales. These teapots are officially know as the "Brilliant Series Group 120 Teapots."

Although the "Thorley" teapots are sometimes found plain, they are most often found with gaudy gold decoration. Some have glass rhinestones imbedded in small pockets formed in the body. Collectors are most interested in the teapots with rhinestones. This line, like the earlier Victorian series, was not highly successful, but these teapots still remained in the catalogs as late as 1968. At that time the wholesale cost was $4.95 each.

As may be seen in the photograph, the "Grape" design teapot was also made with the Classic pattern Bouquet decal. This teapot has also been found with the Game Bird decal. In addition, several pieces of kitchenware were produced in the matching "Grape" pattern. These include a set of three mixing bowls, a round handled casserole, and a cookie jar. These are usually found in yellow.

The "Grape" teapot is the easiest to find. The "Apple" had been the most difficult acquisition for most collectors, but the other four teapots are becoming very hard-to-find.

Teapot	Common Color	Gold Decorated	Rhinestone Decorated
"Apple"	$95.00 – 125.00	$150.00 – 195.00	
"Grape"*	$50.00 – 65.00	$80.00 – 90.00	$95.00 – 125.00
"Regal"	$80.00 – 90.00	$90.00 – 110.00	$90.00 – 115.00
"Royal"	$55.00 – 65.00	$85.00 – 95.00	$100.00 – 125.00
"Starlight"	$55.00 – 65.00	$70.00 – 80.00	$80.00 – 90.00
"Windcrest"	$50.00 – 60.00	$70.00 – 85.00	$90.00 – 100.00

*With Bouquet decal, $115.00 – 130.00; with Game Bird decal, $95.00 – 125.00.

Kitchenware	
Bowl, 6"	$7.00 – 9.00
Bowl, 7½"	$10.00 – 12.00
Bowl, 8¾"	$12.00 – 14.00
Casserole	$20.00 – 25.00
Cookie jar	$30.00 – 40.00

Ad from 1968 Bostwick-Brown Company catalog.

Left to Right: Cookie jar, "Grape"; casserole, "Grape"; teapot, "Grape" with gold band.

Row 1: "Grape," ivory with blue rhinestones; "Grape," yellow with gold band; "Grape," ivory with Bouquet decal.
Row 2: "Regal," maroon; "Regal," apple green/gold; "Starlight," lemon.
Row 3: "Windcrest," lemon/gold; "Apple," sky blue; "Royal," ivory.

"PERT" AND E-STYLE TEAPOTS

"Pert," Chinese red and Hi-white; "Pert," canary/gold.

"Pert" teapots are a part of the kitchenware line. This shape teapot is more commonly associated with some of the decal lines, but gold decorated teapots in this shape also exist. They are usually found in cadet or yellow with gold decoration on the handle, spout, and around the lid opening. The undecorated teapot found most often has a Chinese red body with a Hi-white handle.

E-style teapots which are a familiar shape to collectors of Cameo Rose are showing up decorated with other decals and with gold. Two are pictured below. Other decal decorations have also been found. Although these decorated teapots are not common, there has not been much collector interest in this shape teapot.

Teapot	Chinese Red	Common Colors	Gold Decorated
"Pert," 3-cup	$25.00 – 30.00	$22.00 – 25.00	$30.00 – 35.00
"Pert," 6-cup	$32.00 – 37.00	$28.00 – 32.00	$35.00 – 40.00
E-style			$25.00 – 32.00

E-style teapots, gold decorated and floral decorated.

NO. 1 TEA SET AND NO. 2 COFFEE SET

Row 1: No. 1 Tea Set in Blue Belle color: open sugar; 21 oz. teapot; cream pitcher; tea cup and party plate.
Row 2: No. 2 Coffee Set in Buttercup color: open sugar; 24 oz. coffee pot; cream pitcher; coffee cup and party plate.

The No. 1 Tea Set and No. 2 Coffee Set were both introduced in the early 1950s. Both the Coffee Set and Tea Set came in two colors and with three different floral decorations. The yellow color is called Buttercup and the light blue color is Blue Belle. The three decorations are 80-B, a blue flower, 80-Y, a yellow flower, and 80-P, a pink flower. Both sets are trimmed with gold lines.

The Tea Set uses the morning set teapot and creamer shapes. However, the similarity between the two sets ends there. The shape of the sugar is different and a cup and party plate have been added. The morning set sugar has handles and a lid. The No. 1 Tea Set sugar is open and has no handles. Also the morning set does not have cups and saucers. The party plates have an off-center ring upon which the teacup fits. The party plates to the Tea Set are round while the plates to the Coffee Set are scalloped.

The No. 2 Coffee Set has an open sugar with a ruffled top and a tall creamer with a handle and general shape that matches the coffee pot. This coffee pot shape is also used in the Golden Glo line, and a larger version which bears the Drip-O-lator backstamp may be found decorated with a floral decal.

The Blue Belle Coffee Set and the Buttercup Tea Set have been found advertised in a 1952 Jewel Tea Company catalog.

	Coffee Set	Tea Set
Coffee pot	$75.00 – 85.00	
Creamer	$16.00 – 18.00	$16.00 – 18.00
Cup	$10.00 – 12.00	$10.00 – 12.00
Plate	$7.00 – 9.00	$7.00 – 9.00
Sugar	$16.00 – 18.00	$16.00 – 18.00
Teapot		$80.00 – 95.00

EARLY GOLD DECORATED TEAPOTS

"Johnson," cobalt/gold;
"Naomi," cobalt/gold.

"Columbia," maroon/gold.

The teapots shown on this page are from an early gold decorated line which probably dates to the mid-twenties. The three teapots shown here and the cobalt and gold Ohio shown on page 219 are the teapots we believe were part of the series. Other similar teapots may show up, but they are uncommon enough at this time to prevent lending any insight into their history.

The ten-sided cobalt "Columbia" teapot shown in the individual photo has the #2 backstamp with the numbers 15-80 in place of "MADE IN U.S.A." We have only seen one other teapot like this and it was cobalt with the same gold decoration.

The "Johnson" teapot is an elegantly designed piece with liberal gold decoration. The long spout and gently rounded handle add grace and balance to the finished teapot.

The "Naomi" teapot has six panelled sides. Each panel has a gold decorated emblem and is outlined with a gold border.

Teapot	Gold Decorated
"Columbia"	$275.00 – 325.00
"Johnson"	$275.00 – 300.00
"Naomi"	$250.00 – 285.00

ART DECO TEAPOTS

The teapots shown below are from what appears to be a three teapot series which collectors are calling "Deco." Researchers have assigned the names "Adele," "Damascus," and "Danielle" to these three teapots. The colors which are being found most often are olive green, light blue, maroon, and yellow. Each one turns up most often in one basic color, but all have been found in more than one of the above colors.

Teapot	Price
"Adele"	$90.00 – 110.00
"Damascus"	$125.00 – 150.00
"Danielle"	$110.00 – 140.00

Left to Right: "Adele"; "Damascus"; "Danielle."

MUSICAL TEAPOTS

Left to Right: Musical teapot, blue; musical teapot, ivory with maroon and gold trim.

Hall produced a 6-cup musical teapot in the mid-fifties. The teapot was advertised for $6.95 in a 1954 Montgomery Ward Christmas catalog. It has been found most often in the blue color shown in the picture above, but other colors may be found as well. The teapot has a cavity on the under side into which the wind-up music box fits. Appropriately, the music box plays "Tea for Two." Numerous teapots are being found with their music boxes missing.

Teapot	Price*
Musical teapot	$175.00 – 225.00

*Priced with working music box.

TWIN-TEE, TEA-FOR-TWO, AND TEA-FOR-FOUR TEAPOTS

Row 1: Twin-Tee, Black Garden design; Twin-Tee, Pansy decal; Twin-Tee, rose/gold.
Row 2: Twin-Tee, stock green/gold; Twin-Tee, cobalt; Twin-Tee, daffodil with black trim.

The Twin-Tee sets consist of a hot water pot (short spout) and a pot for holding the brewed tea (long spout). There is also a matching divided tray which serves as a trivet for the hot pots. The Twin-Tee sets were introduced in 1926, and may be found in numerous colors. Collectors like these small sets because of the different decals and interesting gold decorations which have been applied to them.

Tea-for-Two sets also are comprised of two pots and a matching tray. However, these sets differ from the Twin-Tee sets in several ways. The tops of the Tea-for-Two pots are angled rather than straight and the trays do not have the full-length center division like the Twin-Tee trays. There is also a larger version of this set called Tea-for-Four.

Tea-for-Two, pink/platinum decoration.

Tea Set	Common Colors*	Unusual Colors	Gold/Decal Decoration
Tea-for-Two	$65.00 – 75.00	$90.00 – 110.00	$125.00 – 150.00
Tea-for-Four	$80.00 – 100.00	$100.00 – 125.00	$150.00 – 195.00
Twin-Tee	$65.00 – 75.00	$90.00 – 110.00	$125.00 – 150.00

*Stock green and stock brown, 25% less.

CUBE AND DOHRMANN TEAPOTS

Left: Cube, emerald. Right: Cube, black.

Cube, blue/gold.

The Cubes are two-cup teapots made by Hall and several other companies under a British patent. The Hall teapots will have the Hall #3 backstamp, the patent numbers, and the following inscription on the bottom: "CUBE TEAPOTS, LIMITED, LEICESTER." Although the Cube-shape teapots have been found in numerous colors, very few have been found with gold decoration.

Hall produced the teapot shown below for the Dohrmann Company. This company operated in the western states and most of the teapots will be found in that geographical area. The teapots have the following backstamp: "DOHRCO" and the HALL mark in a circle with "MADE IN U.S.A." underneath.

Teapot	Red/Cobalt	Other Colors	Gold Decorated
Cube	$80.00 – 110.00	$50.00 – 70.00	$95.00 – 125.00
Dohrco		$45.00 – 55.00	

Dohrco teapot.

"COVERLET" AND McCORMICK TEAPOTS

Row 1: "Coverlet," canary; "Coverlet," pink; "Coverlet," ivory.
Row 2: McCormick, turquoise; McCormick, maroon; McCormick, light blue.

The "Coverlet" teapot has a metal cover with cut-outs for the handle and spout. The teapot in the center has the metal cover removed to show the shape of the teapot. These teapots are marked "Made exclusively for the FORMAN FAMILY, INC. by THE HALL CHINA CO., U.S.A." The teapot may be found in various colors with either a silver or gold color cover. A matching sugar and creamer set are shown in the photo below.

The McCormick teapot was made as a premium item for the McCormick Tea Company. The teapots are marked "McCORMICK, BALTIMORE, MARYLAND." The most commonly found colors are maroon, turquoise, light blue, and stock brown. McCormicks have been found with gold decoration and in the two-cup size with a large raised "Mc" on the side. A few older McCormick teapots have been reported with a lid which locks into the infusor. In this teapot, the lid completely conceals the infusor when it is in place, and both the lid and infusor are removed from the teapot as one piece. The body of these teapots also differs slightly from a normal McCormick. There is a built-in strainer at the tip of the spout and the lid has a loop handle rather than a knob.

Teapot	Common Colors	Gold Decorated
"Coverlet"	$35.00 – 45.00	
McCormick, 6-cup	$25.00 – 35.00	$75.00 – 85.00
McCormick, 2-cup	$35.00 – 45.00	

"Coverlet" sugar and creamer.

TEAMASTER TEAPOTS

Left to Right: Teataster, turquoise; Twinspout, emerald; Twinspout, warm yellow; Twinspout, canary/gold.

Different shapes of teapots which Hall produced for the Teamaster Company are shown in the photographs on this page.

The Teataster is an oval, two-compartment teapot which was made for Teamaster in the forties. Most of the teapots are plain, but a few will be found with gold decoration. The backstamp states: "TEAMASTER, MADE BY HALL IN U.S.A."

Twinspouts are round two-compartment teapots produced for the Teamaster Company. The teapots are usually marked "TWINSPOUT, TEAMASTER, Pat. No. 2135410." Twinspouts will be found with gold decoration and some have been found with sterling silver overlay.

The later teapots of this shape will be marked "INVENTO PRODUCTS."

The 3-cup diamond-shape Twinspout teapots below, called "Alma," were also two-compartment teapots. They were made for Teamaster and have the same backstamp as the Twinspouts above. We have not seen this teapot decorated.

Teapot	Undecorated	Gold Decorated
"Alma," 3-cup	$125.00 – 150.00	
Teataster	$60.00 – 75.00	$85.00 – 95.00
Twinspout	$60.00 – 75.00	$85.00 – 95.00

Left to Right: "Alma," Chinese red;
"Alma," turquoise; "Alma," maroon.

Row 1: Washington, stock brown with gold French Flower design; Washington, cobalt with early gold design; Washington, Hi-white with orange "Dutch" decal. Row 2: "Deca-flip," Red/Hi-white; "Baron," Chinese red; "Alcony," green.

The Washington coffee pot was introduced in 1919. The retail price of a 9-cup Washington was $1.89 in the Montgomery Ward catalog from that year. This coffee pot is still being made and it has appeared in many different colors and with numerous decorations over the long span of production. Sizes in which the Washington coffee pot has been produced include: 1, 1½, 2, 6, 12, and 15-cup.

Researchers have christened the large red and white teapot on the second row "Deca-flip." It is usually found in this color combination, but may on occasion be found with the color pattern reversed.

The "Baron" is seen most often in Chinese red, but may also be found in other colors. It is not an easy coffee pot to find.

The green "Alcony" coffee pot almost appears to be a large version of the short-spout "Carraway" which was made for Tricolator. The lid and handle on the two coffee pots appear to be identical in design. The coffee pot above has the #3 backstamp.

Coffee Pot	Common Color	Gold Decorated	Coffee Pot	Common Color	Gold Decorated
"Alcony"	$35.00 – 45.00		Washington,		
"Baron"	$40.00 – 50.00		6-cup	$25.00 – 30.00	$30.00 – 40.00
"Deca-flip"	$45.00 – 55.00		Washington,		
Washington,			12 and 15-cup	$35.00 – 40.00	$65.00 – 75.00
1 to 2-cup	$18.00 – 22.00	$28.00 – 32.00			

DRIP COFFEE POT SHAPES

Row 1: #691 drip coffee, ivory with blue band and platinum trim; metal base drip coffee; "Jordan" drip coffee, Crocus pattern.

Row 2: "Kadota" drip coffee, Shaggy Tulip decal; "Radiance" drip coffee, #488 decal; E-style drip coffee, Mount Vernon pattern.

A number of different shapes of all-china drip coffee pots were produced by Hall. The complete coffee pot is comprised of four pieces. There is the base, a china dripper, a china spreader which fits inside the dripper, and a lid. Most of these shapes were used in the decal lines. Some of the more common shapes are pictured here to help with identification and for ease of comparison. A shape which is not shown here is "Medallion." This shape may be seen on page 129.

The #691 is usually found in solid colors or decorated as shown above. The colors may vary, as we have seen red, blue, and green bands. Flamingo and Blue Blossom are the only decals we have seen on this shape, although there may be others.

The middle coffee pot on the top row is unusual in that it has an electric warmer base made of metal. The design on the one in the picture is the only one we have seen on this shape.

The "Jordan" drip coffee pot is most commonly associated with the Autumn Leaf pattern. However, this shape drip coffee pot is also found in a number of other decal patterns. It is not common, but it has also been seen in cadet with a Hi-white handle and lid. The distinguishing feature of this coffee pot is its vertical panels which are separated by distinct vertical ribs.

The "Kadota" coffee pot has a smooth body. We have only seen this in ivory in various decal patterns. Usually the backstamp is the Drip-O-lator mark.

The distinctive feature of the "Radiance" coffee pot is the series of rays which separate the body into vertical panels. This coffee pot may be found in solid colors and is used in the decal patterns.

The E-style coffee pot has only been found in a single pattern — Mount Vernon. This pattern was designed by J. Palin Thorley and was sold by Sears during the fifties.

Prices are only for the colors and decorations indicated. The decal pattern coffee pots are priced with their respective patterns.

Coffee Pot	Price
#691, solid color	$100.00 – 135.00
#691, color band	$90.00 – 120.00
Metal base, as pictured	$100.00 – 125.00
"Jordan," cadet/Hi-white	$85.00 – 100.00
"Radiance," solid colors*	$150.00 – 200.00

*Ivory, $20.00 – 30.00.

DRIP-O-LATOR COFFEE POTS

Hall made coffee pot bodies for the Enterprise Aluminum Company of Massillon, Ohio. Enterprise supplied the aluminum dripper for these coffee pots and marketed the finished product. Some shapes will be found in more than one size. Although many shapes appear to be limited to a single decoration, there are a few coffee pot styles which will be found with numerous decorations. Other companies besides Hall also supplied china bases to the Enterprise Company. In some cases these bodies will bear the backstamp of the manufacturer, but the coffee pots produced by Hall will only have the Drip-O-lator mark. The coffee pot shapes known to be made by Hall will be illustrated and priced on the following pages. All the names of both the shapes and decorations have been contributed by researchers.

Opposite Page: The "Trellis" is pictured in a solid color. It may also be found with a V-shaped, multi-colored floral decoration. The "Bauhaus" is usually found with the two floral decorations pictured. The "Waverly" is shown with the Yellow Rose decal here. On the next page it is also pictured with an iridized gold fleurette design. The major differences between the "Waverly" and the "Wavelet" are the length of the spout and the size of the handle. The "Cathedral" coffee pot is available in two sizes and the same daisy-like decal is also found on a few kitchenware pieces. See the miscellaneous page in the kitchenware section. The "Sash" is also found with a blue band with white stars. This coffee pot is known as the "Orb" with the colored, molded band smoothed over and replaced with a decal. The "Meltdown" is a shape which is very similar to a Drip-O-lator coffee pot produced by Fraunfelter. The biggest difference between the two is a slightly longer spout on the Hall coffee pot.

Drip-O-lator	Price
"Bauhaus"	$32.00 – 37.00
"Bricks and Ivy"	$25.00 – 30.00
"Cathedral," small	$27.00 – 32.00
"Cathedral," large	$27.00 – 32.00
Coffee Set shape	$45.00 – 55.00
"Dart"	$27.00 – 30.00
"Drape"	$22.00 – 27.00
"Duse"	$27.00 – 30.00
"Jerry"	$40.00 – 50.00
"Kadota," all-china	$70.00 – 80.00
"Lotus"	$30.00 – 35.00
"Medallion"	$45.00 – 55.00
"Meltdown"	$35.00 – 40.00
"Orb"	$27.00 – 32.00
Panel	$25.00 – 30.00
"Petal," small	$35.00 – 40.00
"Petal," large	$35.00 – 40.00
"Rounded Terrace"	$18.00 – 22.00
"Sash"	$45.00 – 55.00
"Scoop"	$35.00 – 45.00
"Sweep"	$35.00 – 40.00
"Target"	$32.00 – 37.00
"Trellis"	$35.00 – 40.00
"Viking"	$28.00 – 35.00
"Wavelet," small	$35.00 – 40.00
"Wavelet," large	$35.00 – 40.00
"Waverly," small	$25.00 – 30.00
"Waverly," large	$25.00 – 30.00
"Wicker"	$35.00 – 40.00

Matching Sugar and Creamer	Price
Creamer, Coffee Set shape	$10.00 – 12.00
Creamer, "Dart"	$8.00 – 10.00
Creamer, "Duse"	$8.00 – 10.00
Creamer, "Medallion"	$14.00 – 16.00
Creamer, Panel	$12.00 – 15.00
Sugar, Coffee Set shape	$10.00 – 12.00
Sugar, "Dart"	$12.00 – 15.00
Sugar, "Duse"	$12.00 – 15.00
Sugar, "Medallion"	$20.00 – 25.00
Sugar, Panel	$18.00 – 22.00

Drip-O-lator coffee pot backstamp.

Row 1: "Trellis"; "Bauhaus," Jonquil decal; "Bauhaus," June flower decal.
Row 2: "Waverly," Yellow Rose decal; "Drape," mini-floral decal; "Jerry."
Row 3: "Cathedral"; "Sash"; "Viking," Cactus decal.
Row 4: "Petal," large-size; "Petal," small-size; "Meltdown."

Row 1: "Wavelet," small-size with dome lid and Minuet decal; "Wavelet," large-size with Minuet decal; "Waverly," iridized gold mini-fleurette design. Row 2: "Bricks and Ivy"; "Wicker"; "Rounded Terrace," Pasture Rose decal.

"Panel" with potted flower decal and matching sugar and creamer.

Left to Right: "Rounded Terrace," Bouquet decal; "Target," Dutch decal; "Scoop," Wildflower decal.

Numerous "Kadota" shape all-china drip coffee pots will be found with the Drip-O-lator backstamp. However, not all of the coffee pots of this shape were made for Enterprise. Matching covered sugars and creamers may be found for both the "Dart" and "Duse" shapes.

Left to Right: "Kadota" all-china drip with Morning Flower decal;
"Kadota" all-china drip with Wildflower decal; "Dart," pink rose decal.

"Duse" coffee pot;
"Duse" creamer;
"Dart" creamer.

237

Large-size Coffee Set shape coffee pot with matching sugar and creamer.

Row 1: "Medallion" shape coffee pot with matching sugar and creamer.
Row 2: "Viking," tiered potted flower decal; "Sweep."

"Kadota" drip bottom with metal dripper; casserole with matching decal in metal holder.

FORMAN FAMILY PRODUCTS

Row 1: "Edwards" teapot with blue-trimmed mother-of-pearl body; "Russell" coffee pot with Fuji decal; Fuji decal sugar and creamer. Row 2: "Dutch" teapot with Eden Bird decal; "Double Octagon" casserole with Eden Bird decal; "Ribbed Buffet" casserole with Pastel Floral decal.

Products with the Forman Family backstamp represent the end result of a joint effort between Hall and Forman to produce useful articles from a combination of china and chrome. Teapots, coffee pots, casseroles, and electric percolators are the most common items which were finished by the Forman Family workers.

The "Dutch" teapot is very similar to the "Diver" teapot which Hall produced for Tricolator. The lid of the "Dutch" fits over the top edge, while the lid of the "Diver" fits inside the rim. The shape of the tips of the spouts also differs slightly.

The electric warmer holds three Petite Marmites and was designed to keep foods warm. In another application, ice could also be packed around the marmites to chill food.

Item	Price
Casserole, Art Deco	$35.00 – 45.00
Casserole, black/gold	$20.00 – 25.00
Casserole, "Double Octagon"	$30.00 – 35.00
Casserole, "Ribbed Buffet"	$20.00 – 25.00
Coffee pot, "Russell"	$40.00 – 45.00
Creamer and sugar, black/gold	$25.00 – 35.00
Creamer and sugar, Fuji	$25.00 – 32.00
Teapot, "Dutch"	$45.00 – 55.00
Teapot, "Edwards"	$50.00 – 60.00
Teapot, Tip-Pot	$95.00 – 125.00
Percolator, electric	$75.00 – 85.00
Waffle iron, Fuji	$75.00 – 85.00
Warmer, electric	$55.00 – 65.00

Left: Electric warmer with three Petite Marmites. Right: Art Deco casserole in metal holder.

Forman Family Products

Row 1: Creamer, Straw Weave design, black/gold; electric percolator, Straw Weave design, black/gold; sugar, Straw Weave design, black/gold.

Row 2: Casserole, black/gold; teapot, Tip-Pot, black/gold.

TRICOLATOR PRODUCTS

Hall produced numerous pots for Tricolator. They may usually be identified through their backstamps. Many times "HALL" is embossed in the bottom in large block letters along with the words "Tricolator" or "Pour Right."

The coffee pot shape pictured on the bottom of the next page, which most collectors have been calling "Coffee Queen," actually has different names depending upon the size of the pot. According to packing information enclosed with the coffee pots, the name of the four-cup size is Princess; the six-cup size is Coffee Queen; the eight-cup is Empress. All sizes may be found in seven colors.

Most of the Tricolator coffee pots are being found in more than one color and some have been found with decals. The Carraway has also been found with a short spout. We have seen a picture of a long spout Carraway with enamel decoration.

Tricolator backstamp.

Row 1: "Imperial" with floral decal; "Amory."

Row 2: "Diver," floral vine decal; "Diver," Art Deco decoration.

Coffee Pot	Price	Coffee Pot	Price
"Amory"	$50.00 – 55.00	"Diver," floral	$70.00 – 80.00
"Diver," Art Deco	$75.00 – 90.00	"Imperial," floral	$40.00 – 50.00

Row 1:
"Lincoln," blue;
"Lincoln," pink;
"Crown," brown.

Row 2:
"Ansel," red;
"Buchanan," blue.

A panelled version of the "Wilson" has been found. It is called the "Armory." Notice the screw-lock lid of the "Buchanan." The pot has also been found without the locking lid. It will be found in other colors and with decals.

Coffee Pot	Price
"Ansel"	$40.00 – 50.00
"Buchanan"	$45.00 – 55.00
"Lincoln"	$40.00 – 50.00
"Wilson"	$35.00 – 45.00

Coffee Queen with metal dripper.

Coffee Pot	Price
"Blossom"	$50.00 – 60.00
"Carraway"	$40.00 – 50.00
Coffee Queen	$20.00 – 25.00
"Diver"	$70.00 – 80.00
"Empress"	$25.00 – 30.00
"Hoyt"	$35.00 – 45.00
"Imperial"	$40.00 – 50.00
Princess	$20.00 – 22.00
"Ritz"	$55.00 – 65.00
"Wellman"	$55.00 – 65.00

Row 1: "Blossom," green; "Blossom," iridescent tan with silver decal; "Hoyt," green.
Row 2: "Ritz," red; "Wellman," blue.
Row 3: "Diver," Floral Spray decal; "Carraway," long spout; "Imperial," green.

ELECTRIC PERCOLATORS

The most common shape of Hall electric percolators is the style used for the highly collectible percolator in the Autumn Leaf pattern. Today, this percolator with other decals is becoming more attractive to collectors.

Some of the numerous decals found on electric percolators will also be found on other accessory pieces. This has enabled collectors to put together matching mini-sets of certain decals.

Some of the more popular decals found on the percolators are the series of game bird decals. Other accessory pieces found with the game bird decal are a casserole, New York teapot, Windshield teapot, and a "Thick Rim" bowl set.

In addition to the decals pictured, percolators with floral decals will be found. These decals appear less frequently than the game bird decals.

Another percolator with a gold Rx decoration is sometimes seen. The percolator is part of a set which was given as a premium to pharmacists. Other pieces are available with this decoration. For a more complete listing see the Rx listing in the Kitchenware section.

Electric Percolator	Price
Floral decal	$65.00 – 75.00
Game bird decal	$80.00 – 90.00
Gold Deer	$20.00 – 30.00
Irish setter decal	$85.00 – 95.00
Rx decoration	$45.00 – 55.00
Seal of Ohio	$80.00 – 90.00
Solid color	$40.00 – 50.00

Electric percolator with seal of Ohio and original box.

Left to Right: Electric percolator, geese decal; electric percolator, pink; electric percolator, pheasant decal.

Row 1: Electric percolator, gold deer decoration; electric percolator, Irish setter decal.

Row 1: Coffee urn Hanging Vine; sugar, Hanging Vine; electric percolator, Hanging Vine.
Row 2: Electric percolator, Cattail; creamer and covered sugar, Cattail; coffee urn, Cattail.

Westinghouse added the metal and electrical fixtures to the china percolator and coffee urn bodies produced by Hall. Two of the more successful patterns were Cattail and Hanging Vine. Today, the Cattail pattern is more desirable since it matches the popular Cattail dinnerware pattern produced by Universal.

Item	Price
Coffee urn, Cattail	$90.00 – 110.00
Coffee urn, Hanging Vine	$55.00 – 70.00
Creamer, Cattail	$18.00 – 22.00
Creamer, Hanging Vine	$9.00 – 11.00
Electric Percolator, Cattail	$90.00 – 110.00
Electric Percolator, Hanging Vine	$55.00 – 70.00
Sugar and lid, Cattail	$20.00 – 25.00
Sugar and lid, Hanging Vine	$12.00 – 15.00

"Monk Decal"

BEER SETS

"Abbey Meal Decal"

Beer sets may be found in plain solid colors, with silver overlay, or with decals. Basic sets consist of a tankard and six matching mugs. Decal sets will have three right-handed and three left-handed mugs. The tankard is pictured here with the flagon shape mug. Another style, the barrel shape mug is sometimes found with these sets. The flagon is available in five sizes and the barrel mug comes in two sizes. Two different decals are shown — "Monk" and "Abbey Meal." Another decal depicting hunt scenes has been reported. A matching pretzel jar is also available for some decal sets.

	Solid colors	Decals
Tankard pitcher	$50.00 – 65.00	$95.00 – 125.00
Flagon, 8, 10, 12, 14, 16 oz.	$8.00 – 9.00	$30.00 – 35.00
Barrel mug, 8, 12 oz.	$7.00 – 9.00	
Pretzel jar	$60.00 – 75.00	$95.00 – 110.00

OLD CROW PUNCH SET

The Old Crow punch set contains 10 cups, a ladle, and a large elaborate advertising punch bowl. Initially these sets caused more excitement among collectors of advertising memorabilia than among Hall collectors. Some of the first sets were offered to collectors for as high as $450.00. However, the quantity of available sets has proven substantial. Since the price of these sets has decreased and stabilized at a reasonable level more Hall collectors have become attracted to them.

Set in original box	$150.00 – 175.00
Bowl	$80.00 – 90.00
Cup	$4.00 – 6.00
Ladle	$20.00 – 30.00

TOM AND JERRY SETS

Tom and Jerry sets were introduced in the thirties. They are commonly found ith an ivory or Hi-black body and are usually trimmed with gold. The covered bowls hold five quarts and were sold with the #2044 mug.

Item	Price
Covered Tom and Jerry bowl*	$40.00 – 45.00
Tom and Jerry #2044 mug	$4.00 – 5.00
*Red, $95.00 – 125.00.	

The Tom and Jerry bowl shown on the right holds four quarts and was sold with a five ounce mug. This style set has been found in at least one decal kitchenware line and also in the Eggshell Buffet Service line. The capacity of the Tom and Jerry plum pudding style bowl on the left is eight quarts. This bowl came with a seven ounce mug. This bowl set has also been found with the Hunt Scene decal.

Item	Price
Tom and Jerry bowl, footed	$30.00 – 40.00
Tom and Jerry plum pudding bowl*	$27.00 – 35.00
Tom and Jerry mug, 5 oz.	$3.00 – 4.00
Tom and Jerry mug, 7 oz.*	$4.00 – 5.50
*With Hunt Scene decal, UND.	

TEMPERANCE MUGS

These four 8 oz. pro-temperance mugs may have been produced for the Prohibition Party in 1934. All four mugs contain slogans denouncing the repeal of prohibition. The identity of two of the characters seems certain. One is Carry Nation, a noted temperance leader around the turn of the century. The mug with the caricature of Carry Nation asks the question, "Must I start all over again?" The figure with the mustache is probably Congressman Andrew Volstead of Minnesota who was instrumental in engineering the passage of the National Prohibition Act. His comment is, "They surely crabbed my act." The other two figures are still unidentified, although they may have been prominent members of the Prohibition Party. The figure in blue assures, "It will still be grape juice for me," and the smiling character in red admonishes, "I don't want it, you shouldn't have it."

Mug, 8 oz.   UND

WATERING CANS

The Hall watering can, which was produced in the early 1930s, is pictured here in all the colors we have seen. This early 1930s piece is very hard-to-find and information is not extensive at this time, but red is the color most frequently found. The lavender color appears to be the least common.

Watering can $450.00 – 500.00

PROMOTIONAL PRODUCTS

Row 1: Teapot, Philadelphia, "Momento of East District Ohio Music Ass'n Vocal Audition Festival — East Liverpool High School — April 12, 1947"; jug, "Teacher's Highland Cream"; jug, "Seagram's"; jug, "Vat 69." Row 2: Coffee pot, "Sanka"; mug, "Sanka"; Teapot, Cube, "Compliments and Best Wishes T. M. James and Sons China Co. — Purveyors to the Fine Trade — China, Glass, and Silverware."; big cup/saucer, "Golden Anniversary of the Tea Bag — 1904 – 1954." Row 3: Vase, #630, "Edgewater Beach Hotel"; bowl, Kraft cheese; ashtray, #618, "Palmer Beach Hotel."

Hall China has produced many promotional pieces for private companies through the years. Since Hall China is primarily a hand operation, its facilities are easily adaptable to the special needs of its individual customers. Therefore, many items of this nature are still being made. Collectors should be aware the Sanka set and several other promotional pieces which were originally produced by Hall have been reproduced in Japan.

Item	Price	Item	Price
Ashtray, Palmer	$12.00 – 15.00	Jug, Vat 69	$12.00 – 15.00
Big cup with advertisement	UND	Mug, Sanka	$5.00 – 7.00
Bowl, Kraft cheese	$12.00 – 15.00	Vase, Edgewater	$12.00 – 15.00
Coffee pot, Sanka	$16.00 – 20.00	Teapot, Cube with advertisement	UND
Jug, Seagram's	$12.00 – 15.00	Teapot, Philadelphia with advertisement	UND
Jug, Teacher's	$18.00 – 22.00		

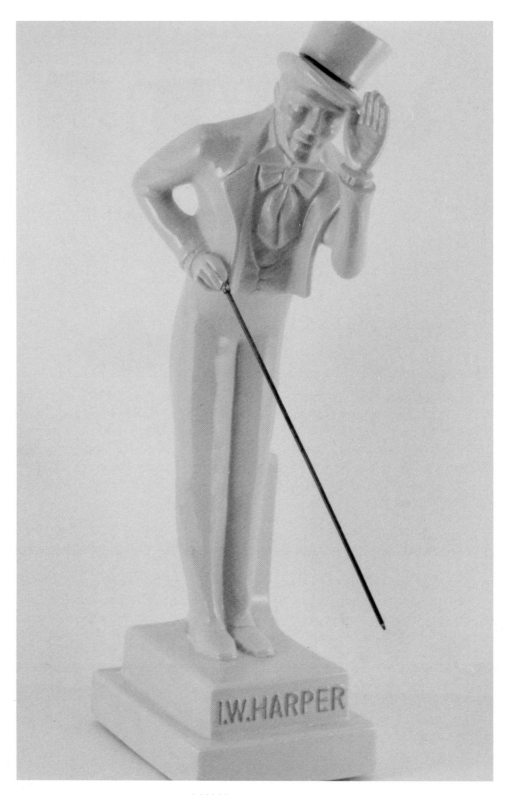

I. W. Harper decanter.

VASES, MUGS, AND ADVERTISING ITEMS

Hall produced a variety of items for hotels and restaurants. Some of these items are shown here.

		Price			*Price*
Row 1:	1. Turkish coffee cup, #1270	$4.00 – 5.00	Row 3:	1. Ashtray	$6.00 – 7.00
	2. Barrel mug, 8 oz.	$5.00 – 6.00		2. Ashtray	$10.00 – 12.00
	3. Mug, footed, #2274	$4.00 – 5.00		3. Ashtray	$9.00 – 11.00
	4. Braniff International mug	$4.50 – 5.50		4. Ashtray, #696	$6.00 – 7.00
	5. Cylindrical mug, #1314	$4.00 – 5.00			
			Row 4:	1. Butter pat, Regency Hotel	$4.50 – 5.50
Row 2:	1. Ashtray, Palmer House	$12.00 – 15.00		2. Ashtray, #679	$5.00 – 6.00
	2. Ashtray	$12.00 – 15.00		3. United Airlines bowl	$12.00 – 15.00
	3. Ashtray	$12.00 – 15.00		4. Spittoon	$20.00 – 25.00
	4. Ashtray	$12.00 – 15.00	Opposite Page:		
	5. Ashtray with matchholder	$12.00 – 15.00		Decanter, I. W. Harper	$40.00 – 50.00

A number of different Hall lamps have been showing up. Identification of the lamps is difficult unless the paper label, which is usually in the shape of an Aladdin teapot, is still intact. Hall produced the china lamp bodies for other companies which added the metal bases and electrical fixtures.

Item	Price
Hall table lamp, solid color	$27.00 – 32.00
Hall table lamp, hand-painted	$40.00 – 50.00
Hall table lamp, decal decoration	$35.00 – 40.00

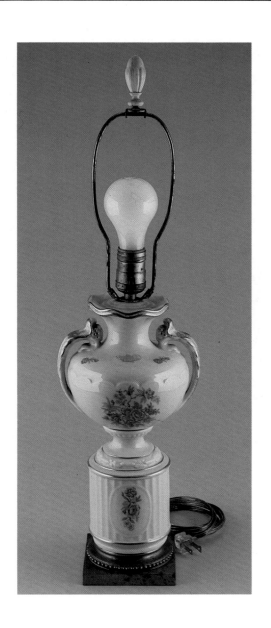

RE-ISSUES AND NEW PRODUCTS

Autumn Leaf Produced for Jewel

In 1976, Jewel discontinued the sale of Hall's Autumn Leaf to allow the Hall China Company to produce sufficient inventory to enable Jewel to fill orders on a timely basis. Production at Hall continued on the 13" platter, the 10" dinner plate, the 5½" fruit dish, the coupe soup bowl, the 7¼" salad plate, and the oval vegetable bowl. In 1978, Jewel announced plans for a major promotion involving those eight pieces which had remained in production and added four discontinued pieces. The additional pieces were the Newport teapot, the cake plate, the 2-handle bean pot, and the 3-piece mixing bowl set. All pieces made by Hall after August of 1978, were to have a new backstamp which included the "1978" date. How-

ever, all pieces of stock produced and stored in the warehouses prior to this date were to be sold in the promotion without the new mark. Old supplies of everything but the Newport teapot were on hand. However, production problems continued to plague Hall and the proposed special promotion was cancelled in mid 1979. Therefore, much of the production with both the old and new marks was disposed of by Jewel in the sale promoted by the poster below. Jewel is no longer selling Autumn Leaf china and the remaining stock is being sold through the Hall Closet (Hall's outlet store at the factory location). Today, there is very little price difference between Autumn Leaf with the old or new mark.

Item	Jewel's Price in 1979
Bean pot	$17.00
Bowl set, 3-pc	$22.00
Bowl, 5½"	$2.00
Bowl, oval	$12.00
Cake plate	$12.00
Cup	$3.00
Plate, 10"	$5.00
Plate, 7¼"	$3.50
Saucer	$2.00

Jewel display sign from 1980 Autumn Leaf special sale.

Hall China Production of Autumn Leaf Commissioned by the National Autumn Leaf Collectors Club

The Hall China Company also produced special pieces of china with the Autumn Leaf decal for members of the National Autumn Leaf Collectors Club. Members are entitled to buy these special club offerings, and the number produced is limited to the number ordered. Members were allowed to order two of the New York teapots. All other issues have been limited to one item per member. These pieces have a special backstamp which identifies them as items made for the NALCC. The following photos show the items which have been produced.

New York Teapot (1984)

Number Produced	Original Price	Current Value
536	$23.00	$500.00 – 600.00

Edgewater Vase (1987)

Number Produced	Original Price	Current Value
626	$16.00	$200.00 – 220.00

	Number Produced	Original Price	Current Value
Row 1:			
Candleholder (1989)	892 pr.	$21.00	$225.00 – 250.00
Philadelphia tea set (1990)	1150	$60.00	$200.00 – 225.00
Row 2:			
Tea-for-Two set (1990)	1300	$45.00	$200.00 – 225.00
Sugar packet holder (1990)	1712	Gift*	$90.00 – 100.00
Candleholder, handled (1991)	2100	Gift*	$90.00 – 100.00
Row 3:			
Casserole (1991)	1400**		$75.00 – 85.00
Solo teapot (1991)	1400**		$100.00 – 125.00
Donut jug (1991)	1400**		$110.00 – 130.00

*These items were given free to members as a Christmas gift from the club.
**Only offered to members as a set; $100.00 per set.

	Number Produced	Original Price	Current Value
Row 1:			
French teapot (1992)	1500*		$75.00 – 100.00
Baby Ball jug (1992)	1500*		$75.00 – 100.00
Chocolate mug (1992)	1500*		$20.00 – 25.00
Row 2:			
Punch bowl, 12-cups (1992)	1148	$160.00	
Donut teapot (1993)	2008	$45.00	

* Items in first row offered to members as a set which included four of the chocolate mugs; $115.00 per set.

In addition to the items pictured, other items produced for the NALCC may find their way into collectors' hands. One item is an oyster cup which was made for members who attended the 1992 NALCC annual meeting. There were 360 of these oyster cups made. Other items which may surface are sample pieces which Hall provides to the club officers who ultimately decide whether to accept or reject the piece for official production for the membership.

Collectors who are interested in Autumn Leaf should consider becoming members of the National Autumn Leaf Collectors Club. Besides meeting and becoming friends with other members who are interested in the same collectible, other benefits include the opportunity to keep up with new developments and to buy, sell, and trade extra pieces. Currently membership is $20.00 per year. Checks should be made out to the NALCC and may be sent to Patti Byerly, 4514 Errington Road, Columbus, Ohio, 43227.

Hall China Production of Autumn Leaf
Commissioned by China Specialties of Ohio

Another source of new Autumn Leaf items produced by Hall China is China Specialties. This private company has commissioned Hall and Libbey to produce limited edition items which were not made in the original production. With a few exceptions, all items are marked with a special backstamp which identifies their origin. The Airflow teapot was the first item produced for China Specialties and will not be found from the Jewel production era. The array of backstamps found on this teapot may result in some confusion among dealers and collectors. To our knowledge there are five different possibilities:

1. No backstamp.
2. Round Hall stamp under glaze in dark ink.
3. Square Hall stamp under glaze in dark ink.
4. Gold stamp "Hall Made in U.S.A."
5. Round Hall stamp in gold.

Other china pieces produced by Hall for China Specialties will generally have one of the following two backstamps:

1. Square Hall mark along with the year of manufacture.
2. Square Hall mark, the year of manufacture and the words "China Specialties Exclusive Limited Edition."

A mistake was made at Hall China on the backstamps of some of the condiment sets produced for China Specialties in 1991. Some of the condiment jars were released with the following backstamp: "Made Especially for the Autumn Leaf Club by Hall China Company." Although an attempt was made to recall the jars with this mark, it was not entirely successful. None of the shakers which complete this set will have any identifying mark. Be aware that the teardrop shape shaker was not made by Hall for Jewel.

	Number Produced	Original Price	Current Value
Row 1:			
Airflow teapot (1990)	1999	$49.95	$125.00 – 150.00
Norris water jug (1991)	1500	$69.95	$100.00 – 150.00
Bud vase (1991)	950	$30.00	
Beer pitcher (1993)	1500	$69.95	
Row 2:			
Onion soup bowl (1992)	1200	$25.00*	
Bean pot, 2½ pt. (1993)	1550	$49.95	
Irish coffee mug (1991)	1700	$22.50**	
Condiment set, 3-pc. (1991)	1500	$49.95	
Row 3:			
Automobile teapot (1993)	1573	$79.95	$150.00 – 175.00
Conic mug, set of 4 (1991)	600	$65.80	
Sherbet, set of 4 (1992)	1400	$39.95	
Ashtray (1992)	1179	$30.00	

*Could be purchased in a set of four for $89.95.

**Could be purchased in a set of four for $79.95.

	Number Produced	Original Price	Current Value
Row 1:			
Hook Cover teapot (1994)	1650	$49.95	
Prayer board* (1992)	1000	$35.00	
St. Louis chocolate pot (1994)	1700	$39.95	
Row 2:			
Reamer (1993)	1550	$59.95	
Relish, 10½" (1993)	1500	$22.00	
Shakers, Flair (1994)	1650	$25.00	
Row 3:			
Ashtray	200	Premium Gift	$135.00
Cruet, Libbey** (1992)	1500	$15.00	
Candy, Libbey	300	Premium Gift	$75.00
Water goblet, Libbey (1992)	1500	$29.95***	
Wine goblet, Libbey (1992)	1500	$29.95***	
Playing cards (1991)		$14.95	

*The prayer board was originally offered in 1992 as a plain board along with a deck of playing cards. A total of 615 plain board were sold. The price was $49.95 with a poker deck and $59.95 with double pinochle cards.

**These are dated by the decal and marked "Canada" on the bottom.

***Priced as a set of four

The Libbey goblets and candy are dated by the decal. The playing cards have a small date, 1991, on the lower right hand corner of the back.

Left to Right: Hurricane lamp; ice tea dispenser; round butter dish.

Pictured above are sample items which are scheduled to be offered by China Specialties in 1994.

Items not pictured:
Pilsner style 15 oz. tumbler in clear glass – 1000 sets of four to be produced.
Retail price is $29.95 per set. Small whiskey in clear glass.

Stainless Steel Tableware

A four place stainless steel tableware service became available to collectors in late 1993. The tableware was produced for a private company by the International Silver Company using original dies which were used to make the silverplate issued by Jewel in 1958. Therefore, the shape of this issue is different from the shape of the stainless sold originally by Jewel in the early 1960s. This offering consists of a five place service — place fork, salad fork, place spoon, teaspoon, and place knife. Each piece is marked, "C & C Collectible® 93" on the back. A 20-piece service for four retails for $167.00.

Non-Hall Autumn Leaf

As with many other popular collectibles, there are numerous items resembling Autumn Leaf pieces which have been fashioned by industrious individuals. In many cases these attempts at imitating or adding to the original collectible has served a useful purpose and there has been no attempt by the maker to defraud the public or misrepresent the article. However, the problems with these articles occur when they reach the secondary market where people are unfamiliar with their origin. Novice collectors who find any unusual china piece, especially if it lacks the Jewel backstamp or shows few signs of age, would be well advised to check the authenticity of the piece with another knowledgeable collector or dealer before paying a high price for such an item. Some of the homemade non-china items are showing up at flea markets and collectors should be aware that these are recent creations which should not command the exhorbitant prices reserved for truly rare items produced for Jewel by the Hall China Company. The following is a list of creations which we have been able to compile and their original prices where they were available.

Item	Original Price
Ceramic dinner bell on a wooden rack	$19.50
Ceramic bottle, pump soap	$27.50
Ceramic bud base	$10.50
Ceramic butter with dome shape ceramic lid	
Ceramic cabinet knobs	
Ceramic candleholder	$10.50
Ceramic footed candy dish	$25.20
Ceramic square ruffled candy and cover	$25.00
Ceramic candy scoop	$32.50
Ceramic child's set, four piece place setting	$100.00
Ceramic dresser box	
Ceramic egg cup	$10.50
Ceramic square hotplate	
Ceramic lamp	$100.00
Ceramic leftover, loop handle	
Ceramic napkin holder	$10.00
Ceramic napkin ring	
Ceramic picture frame	$43.75
Ceramic pie lifter	$7.00
Ceramic wall switch and outlet plates	$8.50
Ceramic large turkey platter	$38.50
Ceramic two-part reamer	$25.00
Ceramic rolling pin, 13" long	
Ceramic soap dish	$7.00
Ceramic soap dish, 2" x 5", oval	$24.50
Ceramic spoon rest	$7.00
Ceramic spooner	
Ceramic tissue box	$25.00
Ceramic toothpick holder	$5.00
Ceramic tureen/underplate/ladle	$38.50
Ceramic vase, 10"	
Clock made from a 10" dinner plate	$65.00
Glass cheese dome/wooden base and inlaid tile	$38.50
Coat rack, six peg oak	$28.50
Colander, white enamel	$38.95
Cutting board, 6" x 11", wooden	$23.95
Match safe, metal	
Paper towel holder, oak	$38.50
Place mats, oval 12" x 18", vinyl	
Quilt, homemade	
Salt/pepper, tall wooden hand-painted	
Sifters, one and two cup metal	
Spice jars with rack	

In addition to the above, there are also reports of the existence of several hand-painted kitchen chairs. Clocks have also been fashioned from 9" plates and cake plates. Other items with the Autumn Leaf decal which have been offered for sale include wrist watches, afghans, napkins, and stationary. Needless to say, almost anything imaginable might be found with this popular decal. This section has been included to help enable you as a collector to make a knowledgeable decision about the origin of the various types of merchandise which may be offered to you. Be aware that new items are being produced constantly, and that this listing may not include all the new items you may encounter.

Crocus and Orange Poppy Re-issues

China Specialties is currently producing or has the following items scheduled for production in the Crocus and Orange Poppy patterns.

	Number Produced	Original Price
Row 1:		
Crocus Pattern		
Automobile teapot (1993)	750	$79.95
Irish coffee mug (1994)	500*	
Reamer (1994)	750	$59.95
Row 2:		
Orange Poppy Pattern		
Airflow teapot (1994)	750	$54.95
Norris covered jug (1994)	750	$54.95

*Total of 2000; sold in sets of four.

Red Poppy and Silhouette Re-issues

The following items in the Red Poppy and Silhouette patterns are being produced as limited edition collectibles by Hall China for China Specialties.

	Number Produced	Original Price
Row 1:		
Red Poppy Pattern		
Reamer (1993)	450	$59.95
Bud vase (1993)	500	$25.00
Airflow teapot (1993)	400	$49.95
Condiment jar (1993)	400	$25.00
Row 2:		
Silhouette Pattern		
Norris covered jug (1994)	500	$54.95
Pilsner tumbler, Libbey (1993)	500	$25.00*
Bud vase (1993)	400	$25.00
Airflow teapot (1993)	350	$54.95
Mustard jar (1993), not pictured	300	$25.00
Beer pitcher (1993), not pictured	300	$49.95

*Price for set of four.

Hall American Line Re-issues

In early 1985, Hall China announced a new retail line for department stores. Most of the 65 items targeted for this promotion were items already in production. These were primarily casseroles, bakers, bowls, and platters. The new items which were part of the re-issue which concerned collectors the most were some teapot and water server shapes. The Airflow, Rhythm, and T-Ball square teapots, the Streamline and Donut jugs, and the "Hercules" and "Nora" shape water servers were included. Another piece which was made and caused some collector concern was the "Sundial" batter bowl. However, this piece was issued with a square base like the one used in the Autumn Leaf decal pattern. Identification of the new pieces is easy for anyone who is familiar with Hall's old color glazes. For others who are less experienced, the backstamp on the new items will be square; old items will have either the round backstamp or the "Superior Quality Kitchenware" mark.

Hall Historical Line Re-issues Produced for China Specialties

Beginning in 1992, China Specialties commissioned Hall China to produce limited edition teapots. The shapes selected were from the Novelty Teapot Line which Hall China had produced originally in the late 1930s. Colors selected are those which are not believed to have been made originally, although some may appear similar to the old colors. All pieces are marked with a special backstamp which indicates they are a limited edition re-issue. In a few instances, new teapots being represented as old have appeared on the resale market with their backstamp removed. Be suspicious of any automobile or football without a backstamp. Inspect the bottom carefully for scratches which may indicate the new mark has been removed. Also look at the spout. The hole in the spout of the new teapots is generally much smaller than in the earlier teapots.

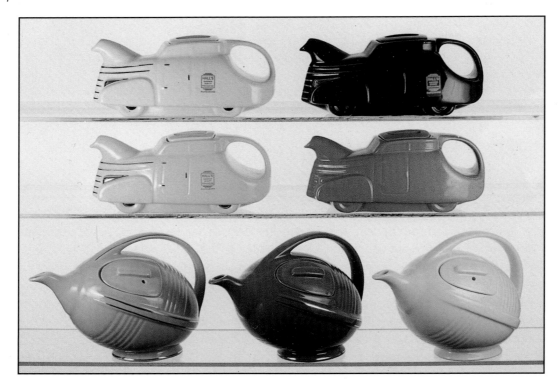

Row 1: Automobile teapot, bone white with platinum trim; automobile teapot, green luster with platinum trim. Row 2: Automobile teapot, sunlight yellow with gold trim; automobile teapot, Holiday Sea Mist. Row 3: Football teapot, sandust with gold trim; football teapot, colonial blue with platinum trim; football teapot, sunlight yellow.

Automobile Teapot

Color	Date Issued	Number Made	Original Price	Current Price
Bone white	1992	300	$49.95	
Bone white/platinum	1992	500	$59.95	$100.00
Green luster	1992	100	$49.95	
Green luster/gold	1992	200	$59.95	
Green luster/platinum	1992	500	$69.95	$79.95
Sunlight yellow/gold	1993	200	$69.95	
Sunlight yellow/platinum	1993	300	$69.95	
Holiday Sea Mist/platinum	1994	500	$59.95	
Holiday Sea Mist/gold	1994		$69.95	

Football Teapot

Color	Date Issued	Number Made	Original Price	Current Price
Sandust	1992	350	$49.95	$100.00
Sandust/gold	1992	150	$59.95	$150.00
Colonial blue	1992	300	$49.95	
Colonial blue/gold	1992	200	$69.95	
Sunlight yellow	1993	300	$49.95	

NOMENCLATURE CROSS REFERENCE

Since Hall did not give names to every item produced, researchers have found it convenient to provide names to help with identification. In some cases more than one name has become associated with the same piece or shape. This listing will cross reference the multiple names for those collectors interested in using numerous references.

Names Used In This Reference	Other Names	Names Used In This Reference	Other Names
Adonis	Prince	Phoenix	Patrician
Apple	Browning	Plume	Disraeli
Baron	Big Boy	Radiance	Sunshine
Benjamin	Albert	Rayed	J-Sunshine
Birch	Darby	Regal	Dickens
Bowknot	Gladstone	Ribbed	Flute
Bowling Ball	Pepper	Rounded Terrace	Step-round
Cathedral	Arch	Royal	Eliot
Connie	Victoria	Rutherford	Alton
Coverlet	Cozy Cover	Shaggy Tulip	Parrot Tulip
Daniel	Rickson	Silhouette	Taverne
Drape	Swathe	Simplicity	Classic
Five Band	Banded	Starlight	Tennyson
Floral Lattice	Flowerpot	Stonewall	Banner 'n Basket
General	Emperor	Sundial	Saf-Handle
Grape	Darwin	Target	Bullseye
Great American	Golden Key	Teardrop	Egg drop
Hercules	Aristocrat	Terrace	Step-down
Jerry	Monarch	Thick Rim	Big Lip
Medallion	Colonial	Viking	Bell
Murphy	Peel	Waverly	Crest
Norse	Everson	Wild Poppy	Poppy & Wheat
Novelty Radiance	Sunshine	Windcrest	Bronte
	Bulge	Yellow Rose	Pastel Rose
Perk	Deca-plain	Zephyr	Bingo
Pert	Sani-Grid		

BIBLIOGRAPHY

Autumn Leaf News. National Leaf Collectors Club: Austin, TX.

Barth, Harold. *History of Columbiana County, Vol. II.* Historical
        Publishing Co.: Topeka-Indianapolis, 1926.

China and Glass Red Book. China and Glass Tablewares, Commoner
        Publishing Company: New York.

Duke, Harvey. *Superior Quality Hall China: A Guide For Collectors.*
        ELO Books: U.S.A., 1977.

Duke, Harvey. *Hall 2.* ELO Books: U.S.A., 1985.

"History of the Hall China Company, East Liverpool, Ohio." Ceramic
        Abstracts and The Bulletin of the American Ceramic
        Society. August 15, 1945.

Jewel Home Shopping Service Catalogs. Jewel Home Shopping
        Service: Barrington, IL.

Sears, Roebuck and Co. Catalogs. Sears, Roebuck and Co.:
        Chicago, IL.

The Jewel News. Jewel Tea Co., Inc. Barrington, IL.